WHEN DID WILD POODLES ROAM THE EARTH?

Other Books by David Feldman:

Imponderables™

How to Win at Just About Everything

Why Do Clocks Run Clockwise?
and Other Imponderables™

Who Put the Butter in Butterfly?
and Other Fearless Investigations
into Our Illogical Language

When Do Fish Sleep?
and Other Imponderables™
of Everyday Life

Why Do Dogs Have Wet Noses?
and Other Imponderables™
of Everyday Life

Do Penguins Have Knees?
An Imponderables™ Book

WHEN DID WILD POODLES ROAM THE EARTH?

An Imponderables™ Book

David Feldman

Illustrated by Kassie Schwan

HarperPerennial
A Division of HarperCollins*Publishers*

A hardcover edition of this book was published in 1992 by HarperCollins Publishers.

HarperCollins books may be purchased for educational, business, or sales promotional use. For information please write: Special Markets Department, HarperCollins Publishers, Inc., 10 East 53rd Street, New York, NY 10022.

First HarperPerennial edition published 1993.

Designed by Cassandra J. Pappas

The Library of Congress has catalogued the hardcover edition as follows:

Feldman, David, 1950–
   When did wild poodles roam the earth? : an Imponderables™ book /
   David Feldman.
     p.   cm.
   Includes index.
   ISBN 0-06-016908-7 (cloth)
   1. Questions and answers. I. Title.
 AG195.F457   1992
 031.02—dc20   92-52593

ISBN 0-06-092432-2 (pbk.)

93 94 95 96 97 CW 10 9 8 7 6 5 4 3 2 1

For Kassie Schwan

Contents

CONTENTS

CONTENTS

CONTENTS   xiii

CONTENTS

Preface

Are you thinking of buying this book? If so, take this simple quiz about food and nutrition. In each category, which question concerns you most, A or B?

> Vitamins. A) Does a well-balanced diet provide one with sufficient vitamins, or should one take a supplement? B) Why is there no Betty Rubble character in Flintstones multivitamins?
>
> Poultry. A) Are free-range chickens superior nutritionally to conventionally raised chickens? B) Has anyone ever seen a *live* Cornish game hen?
>
> Seafood. A) Are lobsters as high in cholesterol as beef? B) Are lobsters ambidextrous?
>
> Decaffeinated Coffee. A) Is there anything dangerous about the decaffeination process? B) Why do decaf pots in restaurants have orange rims?

If you answered A to three or more of the four questions, you are a normal, well-adjusted person, concerned about the important issues of our day. We're proud of you. Buy another book.

But if you are a B-type person, who lies awake wondering why, if moths are attracted to light, they don't fly toward the sun, you have found your spiritual home in this book. Imponderables are the little mysteries of life that drive you nuts until you find out their solution. That's precisely what we're trying to do (solve the mysteries, not drive you nuts).

This, our sixth *Imponderables* book, is a collaboration between our readers and us. Most of the Imponderables in this book came as suggestions from readers. In the Frustables section, our readers take a crack at answering Imponderables that have stumped us. In the Letters section, readers take a crack at our heads, enumerating our imperfections.

As a gesture of our appreciation, we offer an acknowledgment and a free, autographed copy of our next book to the first person who sends in an Imponderable or the best solution to a Frustable we use.

The last page of the book tells you how you can contribute to the enterprise. But for now, sit back and enjoy. There will be no more quizzes.

Imponderables

Are lobsters ambidextrous?

Have you ever noticed, while digging into a lobster, that one claw is significantly larger than the other, as if one claw was pumping iron and taking steroids, while the other claw was used only for riffling the pages of library books? The large claw is called the "crusher" and the smaller one the "cutter" (terms that sound like the members of a new tag team in the World Wrestling Federation). The crusher has broader and bigger teeth but moves relatively slowly. The cutter has tiny, serrated teeth and moves swiftly.

The two claws do not start out distinctly different. Lobsters shed their shells more often than Cher has plastic surgery—they undergo three molts in the larval stage alone. When lobsters are first hatched, the two claws look identical, but with each successive stage in their development, the differences become more pronounced. It isn't until their fifth molt, and second postlarval molt, that the two claws are truly differentiated.

As you may have guessed, the crusher claw is important for the defense of lobsters against predators, and the cutter particularly useful in eating. Claws of lobsters are often torn off in accidents and in fights. Although there are some differences among species of lobsters, most lobsters will regenerate severed claws.

Most bizarre of all, if the remaining claw of an injured lobster is a cutter, many species with "plastic dimorphism" will change the function of that claw from cutter to crusher, presumably because the crusher is more essential for survival. The next regenerated claw of that lobster is capable itself of shifting to the cutter function, so that the positions of the two claws are reversed.

According to Darryl Felder, chairman of the University of Louisiana, Lafayette, biology department, lobsters are not always right- or left-"handed." The crusher may be on the right or left side of a lobster.

The ultimate answer to this Imponderable depends upon how you define ambidextrous. Certainly, lobsters can use either cheliped (the scientific name for claw) with equal ease. Although their regenerative powers give lobsters a certain flexibility, the versatility of each claw is not as great as that of a switch hitter in baseball, who can swing the bat equally well from both sides, or the pickpocket who can pilfer skillfully with either hand.

Submitted by Danny Kotok of New York, New York.

Why is there no Betty Rubble character in Flintstones Multivitamins?

For reasons too unfathomable for even us to delve into, we are thrown this question periodically on radio phone-in shows but have never received it in a letter. Perhaps no one wants to take credit for asking this Imponderable. One radio host said that he

DAVID FELDMAN

had investigated the matter, and found that for technical reasons, it was difficult to manufacture a realistic Betty facsimile.

Ah, we wish that were true, but the real story is far sadder, far darker. We heard from William D. Turpin, director of consumer relations for Multivitamins' manufacturer, Miles, Inc.:

> The current group of Flintstones characters was selected based upon research of the popularity of each character with children. As a result of this research, it was determined that Betty Rubble is not as popular with the majority of the children as the other characters.

Thus, if you investigate the contents of a Flintstones Multivitamins jar carefully, you'll find seven different "characters." As expected, Wilma, Fred, and a lonely Barney are included. Bamm-Bamm, Pebbles, and Dino are there, too, to help round out the nuclear family. But the Flintmobile? Is a car really more popular with children than a fine specimen of womanhood? You'd better believe it.

Truth be told, Betty was never our favorite character either. In fact, we don't think she deserved a great catch like Barney. Nevertheless, her lack of charisma is hardly reason enough to break up the family units that helped make the Flintstones a television and multivitamin supplement institution.

What in the heck is a tumbleweed? Why does it tumble? And how can it reproduce if it doesn't stay in one place?

Three Imponderables for the price of one. The first part is easy. The most common form of tumbleweed, the one you see wreaking havoc in movie westerns, is the Russian thistle. But actually the term is applied to any plant that rolls with the wind, drops its seed as it tumbles, and possesses panicles (branched flower clusters) that break off.

Usually, the stems of tumbleweed dry up and snap away

from their roots in late fall, when the seeds are ripe and the leaves dying. Although tumbleweeds cannot walk or fly on their own, they are configured to move with the wind. The above-ground portion of the thistle is shaped like a flattened globe, so it can roll more easily than other plants.

In his March 1991 *Scientific American* article "Tumbleweed," James Young points out how tumbleweed has adapted to the arid conditions of the Great Plains. One Russian thistle plant can contain a quarter of a million seeds. Even these impressive amounts of seeds will not reproduce efficiently if dumped all at once. But the flowers, which bloom in the summer, are wedged in the axil between the leaves and the stem, so that their seeds don't fall out as soon as they are subjected to their first tumbles. In effect, the seeds are dispersed sparingly by the natural equivalent of time-release capsules, assuring wide dissemination.

Young points out that tumbleweed actually thrives on solitude. If tumbleweed bumps into another plant, or thick, tall grass, it becomes lodged there, and birds and small animals find and eat the seeds:

> Hence, successful germination, establishment of seedlings, and flowering depend on dispersal to sites where competition is minimal: Russian thistle would rather tumble than fight.

Although songs have romanticized the tumbleweed, do not forget that the last word in "tumbleweed" is "weed." In fact, if the Russian thistle had been discovered in our country in the 1950s rather than in the 1870s, it probably would have been branded a communist plot. Thistle was a major problem for the cowboys and farmers who first encountered it. Although tumbleweed looks "bushy," its leaves are spiny and extremely sharp. Horses were often lacerated by running into tumbleweed in fields and pastures, and the leaves punctured the gloves and pants worn by cowboys.

Tumbleweed has also been a bane to farmers, which explains how tumbleweed spread so fast from the Dakotas down to the Southwest. The seeds of tumbleweed are about the same

DAVID FELDMAN

size as most cereal grains. Farmers had no easy way to separate the thistle seeds from their grains; as "grain" moved through the marketplace, thistle was transported to new "tumbling ground."

Today, tumbleweed's favorite victims are automobiles and the passengers in them. We get into accidents trying to avoid it, trying to outrace it, and from stupid driving mistakes when simply trying to watch tumbleweed tumble.

Submitted by Plácido García of Albuquerque, New Mexico.

When a body is laid out at a funeral home, why is the head always on the left side from the viewer's vantage point?

Why are so many readers obsessed with this Imponderable? And why are so many of them from Pennsylvania?

We found no evidence that any religion cares one iota about the direction in which a body is laid out at a viewing. Discussions with many funeral directors confirmed that the arrangement has become a custom not because of religious tradition but because of manufacturing practice.

Caskets can be divided into two types: half-couches, which have two separate lids, either or both of which can be opened; and full couches, whose lids are one, long unit. Full couches are designed to display the entire body at the viewing; half-couches are intended to show the head and upper torso of the deceased, with the option that, if the second lid is opened, the full body can be displayed.

DAVID FELDMAN

The hinges of all caskets allow the lids to be opened only in one direction. When the lids are lifted, they move first up and then back away from the viewers, to allow an unobstructed view for the bereaved. In many viewing rooms, the raised lids rest against a wall during viewing, dictating the direction the casket will be placed in a viewing room.

According to Howard C. Raether, former executive director and now consultant to the National Funeral Directors Association, the half-couch caskets made in the United States are all manufactured so that "only the left side has an interior and pillow for positioning and viewing the body." The two sides of the half-couch are also not symmetrical and thus not totally interchangeable. The left side of the half-couch is shorter than the "leg side," and because it is not normally opened, the bottom of the right side of the casket is usually unfinished. The interiors of full-couch caskets are also designed for the head to be placed on the left side.

Occasionally, however, a funeral director may need to put the head on the right side of the casket, usually when an injury or disease has disfigured the "wrong" side of the deceased's face. Since American-made caskets are rarely tapered, it is easy to rearrange the pillows inside the casket and put the deceased in the opposite direction.

One of our sources, who has worked in the industry for over fifty years and has sense enough to want to remain anonymous, told *Imponderables* that more families are asking for full-body viewings these days. He singled out *Pennsylvania* (along with southern New Jersey and parts of Florida and Ohio) for special mention in their preference for full-couch caskets—everywhere else, half-couches predominate.

What's with these Pennsylvanians?

Submitted by Barbara Peters of Norwood, Pennsylvania. Thanks also to Bridget Hahn of Conneaut Lake, Pennsylvania; Carol Haten of Monroeville, Pennsylvania; Earle Heffley of Springfield, Illinois; Sandy Zak of Pittsburgh, Pennsylvania; and Jason Humble of Starks, Louisiana.

Has anyone ever seen a live Cornish game hen?

We've seen a few dead Cornish game hens in our time, usually on a plate in front of us—and always when we are ravenously hungry at a formal dinner, surrounded by folks we don't know. So we feel we have to eat the bird with a knife and fork. Without picking up the dead hen and eating it with our fingers, we are capable of extracting a good two or three mouthfuls' worth of edible meat before we give up on meeting our protein requirements for the day.

As you can see, we have more than a little hostility toward these little bitty particles of poultry, so we are going to expose a nasty scandal about Cornish game hens (aka Rock Cornish game hens): They are nothing more than chickens—preadolescent chickens, in fact.

That's right. Cornish game hens, despite their highfalutin moniker, are nothing more than immature versions of the same broilers or fryers you buy in the supermarket. A Rock Cornish game hen could theoretically grow up to be a Chicken Mc-Nugget. (At least a Chicken McNugget gets eaten.) We have *all* seen a live "Cornish game hen."

Federal regulations define a Rock Cornish game hen or Cornish game hen as

> a young immature chicken (usually 5 to 6 weeks of age) weighing not more than 2 pounds ready-to-cook weight, which was prepared from a Cornish chicken or the progeny of a Cornish chicken crossed with another breed of chicken.

In practice, most Cornish fowls are crossbred with Plymouth Rock fowls.

Dr. Roy Brister, director of research and nutrition at Tyson Food, Inc., told *Imponderables* that *all* the chicken we eat has the Cornish White Rock as one of its ancestors. Cornish fowl are prized because they are plump, large-breasted, and meaty. Other breeds are too scraggly and are better suited for laying eggs. Most of the Cornish game hens now sold in the United States are actually less than thirty days old and weigh less than one pound after they are cooked.

According to the USDA's *Agriculture Handbook*, Cornish game hens are raised and produced in the same way as broilers. But because they are sold at a smaller weight, the cost per pound to process is higher for the producer and thus for the consumer.

But let's face it. It's a lot easier to get big bucks for a product with a tony name like "Rock Cornish game hen" than it is for "chick" or "baby broiler." If veal were called "baby cow," its price would plummet overnight. Dr. Brister speculates that the creation of "Cornish Game Hens" was probably a marketing idea in the first place.

While we are pursuing our literary equivalent of "A Current Affair," one more scandal must be unleashed. Not all those Cornish game hens are really hens. Legally, they can be of either sex, although they are usually females, because the males tend to be larger and are raised to be broilers. In fact, if immature chicks get a little chubby and exceed the two-pound maximum weight, they get to live a longer life and are sold as broilers.

Submitted by an anonymous caller on the Mel Young Show, KFYI-AM, Phoenix, Arizona.

Why do boxer shorts have straight frontal slits and briefs have complicated "trap doors"?

All that infrastructure on the briefs is what keeps you from indecent exposure charges. Even though most briefs and boxers sold in the U.S. are made out of the same material (cotton-polyester blends), briefs are knitted and boxers are woven. The two techniques yield different wear characteristics.

Boxers are built for comfort and won't stretch unless elasticized bands are added. But as Janet Rosati of Fruit of the Loom's Consumer Services told *Imponderables*, briefs are intended as support garments and are designed to stretch. Without all the reinforcements, or "trap doors," as our correspondent so elegantly put it, the opening on briefs would tend to gape open at embarrassing and unfortunate times. 'Nuf said?

Submitted by Josh Gibson of Silver Spring, Maryland.

DAVID FELDMAN

Why have auto manufacturers eliminated the side vents from front door windows?

As Frederick R. Heiler, manager of public relations for Mercedes-Benz of North America, put it, "Vent wings have gone the way of the starter crank handle." Sure, there are the occasional exceptions, such as the 1988 Mercury, which resurrected this feature. But on the whole, it has now been superseded by the vent setting on air-conditioning systems (the device that propels air onto your shins rather than onto your face).

Why the change? The main reason, believe it or not, is fuel economy. In order to meet the Environmental Protection Agency's fuel requirements, American car manufacturers will change just about anything in order to achieve a better aerodynamic design. Heiler remarks that "designers found they could do without the air turbulence of the extra window post and hardware." Especially at high speeds, air turbulence, including turbulence caused by leaving the "regular" windows down, lowers fuel economy significantly.

Representatives at Ford and Chrysler add that since most automobiles now come equipped with air conditioning and flow-through ventilation systems, the need for vent wings has been obviated (thus reducing the flak the companies received for eliminating them). Our cars are now like modern office buildings —often run without windows ever being opened.

An official at the National Highway Traffic Safety Administration, who preferred to remain anonymous, corroborated the above but listed two more reasons why auto manufacturers dumped vent wings: One, a single, bigger plate of glass costs less than a smaller piece with a vent wing; and two, the vent wing was the perfect place for thieves to insert the old coat hanger.

Submitted by Tom Ferrell of Brooklyn, New York. Thanks also to Ronald C. Semone of Washington, D.C.; H.J. Hassig of Woodland Hills, California; and Richard Nitzel of Daly City, California.

Why do the Oakland Athletics' uniforms have elephant patches on their sleeves?

The elephant may be the symbol of the Republican party, but partisan politics was the last thing on Connie Mack's mind when the legendary owner of the Philadelphia Athletics decided to adopt the white elephant as his team's insignia. Rival New York Giants manager John McGraw boasted that the Athletics, and the fledgling American League, to which they belonged, were unworthy competitors, and indicated that Mack had spent a fortune on a team of "white elephants."

Mack got the last laugh. The A's won the American League pennant in 1902. A few years later, the elephant's image appeared on the team sweater. In 1918, Mack first emblazoned the elephant on the left sleeve of game uniforms.

The elephant image became so popular that in 1920, Mack

DAVID FELDMAN

eliminated the "A" on the front of the jersey and replaced it with a blue elephant logo. Four years later, he changed it to a white elephant. After a few years of playing more like a bunch of thundering elephants than a pennant contender, Mack de-pachydermed his players' uniforms.

No A's uniform sported an elephant again until 1955, when the Kansas City A's added an elephant patch to their sleeves. But when the irascible Charlie Finley bought the A's in the early 1960s, he replaced the elephant with the image of an animal more befitting his own personality—the mule.

But you can't keep a good animal down. According to Sally Lorette, of the Oakland A's front office, the current owners of the A's resurrected the same elephant used by the Kansas City Athletics in time for the 1988 season. The mascot did the job for the Oakland A's just as it had for Connie almost a century ago. Since 1988, the A's have won three American League pennants and one championship.

Submitted by Anthony Bialy of Kenmore, New York. Thanks also to a caller on the Jim Eason Show, KGO-AM, San Francisco, California.

Why is the imperial gallon bigger than its American counterpart?

The English have never been particularly consistent in their standards of weights and measures. In fact, in the eighteenth and early nineteenth centuries, England changed its definition of a gallon about as often as Elizabeth Taylor changes wedding rings. (Before then, Kings Henry VII and VIII and Queen Elizabeth I had also changed the definition of a gallon.)

Colonialists in America adopted the English wine gallon, based on the size of then-used hogsheads (barrels) of 231 cubic inches. The English, who also recognized the larger ale gallon of 282 cubic inches, finally settled the mess in 1824 by eliminating the ale and wine gallons completely and instituting the imperial gallon, defined as the volume of ten pounds of water at the temperature of 62 degrees Fahrenheit, the equivalent of about 277.420 cubic inches.

Meanwhile, Americans were basking in the freedom of a

DAVID FELDMAN

participatory republic but were saddled with an anachronistic wine gallon. In both the English and American systems, one gallon equals four quarts and eight pints, but English portions were significantly larger.

To compound the standardization problem, the British decided to use the same system to measure liquid and dry substances. They redefined a bushel as eight gallons. In the U.S., bushels, pecks, and all those other measurements we hear in Broadway songs but not in everyday speech are used only to measure grains and other dry commodities.

Perhaps this was England's revenge for the American Revolution. By the time the English finally got their act together and laid out a simple, sensible system of measurement, Americans had already committed to the inferior, old English system.

Submitted by Simon Arnold of Los Angeles, California.

Why do painters wear white uniforms?

Often, when we confront practitioners of an industry with an Imponderable about their line of work, they are befuddled. "I'd never stopped to think about that" is a typical reply.

Such was not the case with painters we contacted about this mystery. Nobody seemed to know for sure how the practice started, but we were lavished with theories about why "whites" made sense. In fact, when we contacted the International Brotherhood of Painters & Allied Trades, we were stunned to find out that after they posed the same question to their membership, their *Journal* was filled with responses in the April and May 1985 issues. Our thanks to the many members of IBPAT and other painters we contacted for help in answering what, on the basis of our mailbag, is a burning question of the 1990s.

One advantage that just about everyone could agree on is that white connotes cleanliness. A painter, after all, removes dirt and crumbling plaster before applying paint. Many painters compared the purity of their "whites" to the uniforms of nurses, chefs, and bakers. Philadelphia painting contractor Matt Fox told *Imponderables* that a white uniform is like a badge that says, "There's no paint on me, so I'm doing my job." Obviously, it is as hard to hide paint smeared on a white uniform as it is to hide a ketchup stain on a chef's apron.

The white uniform is also a sign of professionalism, one that distinguishes painters from other craftspeople. One IBPAT member wrote that in the early twentieth century, his father often encountered part-time, nonunion workmen trying to horn in on the painting trade. These workers, usually moonlighting, wore blue bib overalls or other ordinary work clothes not related to the paint trade. By contrast, "Our men certainly looked professional in their white overalls, white jackets, and black ties." Even today, most professionals prefer crisp white uniforms (even if they've shed the tie), while odd-job part-timers might don blue jeans and a T-shirt.

Of course, a color other than white could still look clean and professional. And at first glance, white seems like precisely the wrong color—by wearing white, you "broadcast" any color you spill. True, but remember that the majority of the time (estimates are 70 to 80 percent), painters are dealing with white paint. And what other color uniform is going to look better when splattered with white paint?

Painters deal with other white substances more than likely to be deposited on their uniforms. Painter Jerry DeOtis presumes that the tradition of "whites" began in eighteenth-century England, when buildings were routinely whitewashed. Irving Goldstein of New York City adds:

> Plaster, lime, spackle, and compound are also white. Repairing and sanding existing walls creates a fine white powder; therefore wearing "painters whites" enables these materials to blend into the uniform.

The beauties of white as proper background even inspired one Local 277 member, Liz Weber, to burst into verse:

> ... and although we strive for neatness,
> getting paint on our clothes is our one weakness.
> So what if those colors tend to cling—
> we're in style because . . .
> White goes with everything!

Even if a painter isn't thrilled with pigment-stained whites, compared to other colored garb, they are a washroom delight. Traditionally, painters used bleach or lye to remove paint from their uniforms: Those that started with dark uniforms ended up with bleached-out, dingy, light-colored ones anyway.

Some other painters we consulted mentioned two other advantages of whites: They are cheaper than dyed fabrics and, because of their color, reflect light rather than absorb it, a small comfort to painters working in the sun-drenched great outdoors.

Submitted by Angelique Craig of Austin, Texas. Thanks also to Howard Livingston of Arlington, Texas; Laura Arvidson of Westville, Indiana; Cristie Avila of Houston, Texas; Tom Rodgers of Las Vegas, Nevada; Adam Rawls of Tyler, Texas; and Karen Riddick of Dresden, Tennessee.

HURRY UP! IT'S ALMOST TIME FOR THE HUMAN'S MIDNIGHT SNACK !!

Why do roaches run away when a light is turned on in a darkened room?

Just as a sunflower is genetically programmed to turn toward the sun, many plants and animals are phototropic—they are genetically programmed to turn away from and avoid the sun. Cockroaches are nocturnal animals, and most species instinctively scurry when exposed to light.

The urban roach has adapted well to its environment. While we are asleep, dreaming away, the roach is free to loot our kitchens as if they were no-cost supermarkets. By roaming at night, it also avoids the rodents that might eat it during the day. At night, the only foes roaches have to worry about are Raid and Combat.

It is impossible to know for sure, since we can't interview a roach, to what extent the roaches are bothered by the light per se, or whether the scurrying is a genetically programmed response to help roaches avoid predators. Randy Morgan, entomologist at the Cincinnati Insectarium, told us that the speed of a given roach's retreat is subject to many factors, including its species, the humidity, and how hungry it is.

DAVID FELDMAN

But why assume that the roach is running because of the light? Maybe it is running away from *you!* Cockroaches have poor eyesight; their main method of detecting danger is by sensing vibrations around them. Robin Roche, entomologist at the Insect Zoo in San Francisco, told *Imponderables* that roaches have two hornlike structures on their back called cerci. The cerci have hairs that are very sensitive to wind currents. So when you enter the kitchen for your midnight snack, chances are the roach senses you not from sight, or by sound, but by feeling the air currents your movement has generated.

At the very least, the roach knows something is moving around it; when you flip the light switch on, an automatic physiological response ensues. If it hasn't already bidden a hasty retreat, it decides that the better part of valor is to sneak back into the crevice it came from. When you go back to bed, it knows those bread crumbs will be right where you left them before, and it can snack away later in peaceful darkness.

Submitted by Jill Davies of Forest, Mississippi.

If moths are attracted to light, why don't they fly toward the sun?

There is one little flaw in the premise of this Imponderable. Even if they were tempted to fly toward the sun, they wouldn't have the opportunity—the vast majority of moths are nocturnal animals. When's the last time you saw one flitting by in daylight? Actually, though, the premise of this question isn't as absurd as it may appear. For details, see the next Imponderable.

Submitted by Joel Kuni of Kirkland, Washington. Thanks also to Bruce Kershner of Williamsville, New York.

Why are moths attracted to light? And what are they trying to do when they fly around light bulbs?

Moths, not unlike humans, spend much of their time sleeping, looking for food, and looking for mates. As we've already learned, most moths sleep during the day. Their search for dinner and procreation takes place at night. Unlike us, though, moths are not provided with maps, street signs, or neon signs flashing "EAT" to guide them to their feeding or mating sites.

Over centuries of evolution, moths have come to use starlight, and particularly moonlight, for navigation. By maintaining a constant angle in reference to the light source, the moth "knows" where to fly. Unfortunately for the insects, however, humans introduce artificial light sources that lull the moths into assuming that a light bulb is actually their natural reference point.

An English biologist, R.R. Baker, developed the hypothesis that when moths choose the artificial light source as their reference point, and try keeping a constant angle to it, the moth ends up flying around the light in ever-smaller concentric circles, until it literally settles on the light source. Baker even speculates that moths hover on or near the light because they are attempting to roost, believing that it is daytime, their regular hours. Moths have been known to burn themselves by resting on light bulbs. Others become so disoriented, they can't escape until the light is turned off or sunlight appears.

So don't assume that moths are genuinely attracted by the light. Sad as their fate may be, chances are what the moth "is trying to do" isn't to hover around a porch light—the only reason the moth is there is because it has confused a soft white bulb with the moon. The moth would far rather be cruising around looking for food and cute moths of the opposite sex.

Submitted by Charles Channell of Tucson, Arizona. Thanks also to Joyce Bergeron of Springfield, Massachusetts; Sara Anne Hoffman of Naples, Florida; Gregg Hoover of Pueblo, Colorado;

DAVID FELDMAN

Gary Moore of Denton, Texas; Bob Peterson, APO New York; and Jay Vincent Corcino of Panorama City, California.

Why do some nineteen-inch televisions say on the box: "20 IN CANADA"?

Do televisions grow when exposed to the clean air in Canada? Are Canadian rulers more generous? Do televisions bloat when transported over the border?

None of the above. What we have here are two bureaucratic mechanisms that have agreed to differ. In Canada, the size of a television is measured by determining the size of the picture tube from one corner to its opposite diagonal corner. But in the U.S., the *viewable* picture is measured: from one corner of the picture itself to its opposite along the diagonal. Those cropped corners on the monitors reduce the viewing size by approximately one inch.

The picture tube is always a little bigger than the measurable picture, which is why Canadians might think they are getting ripped off when they try to confirm the measurements of their sets. Steve Sigman, vice-president of consumer affairs for Zenith, told *Imponderables* that the television picture shrinks naturally with age. Luckily, the shrinkage materializes along the edges of the monitor. By supplying a little extra picture tube, the manufacturer insures that the consumer will get the whole image for a long time.

Submitted by Mary Mackintosh of Sacramento, California.

Why does an old person's voice sound different from a middle-aged person's?

To unravel this Imponderable, we spoke to our favorite speech pathologist, Dr. Michael J. D'Asaro, of Santa Monica, California, and Dr. Lorraine Ramig, who has published extensively on this very subject. Both of them named three characteristics of the aged voice and found physiological explanations for each:

1. The elderly voice tends to be higher in pitch. This characteristic is much more noticeable among men because hormonal changes at the onset of menopause work to lower the pitch of older women. As we age, soft tissues all over our body shrink in size. The vocal cords are no exception. As we learned in *Why Do Clocks Run Clockwise?*, there is a direct correlation between the mass of the vocal cords and pitch: The larger the vocal cords, the lower the pitch.

2. The elderly voice tends to be weaker in strength. D'Asaro points out that another characteristic of aging is increased stiffening of joints, which reduces amplitude of motion:

> In the voice mechanism, the result is reduced volume, especially if the respiratory system is also reduced in capacity. The shortness of breath reduces the motive power of the voice, the exhaled breath.

Ramig adds that the degeneration of vocal folds compounds the problem of creating enough air pressure to fuel a strong voice.

3. Many elderly people experience quavers or tremors in the voice. Again, many old people experience tremors in other muscle groups, as they age, as part of a decrease in nervous system control. Tremors in the laryngeal muscles produce the Katharine Hepburnish vocal quavers we associate with old age. Frequently, serious neurological disorders, such as Parkinson's disease, are also responsible for severe tremors in the voice.

Ramig told *Imponderables* that not every old person experiences these symptoms, so we asked her if there could be a psychological component to the stereotyped notion of the aged voice. She responded that in many cases, there very well might be. Certainly, the strong, unwavering voices of numerous elderly actors and singers betray their age. Do these young-sounding performers have different anatomical equipment than others of their age? Does their constant training and projection of their vocal equipment help maintain their laryngeal muscles in fighting trim? Or does their active lifestyle keep them from succumbing to the apathy of some of their age peers? These are the types of further Imponderables that will keep Ramig and her fellow researchers knee-deep in work for years to come.

Submitted by Herbert Kraut of Forest Hills, New York.

Why is there usually no organization in the shelving of soup cans in supermarkets?

Few grocery store experiences are as frustrating as trying to find your can of split pea soup amid a sea of red and white. Ninety percent or more of most soup sections are filled with Campbell Soup Company products, and our correspondent wondered why soup lovers weren't given a break.

Perhaps, our reader speculates, the soups could be arranged alphabetically. But then would cream of mushroom soup be filed under "C" or "M"?

No, organization by genre seems more logical. Indeed, this is what Campbell tries to do. Unfortunately, although Campbell suggests a shelving plan for retailers, grocers ultimately have "artistic control" over how and where the soup is shelved.

We had a long talk with Kevin Lowery, Campbell's manager of corporate communications, who offered us a primer on how the ideal soup section should be organized. A random check of

DAVID FELDMAN

our local supermarkets indicated that they were at least trying to follow the following golden rules:

Rule 1: *The Big 3 must go on the bottom shelf.* The Big 3, of course, are chicken noodle, cream of mushroom, and tomato soup, by far Campbell's best sellers. About 80 percent of cream of mushroom purchasers use it as an ingredient in cooking rather than as an eating soup, such as chicken noodle. Tomato soup is used by about half of all purchasers as an ingredient rather than an end product.

Lowery claims that the Big 3 are the three single fastest-moving dry (i.e., nonbeverage) items in an entire typical supermarket. The Big 3 are placed on the lowest shelves to ease the burden of grocery workers, who usually restock in case lots because of the quick turnover.

Rule 2: *New soups are stocked at eye level.* Eye level is the best placement for impulse purchasing. If you are in doubt about whether a variety is a new product, it can be identified with ease. Whenever Campbell markets a new variety of its regular "red and white" soups, the new product is given a "vignette label," with the contents pictured on the front of the can.

Rule 3: *Cooking soups should be segregated.* All these "cream of" soups should be stocked together.

Rule 4: *Eating soups are the biggest category, so poultry, beef, and vegetarian soups should be placed in separate sections.* In our experience, few markets even attempt this.

Rule 5: *Ready-to-serve and dry soups should be separated from all the others.*

Campbell's shelving plan theoretically produces the best of both worlds, allowing its soups to be organized by food type, preparation, and function, but the company's strategy is usually foiled in practice. How can you expect grocery stores to deploy sophisticated marketing schemes when they have great difficulty bagging your order?

Submitted by Louis Zelenka of Bainbridge, Georgia.

Why has Swanson stopped putting vent holes on the top of its pot pies?

The relentless rise of the microwave oven was responsible for the abolition of those vent holes. All frozen foods, including pot pies, have become popular items for the microwave.

Swanson introduced the first microwavable double-crusted pie on the market in 1989. While developing the product, Swanson determined that the pie baked better without the vent holes.

Joanne Marshall, of the Campbell Soup Company, told *Imponderables* that when a pot pie is prepared in a conventional oven, "We direct consumers to prick the top crust in order to ensure a crisp-textured pastry." One of the side benefits of eliminating the vent holes, if not the original rationale, is that it eliminates spillage of the filling during baking.

We'd add another reason. Even with the vent holes, fewer things are more capable of burning the roof of the mouth than the insides of a pot pie. Anything that allows the pot pie to "let off steam" can't be all bad.

Submitted by Randall Tada of Bellevue, Washington.

Why do TWIX cookie bars have holes in them?

Alas, while one company taketh away holes, another provideth them. We may have lost our beloved pot pie vents, but the folks at M&M/Mars have inserted them in their TWIX Bars.

We assumed that the answer to this Imponderable was that the ingredients in holes were considerably less expensive than those for the cookie bar itself. The more air in the product, the bigger the product seems, and the greater the value of the product is perceived to be (Cheerios and Ivory Soap certainly haven't suffered commercially from their airy constitutions).

DAVID FELDMAN

But it turns out we were paranoid. Hans Fiuczynski, external relations director of M&M/Mars, explains that the different ingredients in the TWIX cookie bar vary in their reaction to heat:

> As storage conditions in shops and in cupboards vary a bit, there is the chance that the topping on top of the cookie (such as caramel) would expand and create hairline cracks in the chocolate coating, thus allowing oxygen to enter the product. This would reduce the shelf life.
>
> To prevent this from happening, or at least to mitigate this effect, holes are put into the cookie so the topping can expand into the holes, internally, rather than crack the coating.

Submitted by Corrine Levering of Highland, Michigan.

What are those wavy marks on the bottom of Snickers bars?

What's with you guys? Holes in TWIXes? Wavy lines on Snickers? Don't you know you are supposed to be scarfing, not scrutinizing, candy bars?

We obtained Snickers specimens and found that, indeed, there were wavy marks on the bottom of each bar. The marks were not applied to the surface of the chocolate but were in the form of thin indentations, as if someone ran a needle through the epidermis of the chocolate on the bottom of the bar. To uphold our rigorous scientific principles, we also purchased a Milky Way bar. It, too, had markings on its bottom, but they formed a honeycomb pattern.

Despondent correspondent Jennifer Martz has been begging us to get to the bottom of this Snickers Imponderable for years, so we contacted M&M/Mars once again. We feared that we were risking overexposing Hans Fiuczynski to his growing legion of fans (but don't despair, Fiuczynski groupies—see the Letters section for Hans's bombshell announcement about

M&Ms), so we asked Marlene Marchut, external relations manager, for help.

She unlocked the mystery of the wavy lines. Marchut explained that there are two ways of preparing commercial chocolate bars: molding and enrobing. To mold a bar, the chocolatier pours liquid chocolate into a plastic or metal mold, where it conforms to the shape of the mold. Most solid chocolate bars are molded, because the process is simple and produces a bar of uniform shape and a pleasing, glossy finish. Although bars with fillings (e.g., caramel, nougat, nuts) can be produced by molding, most commercial candy bar makers use the enrobing process (M&M/Mars enrobes all of their bars except for the new solid chocolate Dove Bar). Enrobing is more complicated:

> The process begins with a filling, which is laid in a wide band on a continuous stainless steel belt. In the case of "layered" fillings, there are two bands, one on top of the other. The wide band is then sliced into long, continuous strips and eventually cut to the desired length, forming "centers." The actual enrobing process begins when these centers pass through a continuous curtain of liquid chocolate, which coats the top and sides of the bar. At the same time, a rotating chocolate-covered wheel beneath the mesh belt coats the base of the bar. To ensure an attractive, glossy, smooth coating, the chocolate must be at just the right temperature. The fully enrobed bar is then cooled and prepared for wrapping.

During enrobing, the chocolate is placed on a mesh belt rather than a solid one, so that excess liquid chocolate can be collected. In order for the chocolate to harden properly, it must pass through a cooling tunnel, where the cocoa butter crystallizes.

All fine and dandy, except for one potential problem: The liquid chocolate, once enrobed, does not transfer easily from the wire-mesh belt to the solid belt used to carry the bar through the cooling tunnel. Nothing could hold up the production line more annoyingly than splattered liquid chocolate. Mars came up with an elegant solution to clear the potential hurdle—one that coincidentally also creates the wavy lines. Marchut explains:

DAVID FELDMAN

The solid belt [that picks up the chocolate from the enrober and sends it through the cooling tunnel] has a pattern on its surface which helps us to "pull" the wet bar off the wire belt. The patterns create a rough, irregular surface, just as the chains on tires help pull the car over wet surfaces.

When the chocolate bar has hardened, it is released from the patterned, solid belt as it is transferred to be wrapped. Once again, the pattern on the belt aids in the release of the bottom surface. The physics of the pattern allow the irregular surface to more easily "snap" off the belt than a completely smooth bottom, which has a tendency to create more suction.

Not all the bars of any given brand necessarily have exactly the same pattern (although we've never seen an unwavy Snickers bar)—it depends upon the individual plant or enrobing line.

From what we can tell, the folks at M&M/Mars aren't obsessed about the aesthetic pleasure offered by the bar bottoms. They just want their chocolate to melt in your mouth, not on their assembly line.

Submitted by Jennifer Martz of West Chester, Pennsylvania. Thanks also to Marguerite MacLeod of Braintree, Massachusetts; and Stacia Leary of Saunderstown, Rhode Island.

What is one hearing when one hears a house "settling" or creaking?

We like to think of a home as a bulwark, a refuge from the vicissitudes and capriciousness of the outside world. The infrastructure of a house consists of elements like beams, pillars, and foundations, words that connote steadiness, permanence, and immutability.

But architects we talked to soon disabused us of this notion. In fact, talking to an architect about the stability of houses is a little like talking to Norman Bates about shower safety. In particular, we were startled by a book called *How Buildings Work: The Natural Order of Architecture*, written by Edward Allen, and passed on to us by James Cramer, executive vice-president/CEO of the American Institute of Architects. In one chapter, "Providing for Building Movement," Allen details the many ways in which buildings move, and if we weren't averse to

DAVID FELDMAN

clichés and bad puns, we would say that the opening rocked us to our very foundations:

> A building, even a seemingly solid, massive one, is never at rest. Its motions are usually very small ones, undetectable by the unaided eye, but most of them are of virtually irresistible force, and would tear the building to pieces if not provided for in some way.

Allen states that in an average house, all of these components can and do move:

1. The soil underneath the foundation buckles under the weight of the new foundation.
2. Materials that are put in place while wet, such as mortar, concrete, and lime plaster, shrink as they harden.
3. Some dry materials, such as gypsum plaster, tend to expand and push against adjoining elements.
4. Most lumber used in houses is not completely dry when put in place. Wet lumber shrinks.
5. Structural elements that carry weight loads, such as beams, pillars, and columns, deflect under the weight.
6. Wind and earthquakes cause more "natural" deflection.
7. Wood and concrete sag.
8. Wood, in particular, tends to expand when exposed to high humidity and contract in dry conditions. When humidity decreases noticeably, such as when heat is put on to warm a room in winter, the wood creaks noticeably.
9. Any material adjoining another material with different movement characteristics is in danger of scraping against another or moving away from the other, which can cause movement and noise.
10. All of the above movements can and do cause noise, but the most common noise associated with "settling" is the actual expansion and contraction of the building. Allen explains:

Back-and-forth movements caused by thermal and moisture effects occur constantly. A building grows measurably larger in warm weather, and smaller in cold weather. A roof, heated by the sun, grows larger in the middle of the day while the cooler walls below stay the same size. At night the roof cools and shrinks.

And so on and so on. The architect's planning compensates for the inevitable movement of these materials. Or at least we hope that it does. Otherwise, the creaking noises might lead us to the same fate as Janet Leigh's in *Psycho*.

Submitted by Joanne Walker of Ashland, Massachusetts. Thanks also to Dr. Emil S. Dickstein of Youngstown, Ohio.

Why do dogs drool? And why do some dogs drool much more than other dogs?

In order to execute a proper drool, a dog must have two weapons at its disposal: a lot of saliva and a lot of lip. Getting a dog to salivate is as easy as exposing it to food—the smell of it, the taste of it, the anticipation of it, the consumption of it—and, as Pavlov proved, to any conditioned reflexes associated with feeding.

Drooling is simply the inability of a dog to dam the flood of saliva it manufactures. Salivation serves a useful function, helping the dog to swallow, and to lubricate the alimentary canal, the passageway from the mouth all the way through the esophagus and stomach that food must travel through before it is excreted. Individual dogs vary in their capacity to manufacture saliva, but some breeds manage to contain all saliva flow under normal conditions.

The dog experts we consulted agreed that some breeds drool more than others. Dogs with loose lips (and we're not talking about dogs who gossip too much), such as Saint Bernards, mastiffs, bloodhounds, and boxers, are prodigious droolers. The hanging parts of these dogs' lips, called flews, are usually the tell-tale sign of droolers. Dog breeder Fred Lanting reminded us of the old World War II slogan "Loose flews sink ships." Lanting says that the pushed-in faces of some breeds, such as bulldogs, create loose flews. He adds:

DAVID FELDMAN

Other breeds may drool because of poor breeding. . . . The looser and longer the lips, the more the loss of saliva outside rather than inside the throat.

Anatomist Robert Habel, of Cornell University's College of Veterinary Medicine, wrote *Imponderables* that medical problems can also cause excess drooling. Many drugs "artificially" stimulate salivation. Rabies can cause nerve damage leading to paralysis of the throat and tongue that prevents dogs from swallowing.

Habel reports that his own coonhound "slobbers foam when he is running a trail with his nose to the ground. I think that is the effect of gravity." He added: "Did you see the movie *Turner & Hooch?* You should, before you write about drooling."

Indeed. If you want a graduate course in drooling, drop this book and run to your local video store. We've heard they are doing a sequel to *Turner & Hooch.* It's called *Flews 2.*

Submitted by Catherine Price of New York, New York.

Why do dogs eat cat feces? Why do they sometimes eat their own feces?

And you thought the chapter about drooling was disgusting? Read on.

The nasty habit of eating feces is called "coprophagia" (wasn't that a Stephen King title?). Many puppies have a preoccupation with their own or their, pardon the expression, littermates', feces. But many canines continue to expand their culinary horizons as they get older, and experiment with the feces of other animals. Cat feces tend to be most easily available to domestic dogs, and more readily apparent to dog owners, but dogs won't stop with cat litter.

Why do dogs continue to eat food that, at best, gives them

bad breath, and at worst, leads to parasites and illnesses? Sometimes, undigested food can be found in animal stools. With their keen sense of smell, dogs can spot these "opportunities."

But more often, coprophagia is a symptom of a poor diet or nutritional deficiency. Carol Barfield, an official of the United Animal Owners Association, wrote *Imponderables* that her female Keeshond, Mattie, used to "clean up the cat litter box at any opportunity." After Barfield drastically upgraded Mattie's diet, the feces fetish disappeared almost immediately. Barfield is delighted that now she removes litter, rather than Mattie, from her cat litter box.

Our favorite lecturer on canine topics, Fred Lanting, sent us a delightful letter on the subject of coprophagia. Although he, too, mentioned nutritional deficiencies as an explanation for this habit, he has a simpler explanation for dogs' behavior:

> Dogs eat cat feces simply because they like the taste. Many animals eat (or at least sample) feces. They also lick urine markings to tell them something about the animal they are "researching," but the eating of feces is more than territorial data-gathering. It's also a gourmet delicacy—they think. Can you imagine a dog not liking ripe olives or oysters and wondering about that dumb human who's eating bitter berries and a mollusk that looks like snot? Sounds like a Gary Larson "Far Side" anthropomorphism, doesn't it?
>
> Dogs also eat the traces (droppings) of other species. They are positively *addicted* to rabbit "pellets," *love* deer "nuggets," horse "road apples," etc. On the other hand, they don't come more than a millimeter close to possum, goose, and many other droppings. They will pass up fox feces, as a rule.

Why do they eat their own feces? Or the feces of other dogs? Lanting continues:

> If they eat dog feces, it's due to a number of possible reasons: boredom; pancreatic insufficiency; or temperamental or hormonal problems in the dropper or droppee, depending on the details.
>
> Wild canids (chromosomally compatible with domestic dogs) also eat feces of other species. Sparrows feast on the undigested grain in horse feces. Dung beetles' only *raison d'être* is feasting

DAVID FELDMAN

on feces. Was it Cole Porter who said, "Birds do it, worms do it, dogs and fish and maybe cats do it . . ."? I doubt if anyone has made a study of the catholicity of coprophagy. Usually, pet owners want to know how to *stop* it, not who else is doing it.

Submitted by Nadia Norris of Saint Paul, Indiana. Thanks also to Vince Tassinari of Van Nuys, California.

How do they keep the water in water towers from freezing in the wintertime?

We were on the road promoting our last tome, *Do Penguins Have Knees?*, and radio host Mike Rosen was asking about one of the Imponderables in the book: Why are water towers built so high? We provided our concise, prefabricated answer, sounding, we hoped, as if the study of water towers was one of our driving passions in life.

When it came time to answer phone-in questions, and a caller asked about how they kept the water in towers from freezing, we replied with a resounding "Duh."

Callers soon pounced in with different theories. One caller was sure that there were heating elements in the water tower. Another swore that often water did freeze inside the tower. A third caller claimed that the constant movement of the water inside the tower kept it from freezing.

Time to contact our water tower sources again. Who would

DAVID FELDMAN

have ever thought there would be an Imponderable about water towers in successive books?

It turns out there isn't a single, simple answer to this Imponderable, but most of the time the third caller got it right. SUNY Professor Peter Black, affiliated with the American Water Resources Association, told *Imponderables* that in all but sparsely populated agricultural areas, water inside the tower is moving all the time. He added that wood is a good insulator, and that freezing is rarely a problem.

Thomas M. Laronge, whose Thomas M. Laronge, Inc., consults on water treatment and other environmental issues, isn't quite as sanguine. He points out that water usage tends to be lower in winter than in summer, especially in agricultural areas, and that evaporation consumption is much lower. If the demand is low enough so that water isn't constantly flowing within the tower, the water can easily freeze.

Many water towers are equipped with a cathodic protection system, designed to counteract corrosion. The natural corrosion tends to make the water inside the tower flow in one direction; the cathodic protection system acts as a bucking mechanism to send the current flow in the opposite direction. A byproduct of this system is the constant movement of water, and a cessation of any tendency toward freezing.

Even the first caller wasn't entirely wrong. Thomas Laronge says that in rare instances, in small water systems, water towers may be insulated and/or heated by a jacketing system, in which warm water flows on the outside of the jacket and cool water flows on the inside of the jacket to prevent freezing.

Even if the water in the tower does freeze, service may continue without any problems at all. Laronge explains:

> The density of water is greater than the density of ice. Therefore, if an ice plug forms, it will tend to form on the top of the water surface. Water can still flow through the bottom of the tower. Only the volume is restricted.
>
> Another reason why water towers may not freeze completely is that sometimes an insulating layer of ice forms within the tower.

The ice actually transfers heat slower than does the metal of the tower. Therefore, the ice barrier actually reduces the tendency for water towers to freeze.

Submitted by an anonymous caller on the Mike Rosen Show, KOA-AM, in Denver, Colorado.

Why do quarterbacks call the snap with the exclamation "hut"?

Put men in a uniform. Give them a helmet. And they all start speaking alike. At least, that's what all of our football sources claimed. Pat Harmon, historian at the College Football Hall of Fame, was typical:

> In Army drills, the drill sergeant counts off: "Hut-2-3-4." He repeats "Hut-2-3-4" until the men get in right. Football language has copied the drill sergeant.

We'll have to believe our football authorities, since no evidence exists that the "hut" barked by quarterbacks has anything to do with little thatched houses.

In fact, "hut" wasn't always used as the signal. Joe Horrigan, of the Pro Football Hall of Fame, sent us a photocopy of a section of the 1921 *Spalding's How to Play Football* manual that indicates that perhaps we aren't as hip as our forbears:

> When shift formations are tried, the quarter-back should give his signal when the men are in their original places. Then after calling the signal [he] can use the word "hip" for the first shift and then repeat for the players to take up their new positions on the line of scrimmage.

Our guess is that the only important virtue of "hut" is that it contains one syllable.

Submitted by Paul Ruggiero of Blacksburg, Virginia.

Why are elections in the United States held on the first Tuesday after the first Monday in November rather than on the first Tuesday in November?

We had almost given up trying to answer this Imponderable when we contacted Professor Robert J. Dinkin, of California State University, Fresno, who specializes in the history of U.S. elections. Although Dinkin says he has never seen anything written on this subject, he does have an interesting conjecture.

Hallowmas, also known as All Saints' Day, was celebrated in most locales on November 1. Although candy companies have now insured that Hallow's Eve is the bigger holiday, All Saints' Day was a major celebration in the past. Therefore, as Dinkin speculates: "By making elections on the first Tuesday after the first Monday, no such scheduling conflict could occur." We could only find one other conjecture, from Megan Gillispie, of the League of Women Voters, who claims that the contorted "first Tuesday after the first Monday" language was simply an attempt to prevent elections from landing on the first day of the month "because merchants were busy closing their accounting books and courthouses were often busy with beginning of the month business."

No one seems able to find any primary sources to bolster their arguments. Can any of our enterprising readers?

Submitted by Barry Gluck of Rio de Janeiro, Brazil. Thanks also to Lynda Frank of Omaha, Nebraska.

How do dehumidifiers sense the humidity level in the air and "know" when to shut off automatically?

Not all dehumidifiers shut off automatically. But most that do work like this: Ambient air is drawn into a chamber or pipe via a fan. The outside air passes over a sensor in the humidistat, the device that determines whether or not the air exceeds the humidity you've set as your standard. If the air meets with your requirements, the air will pass through. But if the air in the room exceeds your desired humidity level, the air is heated by a hot-air dryer (or, less frequently, a desiccant chamber) before it is sent back into the room.

How does the humidistat determine the humidity of the ambient air? J. C. Laverick, technical director of dehumidifier manufacturer Ebac Ltd., explains:

> At the heart of the humidistat [behind the console] is a sensing element in the shape of an endless belt made from Nylon 6. This material has the characteristic of changing length in proportion to the amount of moisture it contains. At higher humidity levels its length expands, and it contracts at lower humidity levels. This change of length is converted into the force required to operate the [snap-action] microswitch and hence the dehumidifier.

Submitted by Alan Wright of Mansfield Center, Connecticut.

What do you call that little groove in the center of our upper lips?

Sorry, we can't answer this question. It is hardly an Imponderable, since it has been answered in scores of trivia books. Heck, this question has been posed by so many stand-up comedians on bad cable television shows, we refuse to answer on principle.

Submitted by too many readers.

DAVID FELDMAN

What is the purpose of the little indentation in the center of our upper lips?

If you rephrase your Imponderable in the form of a proper question, you can weasel just about anything out of us. How can we write about the indentation without mentioning its name? OK guys . . . it's called the *philtrum*. You'll be proud to know that we have a groove running down our upper lip for absolutely no good reason, as William P. Jollie, professor and chairman of anatomy at the Medical College of Virginia, explains:

> The indentation in the center of our upper lip is a groove, or raphe, that forms embryonically by merging paired right and left processes that make up our upper jaw. It has no function, just as many such midline merger marks, or raphes, have no function. We have quite a few merger-lines on our bodies: a raphe down the upper surface of our tongues; a grooved notch under the point of our chins; and a raphe in the midline of our palates. There are also several in the genital area, both male and female.
>
> Anatomically, the raphe on our upper lip is called the *philtrum*, an interesting word derived from the Greek word *philter*, which even in English means a love potion. I confess I don't see a connection, but many anatomical terms are peculiar in origin, if not downright funny.

Speaking of funny, it is our earnest hope that after the information in this chapter is disseminated, every stand-up comedian, standing before the inevitable brick wall, will stop doing routines about philtrums. Enough is enough.

Submitted by Bruce Hyman of Short Hills, New Jersey. Thanks also to three-year-old Michael Joshua Lim of Livonia, Michigan.

What happens to an ant that gets separated from its colony? Does it try to relocate the colony? Can it survive if it can't find the colony?

As we all learned in elementary school, ants are social animals, but their organization doesn't just provide them with buddies—it furnishes them with the food and protection they need to survive in a hostile environment.

All the experts we consulted indicated that an isolated worker ant, left to its own devices, would likely die a week or two before its normal three-week lifespan. And it would probably spend that foreshortened time wandering around, confused, looking for its colony.

Ants help each other trace the path between food sources and the colony by laying down chemical trails called pheromones. Our hypothetical solitary ant might try following pheromone trails it encounters, hoping they will lead it back home. Worker ants in a given colony are all the daughters of the original queen and can't simply apply for admission to a new colony.

Three dangers, in particular, imperil a lost ant. The first, and most obvious, is a lack of food. Ants are natural foragers but are used to receiving cues from other ants about where to search for food. A single ant would not have the capacity to store enough food to survive for long. Furthermore, ants don't always eat substances in the form they are gathered. Cincinnati naturalist Kathy Biel-Morgan provided us with the example of the leaf-cutter ant. The leaf-cutter ant finds plants and brings leaves back to the nest, where the material is ground up and used in the colony's fungus garden. The ants then eat the fruiting body of the fungus. Without the organizational assistance of the colony, a leaf does nothing to sate the appetite of a leaf-cutter ant.

The second danger is cold. Ants are ectotherms, animals that need heat but are unable to generate it themselves. When it is cold, ants in colonies will seek the protective covering of the nest. If left to its own devices, a deserted ant would probably try to find a rock or the crack of a sidewalk to use as cover, which

DAVID FELDMAN

may or may not be enough protection to keep it from freezing.

The third problem our lonesome ant would encounter is nasty creatures that think of the ant as their dinner fare. Collectively, ants help protect one another. Alone, an ant must fend off a variety of predators, including other ants. Biel-Morgan compared the vulnerability of the ant, on its own, to a single tourist in New York City. And that is vulnerable, indeed.

Submitted by Cary Hillman of Kokomo, Indiana.

Why is the color purple associated with royalty?

Although pagans once believed that purple dye was the creation of Satan, we actually have the Phoenicians to thank for the association of purple with royalty. Somehow, and we always wonder how anyone ever stumbles upon this sort of stuff, an anonymous Phoenician discovered that the spiny shell of the murex sea snail yielded a purple substance perfectly suited as a dye base. Phoenicians, the greatest traders and businessmen of the ancient world, soon developed purple cloth as one of their most lucrative trading commodities.

Since purple cloth was more expensive than other hues, only aristocrats could afford to wear it. But the Romans codified the practice, turning the color of clothing into a status symbol. Only the royal family itself could wear all-purple garments. Lesser aristocrats wore togas with purple stripes or borders to designate their rank—the more purple on the clothing, the higher the status.

The original "royal purple" was a different color than what we call purple today. It was a dark wine-red, with more red than blue. Many written accounts liken the color to blood. Indeed, the Phoenician dye was prized because it symbolized the unity, strength, and bonding of blood ties, and the continuity of royal families based on bloodlines. The spiritual quality supposedly imparted by the purple color is suggested by its Roman root, *purpureus* ("very, very holy").

The association of purple with royalty crossed many cultures and centuries. Greek legend explained royal purple as the color of Athena's goatskin dyed red. Kings in Babylonia wore a "lanbussu" robe of the same color. Mark's Gospel says that Jesus' robe was purple (although Matthew describes it as scarlet). In many churches, purple became the liturgical color during Lent, except for Good Friday. Consistently, in the succeeding centuries, the color purple was always identified with blood, as late as the time of Shakespeare, for the Bard himself referred to the "purpled hands" of Caesar's assassins, "stained with the most noble blood of all the world."

Curiously, marketing research indicates that today, purple is one of the least popular colors, which helps explain why it is so seldom used in packaging. Is the current aversion to purple stirred by a rejection of the patrician origins of the color, its close approximation to the color of blood, or a rejection of our contemporary purple royalty, Prince?

Submitted by Raymond Graunke of Huntersville, North Carolina. Thanks also to Sharon M. Burke of Los Altos, California; and Brian Dunne of Indianapolis, Indiana.

Was Ben Gay?

We don't have the slightest idea. But we do know how the product got its name.

Ben-Gay was created by a French pharmacist, whose name was, conveniently enough, Dr. Ben Gué. He introduced his product in France in 1898, and called it *Baume Gué* (*baume* means "balm" *en français*).

When the analgesic was launched in the United States, it was decided that the unwashed masses of North America couldn't contend with a French word like *baume* or pronounce

DAVID FELDMAN

one of those nasty accent *acutes.* So marketers settled on naming their product after an Anglicization of its creator's name.

Submitted by Linda Atwell of Matthews, North Carolina.

Why are haystacks increasingly round rather than rectangular?

Everything old is new again. Round stacks were the fashion in the early twentieth century, as Oakley M. Ray, president of the American Feed Industry Association, explains:

> Fifty to one hundred years ago, it was the usual practice for the wheat farmer to "thresh" wheat (separate the grain from the straw). The threshing machine discharges the straw in one location for a given field so that the result was normally a round stack of straw.
>
> Some years later, the hay baler was invented, which compressed either hay or straw into a much smaller space, much as a household trash compactor does in many houses today. The bales were commonly three feet or so in length, perhaps eighteen inches wide, and perhaps eighteen inches high. They were held together by two wires or two strong pieces of twine. Each bale would weigh fifty to one hundred pounds, with the baler set in such a manner that all of the bales in a given field were essentially the same size.

Obviously, the uniform, rectangular shape made it easier to stack rectangular bales neatly and efficiently, first lengthwise in the wagons used to pick up the stacks, and then later in boxlike fashion in warehouses or barns.

But in the last fifteen to twenty years, "swathers" have gained popularity. These machines feature a sickle in front that cuts the hay and a belt that dumps the fodder in nice neat rows —a separate machine rolls it up—where it is left out in the sun to dry. The swather produces "wind-rowed" hay, which rarely blows away, a great advantage, considering the fact that wet hay gets moldy if moist. The ability to allow hay to cure before baling reduces spoilage.

Round bales are much larger than square ones, often about a thousand pounds, ten to twenty times heavier than rectangular bales, so they must be picked up by machine. Still, there are economies of scale achieved by assembling larger units of hay, and mechanically, there are fewer technical problems—there are fewer moving parts in the machinery that produces round bales. Kendell Keith, of the National Grain and Feed Association, told *Imponderables* that the wire and twine used to secure each bale of rectangular hay and the labor involved in packing and securing it were costlier than those for producing round haystacks.

Perhaps the most important advantage of "round hay" is that it weathers better than its compressed rectangular counterpart, as Gary Smith, of the University of Maryland's Agricultural Engineering department explains:

> The round bales shed the weather better. They reduce the need for storage space indoors, depending on what part of the country you are in, they can be left outdoors with minimum loss. Out West there is virtually no loss. In Maryland, there is about a 15% loss. This is cheaper than having to build storage for rectangular bales.

Submitted by Rosemary Arseneault of Halifax, Nova Scotia.

DAVID FELDMAN

What are the little white particles found on the bottom half of English muffins?

The particles are farina. Farina helps add to the taste of the product, but the main function of farina particles, and the reason why they are placed only on the bottom half of the muffin, is to prevent the ball of dough from sticking to the oven plate during cooking.

Submitted by Jessica Ahearne of Madawaska, Maine.

How do they assemble tall cranes without using another crane?

George O. Headrick, director of public relations and administrative services at the Construction Industry Manufacturers Association, was kind enough to direct us to several manufacturers of cranes. While they were uniformly generous in sharing their knowledge of how cranes are erected, they tended to provide us not with more than we wanted to know but a great deal more than we were capable of understanding. So we are indebted for the following explanation to the former secretary-treasurer of the Construction Writers Association, E.E. Halmos, Jr., who is now majordomo of Information Research Group, an editorial consulting group in Poolesville, Maryland:

> The tall cranes, which often carry booms (known to the trade as "sticks") of 120 feet or more, are assembled on the ground, at the construction site. If you'll notice, most of the tall booms are built as steel lattice-work structures, and are thus comparatively lightweight. Usually, the machine arrives on the scene on its own, carrying only the base stub of the boom.
>
> The sections for the full length of the boom usually arrive separately, via trailer-truck. At site, the stub of the boom is lowered to a horizontal position, and the sections of the finished boom laid out on the ground, attached together (much like a child's erector set), then mounted on the stub, and raised into position by cables attached to the crane body.

Likewise, extensions can be added when needed by laying the boom on the ground.

The use of these conventional rigs has been steadily declining, however, in favor of the "tower crane." These are the cranes that sit in the middle of a site and can be raised after they have been erected. The center column on which the control cab and the moving "head" sit is built up to three or four stories. As the building rises around the crane, added height is built onto the center column, and the whole top assembly is "jumped" upward.

Halmos reports that tower cranes have largely eliminated the need for elevators (known as "skips") and the lifting of loads from the ground by mobile cranes. "The tower crane operator can see not only what he's picking up, but can spot the load

DAVID FELDMAN

almost anywhere on the job, without a lot of elaborate signaling."

Submitted by Laura Laesecke of San Francisco, California. Thanks also to Paula Chaffee of Utica, Michigan; Lawrence Walters of Gurnee, Illinois; James Gleason of Collegeville, Pennsylvania; and Robert Williams of Brooklyn, New York.

What is "single-needle" stitching, and why do we have to pay more for shirts that feature it?

You'd think that at fifty dollars or more a pop, shirtmakers could afford another needle or two. Actually, they can.

"Regular" shirts are sewn with one needle working on one side of a seam and another needle sewing the other side. According to clothing expert G. Bruce Boyer, this method is cheaper and faster but not as effective because "Seams sewn with two needles simultaneously tend to pucker. Single-needle stitching produces flatter seams."

Submitted by Donald Marti, Jr., of New York, New York.

KIDS! HOW YOUR **DOG** CAN GET YOU A **COOKIE** BETWEEN MEALS!

Ⓐ TELL GRANPOP THAT FIDO WANTS A BELLY SCRATCH
Ⓑ FIDO'S LEG TWITCHES AND PULLS THE STRING
Ⓒ STRING OPENS UP THE JACK-IN-THE-BOX
Ⓓ JACK FLIES OUT, KNOCKING WEIGHT OFF SHELF
Ⓔ WEIGHT FALLS DOWN ON SEESAW HOLDING COOKIE JAR
Ⓕ SEESAW SEESAWS, COOKIE FLIES UP INTO YOUR MOUTH!
IT'S EASY!

Why do dogs wiggle their rear legs when scratched on their belly or chest?

Maybe there is a Labrador retriever out there writing a book of canine Imponderables, trying to answer the mystery: Why do humans kick their legs up when you tap the area below their kneecaps? The leg wiggling of dogs is called the scratch reflex, the doggy equivalent of our involuntary knee-jerk reflex (or, as it is known to doctors, patellar reflex).

Anatomist Robert E. Habel, of Cornell University's College of Veterinary Medicine, wrote *Imponderables* that the scratch reflex allows veterinarians to diagnose neurological problems in dogs:

> Because the same spinal nerves pass all the way down to the midline of the chest and abdomen, you can stimulate the scratch reflex anywhere from the saddle region to the ventral midline. You can test the sensory function of many spinal nerves and the motor function of the nerves to the hind limb (they don't wiggle

their forelimbs). If the dog moves the hind limb, it means the spinal cord is not severed between the origin of the nerve stimulated and the origins of the lumbar through first sacral nerves, but the cord may be injured above the level stimulated.

A dog is not necessarily injured if it doesn't exhibit the scratch reflex. In fact, Dr. Habel reports that his hound doesn't respond at all.

What function does the scratch reflex serve? Nobody knows for sure, but that doesn't stop dog experts from theorizing. Breeder and lecturer Fred Lanting believes that the wiggling might be a "feeble or partial attempt" to reach the area where you are scratching. Just as scratching ourselves sometimes causes the itch to migrate to other parts of the body, Lanting believes that scratching a dog may cause itchiness in other regions.

Dog expert and biology instructor Jeanette Hayhurst advances an even more fascinating theory, which is that the scratch reflex might help dogs survive. The movement of the back legs during the scratch reflex resembles the frantic movements of a puppy learning to swim. The scratch reflex might be an instinctive reaction to pressure on the abdomen, the method nature provides for a puppy to survive when thrown into the water. Newborn pups also need to pump their back legs in order to crawl to reach their mother's teat.

We'd like to think that our human knee-jerk reflex might also have a practical purpose, but we'll leave it to the dogs to solve this particular mystery.

Submitted by Shane Ellis of Mammoth Lakes, California.
Thanks also to Kurt Perschnick of Palatka, Florida; Sonya Landholm of Boone, North Carolina; Alina Carmichael and Pat Kirkland of Lake St. Louis, Missouri; Sherry-Lynn Jamieson of Surrey, British Columbia; Sofi Nelson of Menomonie, Wisconsin; and Scott Wolber of Delmont, Pennsylvania.

Whilst strolling alone in a garden, Robert quietly pulls out his notebook.

SUCH A CHARMING VERSE! AND ~ WHO'S TO KNOW ?!

OOOOH!

GROW OLD WITH / THE BEST / YET TO BE

Why do so many sundials have Robert Browning's lines "Grow old along with me! The best is yet to be" inscribed on them?

Although not every sundial has a motto on it, most do; the tradition dates from antiquity. None of the many sundial makers and books about sundials we consulted could explain the reason for putting the motto on the sundial in the first place. Timothy Lynch, president of the sundial maker Kenneth Lynch & Sons, speculates that it was originally put there "for the personal gratification of either the maker or the receiver."

The sundial makers we spoke to have standard mottoes or will custom-inscribe a customer's personalized motto. They unanimously agreed with Lee Brown, a designer at Whitehall Products, who told *Imponderables* that virtually all mottoes refer to the passage of time.

Why are Browning's lines the most popular? (Their only competitor in popularity is *Tempus Fugit*—"time flies"—a pithier if less poetic motto.) Ben Brewster, president of Colonial Brass, the largest manufacturer of sundials in the United States, has a simple theory with which the other sources agreed: Most quotations about time are depressing, or at least downbeat. A look at some of the suggested inscriptions used by Colonial Brass will give you the idea:

> "Time takes all but memories."
> "Time waits for no man."
> "You ask the hour, meanwhile you see it fly."
> "Watch for ye know not the hour."
> "Time passeth and speaketh not."

Not the kind of words to send your losing football team bursting out of the locker room in renewed spirits, are they? But Browning's words are reassuring, making old age seem secure and downright romantic.

In her book *Sun-Dials and Roses of Yesterday*, Alice Morse writes:

> One almost unvarying characteristic of the sun-dial motto might be noted—its solemnity. A few are jocose, a few are cheerful, nearly all are solemn, many are sad, even gloomy. They teach no light lesson of life, but a regard of the passing of every day, every hour, as a serious thing.

Morse's book was written in 1922, when most mottoes were biblical quotations. (Her favorite was this far-from-upbeat citation from Chronicles: "Our days on earth are as a shadow, and there is none abiding.")

For better or worse, we live in a society that has a relentless need to find optimism in any situation. Perhaps our fondness for the Browning quote shows a deep-seated psychological need to evade not only death but some of the hardships of old age. After all, better to spout platitudes than to confront the pain in this actual motto sent to us by Brewster, who remarked that its message was a little less uplifting than Browning's bromide:

> What Cain did to Abel
> Brutus to Caesar was quick.
> What Kip B. and Esther's sister

Edith did to Esther and me
Was Torture—slow and fatal
May God forgive them.

Submitted by Sheryl Aumack of Newport Beach, California.

For a whole collection of sundial mottoes, see *The Book of Sun-Dials* by Mrs. Alfred Gatty.

Why do babies sleep so much? Why do they sleep so much more soundly than adults or older children?

This is Mother Nature's way of preserving the sanity of parents.

And there's an alternative, less cosmic, explanation. Dr. David Hopper, president of the American Academy of Somnology, told *Imponderables* that sleep is crucial to the brain development of infants. After birth, the average infant spends sixteen to eighteen hours asleep per day. Up to 60 percent of that time is spent in REM (rapid eye movement) sleep, more than twice the percentage of adults. What is the significance of their greater proportion of REM sleep? Dr. Hopper explains:

> REM sleep is the stage of sleep that dreams are associated with. Brain wave activity is very active during this stage and closely resembles an awake state. It is sometimes called paradoxical sleep because the brain is very active as if awake but the individual is deeply asleep. By one year of age, the brains of babies are sufficiently developed to begin cycling of four distinct NREM (non-rapid eye movement) sleep stages with REM sleep.

Although sleep researchers still do not understand precisely how this works, REM sleep seems crucial to the development of the central nervous system of infants. The NREM "quiet sleep" is far from a waste of time, though, for the pituitary hormones, crucial for growth, are released during this phase of sleep.

Parents will be glad to inform anyone willing to listen that their babies don't always sleep soundly, yet the cliché persists

DAVID FELDMAN

that anyone who can withstand interference from sound or light while snoozing is sleeping "like a baby." The solution to this paradox lies in the unique sleep cycle of newborns. The reason why babies sleep like a log much of the time, as we learned above, is because they are in REM sleep 50 to 60 percent of the time. It can be difficult to rouse an infant during REM sleep; yet the same baby might awaken quite easily when in any stage of NREM sleep.

The proportion of REM to NREM sleep gradually decreases during the first year of life, and babies sleep for longer periods at a stretch. Still, they may be fussier and wake up more easily, especially if they are being weaned from breast milk, which studies show truly does help babies "sleep like a baby."

Submitted by Father Gregory A. Battafarano of Niagara Falls, New York.

What causes the film that forms on the top of the chocolate pudding I cook? Does this film appear on any kind of pudding?

We went straight to the makers of Jell-O brand pudding. The General Foods Response Center replied:

> When pudding has been heated and then allowed to cool while directly exposed to air, the starch on the surface releases water. This evaporation hardens the texture of the top and causes a film to form on *any* pudding that requires cooking. Incidentally, if plastic wrap is placed directly on the surface of the pudding, while cooling, it prevents the water vapor from escaping and the film from forming.

General food researcher Noel Anderson told *Imponderables* that pudding film is actually a "starch gel," a combination of sugar and starch that forms a moisture barrier that will not break down unless subjected to intense heat.

Submitted by Linda Wiley of Berlin, New Jersey.

Why does milk obtain a skin when heated, while thicker liquids, like gravy, lose their skin when heated?

Proteins and starch react differently to heat. When heated, the protein in milk coagulates; the fat globules no longer can be suspended in water and, being lighter than water, float to the top. Bruce V. Snow, a dairy consultant, told us that the fat globules "adhere and form a surface skin when the liquid ceases to boil or simmer heavily."

But when gravy is heated, the starch, which has formed the skin in the first place, breaks down. Since starch is more soluble than protein, the result is that the ex-skin is reabsorbed into the rest of the gravy. The same process can be seen when soup is reheated after a skin has "grown" in the refrigerator.

Submitted by Beth Oakley of Ishpeming, Michigan.

DAVID FELDMAN

Why do the tags on the left side of the right back pocket of Levi's jeans come in different colors? What is the code?

If you haven't noticed the different colors on the tags on the back pockets of Levi's jeans, you just haven't been looking at enough rear ends lately, or else it's time for that eye check-up you've been avoiding for the last five years or so. Actually, the folks at Levi Strauss & Co. call them "tabs," not tags.

Lynn Downey, the company historian, says that tabs were originally created to make Levi's stand out from the competition. Tabs were the brainchild of an in-house advertising manager in 1936, and have been on all Levi brand jeans ever since. The design of the tabs and their position on the jeans are registered trademarks of Levi Strauss & Co.

There are now four different colored tabs (red, orange, silver, and cream) and they do indeed signify something—the type of construction used to manufacture the jeans. Although the consumer may not be aware of it, Levi Strauss spokesperson Jill Novack told *Imponderables* that many stores place all of the red-tab Levi jeans together, the orange together, etc. Here, in descending order of sales, are the four different colored tabs and what they mean:

1. *Red.* Red-tab Levi's feature the classic, detailed construction: five high-sloped pockets; six rivets in the front pocket; single-needle work on the top stitching; double stitching on the back pocket, which flares slightly. All 501s have red labels, but so do many other popular styles: 505, 506, 509, 517, 550, 583, 584, etc.

2. *Orange.* Orange-tabs often look superficially like their red-tab counterparts. In fact, some lines, such as the 505 and 550, have both red- and orange-tab versions. But orange-tab jeans have slightly less expensive finishing and tend to cost a few dollars less than red-tab Levi's. Here's why: Orange-tabs have five rather than six rivets in front; more gradually sloping pockets; double-needle rather than single-needle work on the top stitching; and their pockets are simpler, with the stitching on the back pockets parallel rather than flared. Most of the 500 series not named above have orange tabs.

3. *Silver.* Levi's "fashion forward" contemporary jeans line features silver tabs. These jeans are identified by names rather than numbers, and are often available only on a seasonal basis. Baggy jeans, anti-fit, and sport jeans are all placed in the silver line. The silver line tends to contain the most expensive Levi jeans.

4. *Cream or Natural.* The rarest of the tabs is the so-called natural tab, with a cream color that is the untreated natural color of the tab fabric, with brown lettering. The natural tab can be found only on Levi's "Naturals" line, jeans that are, appropriately enough, naturally colored. Levi Strauss spokesperson Brad Williams told us that Naturals are softer to the touch than all their other jeans because they are the only ones that contain no dye. For technical reasons, starch must be used when applying dyes to jeans. As the consumer continues to wash most jeans, the starch gradually is eliminated from the garment. This lessening of the starch content is the reason why jeans get more comfortable after repeated washings.

Or course, *we* knew nothing about this color coding before we started researching this Imponderable. So the next time we are in the market for 501's, we will undoubtedly become para-lyzed with self-consciousness. Do we buy the red-tabs and prove that we are fashion snobs of the worst order, demanding con-struction details that we never noticed in the first place? Or do we try orange-tabs, and advertise to the rest of the world how cheap we are?

Submitted by Cathy Pearce and Heather McCausland of Lakeland, Florida.

How did Levi's 501 jeans get their number?

Levi Strauss (yes, there *was* a real Levi Strauss) was a dry goods merchant in California and sold a wide range of products. The original Levi jean was the 501, and this number was simply its arbitrary stock number, according to Levi Strauss & Co. spokes-person Brad Williams.

Strauss disliked applying the word "jeans" to his garment, so he promoted the 501 as "waist-high overalls." Just think, if his company kept that name into the 1970s, chances are that high-fashion designers like Gloria Vanderbilt and Calvin Klein wouldn't have foisted "designer waist-high overalls" on a gulli-ble public at triple the prices of Mr. Strauss.

Submitted by Sharon Michele Burke of Los Altos, California. Thanks also to John Hyatt of Boise, Idaho.

Why do the bricks used in constructing houses come with three holes in them?

We have the feeling that when Lionel Richie and the Commo-dores sang "Brick House," this wasn't what they had in mind. In fact, we didn't even know there were holes in bricks until reader Sandra Sandoval brought this to our attention.

When we get a brick Imponderable, we know where to head —to the Brick Institute of America and its director of engineering and research, J. Gregg Borchelt. He informed us that these holes are known to brickophiles as "cores," and that there can be zero to twelve cores in a "unit," or individual brick. The main reason for the cores, according to Borchelt,

> is to improve the drying and firing process of the unit. The clay dries more easily and reaches a more uniform firing temperature with the cores present. Tests were conducted to show that the presence of cores does not reduce the overall strength of the brick.

But the cores serve many other purposes. Construction writer and consultant E.E. Halmos, Jr., of Poolesville, Maryland, told *Imponderables* that one of the main benefits of cores is that they provide a way for the mortar to penetrate the brick itself,

> thus making a better bond between layers (or courses) of brick, without the need for metal ties or other devices. A brick wall derives virtually no strength from the mortar—which is only to tie courses together. That's why the so-called Flemish or Belgian bonds were developed, to tie the outer and inner columns of brick (called "wythes") together in early construction—resulting in the interesting patterns you see in Williamsburg and older structures in other cities. The little holes provide a better vertical bond between the bricks.

Borchelt enumerated other advantages of cores: They lower the weight of the bricks without sacrificing strength; they are a receptacle for steel reinforcement, if needed; they make it easier to break units into brick bats; and they can aid in lifting large units. Bet you never guessed three holes could be so talented.

Submitted by Sandra Sandoval of San Antonio, Texas.

DAVID FELDMAN

Why do dogs eat standing up, while cats often eat sitting down?

No dog or cat would volunteer to answer this Imponderable, so we were forced to consult human experts. All agreed that the answer goes back to the ancestors of our pets, who lived in the wild.

Our most interesting response came from Dr. James Vondruska, research veterinarian and senior developmental scientist for pet food giant Quaker Oats Company. Vondruska reminds us that dogs are by nature pack animals. In the wild, they hunted in packs. In homes, they adopt the household as their pack and their owners as dominant members:

> In their prehistoric years, dogs lived with others of their type, and hunted or scavenged for food together. Many of their type, such as the African Cape Hunting Dog and the hyenas, still do. Scavenging dogs must compete with the pack members for their food, which often leads to fighting. For this reason, dogs will eat standing up, so that they can better protect their food. Even though they usually don't have to fight over their food anymore, the behavior persists in modern dogs.

Vondruska contrasts the dog's behavior in the wild with that of our house cat's ancestors. Most cats, even in the wild, are solitary creatures, and are hunters rather than scavengers. Susie Page, of the American Cat Association, compares the eating posture of cats to that of other hunting predators who "hunch" over their prey while devouring it.

With the exception of African lions, who live in prides, cats rarely had to contend with eating companions/rivals in the wild. This probably explains not only why cats today would feel secure eating in a more relaxed crouched or sitting position but also why cats eat languorously, while dogs eat at a pace that suggests that any meal might be their last.

Of course, cats as well as dogs often eat standing up, even while eating in comfortable surroundings from a bowl. Vondruska points out one big advantage to eating in a crouched position for both dogs and cats: "This is the only way in which they can use their paws to hold their food, and this is sometimes necessary when chewing bones."

Submitted by a caller on the Ray Briem Show, KABC-AM, Los Angeles, California.

Why do all the Christmas tree lights burn out when one burns out?

Many a Yuletide has been ruined by the blight of premature Christmas light burnout. So for those who have experienced the trauma of having one burnt-out bulb turning your rainbow of illumination into a cavelike darkness, we have one word of advice for you. Upgrade.

If you experience this problem, your Christmas lights are *series*-wired. In series wiring, each bulb acts like a fuse; if one bulb burns out, the circuit is broken. Some sets have a shunt wire that allows the electricity to pass into the next socket if one bulb burns out, but no series-wired set will work if a bulb is removed from its socket. If your set does not have a functioning shunt wire, all you need to do is locate the missing bulb and replace it in order to close the circuit.

E. H. Scott, of J. Hofert Co., a leading supplier of Christmas trees and decorations, told *Imponderables* that many consumers are confused about how to replace bulbs in series-connected sets. To find the appropriate bulb, you merely divide the voltage standard (120 volts) by the number of bulbs in the set. If you have a set of 20 lights, you would need a six-volt bulb.

Of course, most families keep Christmas lights originally bought during the Stone Age. Most contemporary Christmas light sets have forsaken series wiring for *parallel* wiring. In this configuration, each bulb burns independently, so that 120 volts are directed to each bulb. The current will flow even if one or more bulbs burn out.

Why did manufacturers use series wiring when parallel wiring was so much more convenient? Hy Greenblatt, representative of the Manufacturers of Illuminating Products, gave us the answer we expected: Parallel wiring is harder to manufacture and considerably more expensive to produce.

Submitted by O.J.J.R. Jennings of Henderson, Nevada. Thanks also to Gregg Gariepy of Muskego, Wisconsin.

Why are Yellow Freight System trucks painted orange?

Consistency is the refuge of small minds. Let Yellow Cab Companies all over North America paint their fleets yellow. Trucking giant Yellow Freight System has a more highly evolved imagination.

We got the answer to this Imponderable from Mark J. Spencer, a friendly man with an unlikely job—art curator for Yellow Freight. Spencer is also, as he puts it, "the unofficial archivist of the unofficial archives and thus the unofficial historian" of his company.

Yellow Freight was founded by A. J. Harrell, who ran a taxi service, the Yellow Cab Company of Oklahoma City, in the early 1920s. A.J. started the Yellow Cab Transit Co., a bus service, in 1924, and, more important for our purposes, opened a truck ter-

DAVID FELDMAN

minal in Oklahoma City. Starting with two trucks, what was then known as the Yellow Transit Company, and later Yellow Transit Freight Lines, gobbled up several other companies and became the Yellow Freight System, now one of the three largest freight companies in the United States, with more than 600 terminals and 30,000 employees.

So why did Harrell, who named all of his companies "Yellow," paint his trucks orange? The evidence indicates that at the very beginning of his freight company, the trucks were not painted any particular color. But Harrell was obsessed with safety, and in the late 1920s or early 1930s, he commissioned the E. I. Dupont Company to determine precisely which shade of color was most visible from the farthest distance. Dupont's answer: the "swamp holly orange" color you see on all of the tractors of Yellow Freight System.

Faithful readers of *Imponderables* already know that the amber and red shades found on traffic stoplights were selected for the same reason. Yellow Freight's orange looks like a blend of those two stoplight colors.

Submitted by Paola Sica of Lawrence, Kansas. Thanks also to Bethany Franko of Spring Valley, Ohio; and Jared Martin of Kokomo, Indiana.

Why has the orange-colored coffee pot become the symbol for decaffeinated coffee in restaurants?

Obviously, it behooves the customer and restaurateur to have easily identifiable coffee pots on hand, for no waiter or customer can discriminate visually between "regular" and decaffeinated coffee. But the orange rim on restaurant coffee pots is no accident—it is the color associated with Sanka brand decaffeinated coffee, the first and best-selling decaffeinated coffee in North America.

The developer of Sanka coffee, European coffee magnate

Ludwig Roselius, realized the commercial potential of a coffee that didn't produce nervousness, sleeplessness, and indigestion in caffeine-sensitive coffee drinkers, but his chemists could not devise a process to remove more than half the caffeine while retaining the richness of ordinary coffee.

Supposedly, when a shipment of coffee was traveling between South America and Europe, a storm flooded the coffee with sea water. Although the coffee was ruined for commercial purposes, Roselius's researchers discovered that the salt water had naturally leached the caffeine out of the coffee but kept the taste intact. Roselius soon marketed a 97 percent caffeine-free product under several different brand names throughout Europe and called the product Sanka (a contraction of *sans caffeine*— "without caffeine") in France.

When Roselius brought Sanka to the United States in the 1920s, the product was introduced in restaurants in New York City, and packaged Sanka was sold over the counter for home consumption. (Only later, when customer incredulity that the taste of a decaffeinated coffee could be palatable waned, was Sanka sold in grocery stores.) Institutional sales of Sanka have represented a substantial part of the brand's sales ever since. When General Foods bought the company from Roselius in 1932, it not only advertised to home consumers but aggressively marketed Sanka to restaurants, institutional food services, and offices.

General Food's Sanka food service division developed the orange pots you see in restaurants and in the coffee room in your office. Subliminally, General Foods hopes, you will equate orange with decaf. This identification is important enough to General Foods that, according to Nan Redmond, director of corporate affairs, the integrity of the color has been assured by trademarking the "Sanka Orange."

In many cases, Sanka/General Foods provides both the coffee maker and orange pots for free to institutions that buy Sanka brand coffee, ensuring that most of the time when we pick up a cup of Sanka brand outside our homes, the drink has been poured from a "Sanka orange" coffee pot. Although General

DAVID FELDMAN

Foods wishes that every drop of decaffeinated coffee served in restaurants were Sanka brand, the company can't keep establishments from serving other brands in orange-rimmed pots. If you see a green-colored pot, it means that Folger Decaf has invaded Sanka territory.

Submitted by K. David Steidley of Short Hills, New Jersey.
Thanks also to Craig Kirkland of Greenville, North Carolina,
and April Williams of Richton Park, Illinois.

Why are "contemporary" or slightly risqué greeting cards invariably long and narrow in shape?

This size is known in the greeting card trade as a "studio" card because their earliest merchandisers were Greenwich Village artists who worked out of their studios. Studio cards emerged just after the end of World War II, created by returning veterans, and could be found in any greeting card section by the 1950s. The long, narrow configuration of the studio card attracted attention on the retail shelf; it differed drastically from the boxy, conventionally sized card. To this day, when we see a group of long, narrow greeting cards in a shop, we assume that they are "funny" or "contemporary."

Although no one seems to know the identity of the inventor of the studio card, chances are he or she was attracted to the size more by financial considerations than marketing ones. Product could be cut from conventional card stock with only one fold. Perhaps even more importantly, the studio card fit snugly into standard number 10 envelopes, which meant that the artists could obtain readily available envelopes inexpensively. Michael DeMent, product spokesperson for Hallmark, told *Imponderables* that many early artists sold studio cards to retail accounts without envelopes. With lower costs, artists could pass the savings on to their retail accounts, and consumers didn't mind—they simply placed the card in one of their own number 10 envelopes at home.

You can no longer assume that all funny cards are studio size. Hallmark has a division called Shoebox Greetings, which it facetiously calls "a tiny little division of Hallmark," which is like a guerrilla operation within the conservative giant. Although Shoebox cards are always humorous, their conventional size does not betray their offbeat attitude.

In a business totally dominated by Hallmark in the 1950s, artists saw a niche: greeting cards, heretofore, were almost exclusively a women's product. Even today, according to DeMent, about 90 percent of the products sold in Hallmark stores are bought by women. Hallmark's rival, American Greetings, was the first major card company to capitalize on the studio card format, with its Hi-Brows line, begun in 1956.

Many of the original studio cards were sarcastic in tone and often off-color in subject matter. Some featured unclad or scantily clad females, which gave any card of that size a risqué reputation that persists even today. That's why although you'll now see many humorous cards in conventional sizes, you'll never find that Mother's Day card, full of sweet roses on the outside and even sweeter verse inside, in the naughty studio size.

Submitted by Caryl Jost of Cleveland, Ohio.

What good does a "Falling Rock" sign do? How are we supposed to adjust our driving when we see a "Falling Rock" sign?

We know what Laurie Hutler means. Driving along a mountain pass and seeing a "Falling Rock" sign always leaves us with free-floating anxiety. Are we supposed to crane our necks and look up at the mountain to spot tumbling rocks? If so, how are we supposed to keep our eyes on the road?

"Falling Rock" signs are usually placed on roadways adjacent to rocky cliffs. You are supposed to worry about rocks on the road, not rocks tumbling down slopes.

Of course, traffic engineers know that we are going to be more anxious once we see a "Falling Rock" sign, and that is one of the reasons the sign is there in the first place. Anxious drivers proceed more slowly than complacent drivers. The chief of the traffic engineering division of the Federal Highway Administration told *Imponderables* that "By alerting the motorist to the

DAVID FELDMAN

potential hazard, the motorist should be able to react more quickly if a rock is encountered." If the motorist slows down, he or she can choose to drive over small rocks; at faster speeds, accidents are created when drivers swerve to avoid such obstacles. At slow speeds, the option of driving around a larger rock is more feasible.

The "Falling Rock" sign is one of the few warning signs for which there are no federal standards. Some jurisdictions use more accurately worded signs, such as "Caution Rocks May Be on Road" or "Watch for Rocks on Road." New York State chooses to use the wording "Fallen Rocks," which manages to be briefer than these other alternatives while simultaneously making it clear that the greater danger is rocks on the road rather than rocks from above.

The State of New York's Department of Transportation indicated how important brevity is in the effectiveness of warning signs. After reiterating the greater semantic precision of "Fallen" over "Falling," the director of the traffic and safety division, R. M. Gardeski, elaborates:

> Naturally we want sign legends to be as precise as possible, but absolutely precise legends often would be too long and complicated to be effective. Drivers have only a few seconds to read, understand, and react to each sign. Precision has to be balanced with the length and size of the legend to produce signs that can be read and understood quickly and easily. Even if it were more grammatically correct to do otherwise, we might still have chosen "Fallen" over "Falling" so the legend could be larger and more readable.

That's right. New York's "Falling" vs. "Fallen" decision was made partly because "Fallen" contains one less letter than "Falling."

Donald L. Woods, a research engineer at the Texas Transportation Institute, has a refreshing perspective on the problems with warning signs:

> Unfortunately, the public presses for warnings of all kinds and the tort liability situation forces government to install far too many warning signs. This results in far too many warning signs

being used on our nation's street and highway system. My favorites are "Church" and "Slow Children."

The "Church" warning sign must mean to watch out because that church is really something. Possibly Brother Swaggart's church should have had such a sign. The "Slow Children" warning sign completely mystifies me. Why should folks want to advertise that their children were not too bright?

Obviously, Mr. Woods's tongue was planted firmly in cheek, but his point is well taken. By oversigning, traffic planners risk desensitizing motorists to the danger implicit in the sign.

Submitted by Laurie Hutler of Boulder Creek, California.

DAVID FELDMAN

Why is there no apostrophe on the flashing "DONT WALK" traffic signal?

Because an apostrophe just uses up space. If you can believe that one of the main reasons New York uses "Fallen Rocks" rather than "Falling Rocks" is because "Fallen" is one letter shorter, why wouldn't you believe that an apostrophe is dead weight?

After all, traffic signs are designed for motorists in moving vehicles who are some distance away. Research has shown that punctuation marks aren't even perceived from a distance. If a punctuation mark isn't noticed, then it is redundant. Any word, mark, or even letter that doesn't add to the meaning of the sign will be eliminated. By using "PED XING" rather than "PEDESTRIAN CROSSING" on signs, the letters can be made larger without a lessening of motorist comprehension.

According to Victor H. Liebe, director of education and

training for the American Traffic Safety Services Association, punctuation "is rarely used on any traffic sign or signal except for certain parking signs, which are usually read from a very slowly moving or stopped vehicle."

Submitted by Bruce W. Miller of Riverside, Connecticut.

DAVID FELDMAN

Why does rinsing with hot water "set" a stain? Why is rinsing with cold water more effective in eliminating the stain?

First the good news. As you increase the temperature of the water applied to a stain, the solubility of the stain also increases. Obviously, dissolving the stain is a good first step in eliminating the stain.

Now the bad news. In practice, most of the time, "dissolving" the stain translates into *spreading* the stain. Usually, hot water helps break up the stain, but it doesn't lift the stain; rather, it allows stains to penetrate deeper into the fiber. Oily stains, especially on synthetics, have this reaction. Once the stain sets deeply enough in a fabric, detergents or dry cleaning are often ineffective.

In other cases, hot water can actually create a chemical change in the stain itself that hampers removal. Protein stains

WHEN DID WILD POODLES ROAM THE EARTH?   77

are a good example of this problem, as Lever Brothers spokesperson Sheryl Zapcic illustrates:

> One common type of stain that can be set by hot water is a protein stain. If protein is a component of the stain, rinsing with hot water will coagulate the protein. For example, egg white, which is a protein, can be loosened with cold water without coagulating; however, hot water will immediately coagulate the egg white. Technically, this is called denaturation of the protein. In any event, the stain becomes insoluble or set.

On some stains, it won't matter much whether hot or cold water is used.

Our own rule of thumb on this subject is: Nothing works. We have been in fancy French restaurants where our dining companions insist that "only club soda can get that stain out of your tie." Of course, we never have club soda at hand. To placate our true believer, we end up ordering a glass. And, *naturellement,* the stain lingers as an enduring testament to our naïve belief that we will one day get a stain out of a garment successfully.

Submitted by Pamela Gibson of Kendall Park, New Jersey.

Why is the bark of a tree darker than the wood inside?

Depends on how and where you slice it. Actually, there is more than one bark in a tree. A living inner bark, called the phloem, is relatively light in color and is composed of the same cells as wood. When the enzymes in phloem are exposed to air, oxidation darkens it, just as a peeled apple or banana discolors when exposed to air.

The outer bark of a tree, called the rhytidome, is dark. Dark and dead. The main purpose of the rhytidome is to protect the inside of the tree, so it contains tannins (acids used in tanning and in medicine), phenols, and waxes, which help form a barrier to protect the tree from invading fungi and insects. These protective substances are the source of the outer bark's dark color. The degree to which the color of outer and inner barks of trees compare to their wood varies considerably, as John A. Pitcher, of the Hardwood Research Council, explains:

> The concentration of tannins, waxes, and phenols varies from tree to tree and between species. Tannins are still extracted from bark for use in the leather curing process (e.g., genuine oak-tanned leathers). On the other hand, [lighter-colored] wine bottle corks come from the dead inner bark of the corkbark oak, *Quercus suber*. The bark is nearly the same color as the wood itself.

Submitted by Jill Davies of Forest, Mississippi.

Why do seven-layer cakes usually have fewer than seven layers?

We faced this investigation with the seriousness of Geraldo Rivera. But the bakers we spoke to laughed about the "scandal of the missing layers."

A survey of bakeries in the City of Brotherly Love, Philadelphia, yielded not only guffaws but the startling revelation that the true seven-layer cake is an endangered species. The baker at D'Elain Pastries simply said, "People call it seven-layer cake, but it's not seven layers. It's four or five." The closest the Swiss Bakery could come up with is a Dobosh cake, which has four layers of cake and three layers of frosting. Seven layers would "make too big of a cake." At least the Eclair Bake Shoppe makes true seven-layer cakes at Passover, but its spokesperson indicated that most other bakeries don't make them anymore. They take too much time to lay out.

We understand why, in the world of commerce, cakes might become inflated in price and deflated in layers, but even cook-

DAVID FELDMAN

books designed for home bakers conspire to eliminate the purity of the seven-layer cake. In his book *Practical Baking*, William Sultan begins his recipe with "Prepare 7 sheet pans . . .", clearly indicating the intent of producing a true seven-layer pastry. But then why does the accompanying picture show a cake with only six layers?

At least Susan Purdy, author of *A Piece of Cake*, owns up to the confusion. Before presenting her recipe, she muses:

> . . . I remember, as a child, always counting the layers just to check, feeling triumphant when the number varied, as it often did and still does, from the seven we consider traditional to nine or even twelve, depending upon the whim of the chef. Now the choice is yours . . .

We really couldn't find anyone in the bakery trade who was upset about the misnamed seven-layer cake. Bakery engineering consultant Dr. Simon S. Jackel told us that most cakes have thick layers. The idea of the seven-layer cake was to create not a thicker cake but a normal-sized cake with extremely thin layers. To Jackel, all that is important in creating an authentic seven-layer cake is to make sure that each layer is separated by icing or filling.

May we offer a humble suggestion? How about bakeries simply calling their offerings "layer cakes"?

Submitted by Gerald Stoller of Spring Valley, New York.

Why is the part of bills that needs to be sent back by customers often too large for the envelope it is to be sent back in, forcing customers to fold the bill stub?

Harper Audio makes cassette versions of *Imponderables* books in a quiz format. A question is posed by Dave "Alex Trebek" Feldman, and three characters, A, B, and C, provide possible answers. Two of them are bluffs, and one is the correct answer.

The task of the listener is to identify which of the three alternatives is correct.

Obviously, in order to use an Imponderable on the tape, we need to conjure up two viable bluffs. This subject is a particular peeve of ours, and the fact that seven readers felt strongly enough about it to write to us indicates that it is plaguing men, women, and children throughout the Western world. One problem arose in using it on the tape: We couldn't think of two decent bluffs.

Why in the world would any company, a utility or phone company or credit card company, ever supply an envelope too small for the stub? The only sensible explanation we could come up with was that chintzy companies were trying to save money by not purchasing larger envelopes.

We are overjoyed. After consulting several business forms and stationery manufacturers, and all of the relevant trade associations, we are pleased to report that the answer to this Imponderable is simple: Our gut instinct was right—there *is* absolutely *no* reason for providing a stub that doesn't fit into the envelope (many envelopes provided for paying bills are also too small to accommodate a check without folding it over, but we'll let this pass). These companies have simply screwed up!

Not since we tackled the insanity of the issue of why there are ten hot dogs in a package but only eight hot dog buns in a package in *Why Do Clocks Run Clockwise?* have we encountered an Imponderable with less reason for being or that makes grown men and women look so silly.

Several of the authorities we contacted were as befuddled and frustrated by this incompetence as we are—for example Maynard H. Benjamin, executive vice-president of the Envelop Manufacturers Association of America:

> The reason that the bills are larger than the envelopes is tha the individuals who procure the envelopes sometimes do not talk to the individuals that work in the billing department. As a result, in some cases the bills are larger than the envelopes; in other cases, the envelopes are much larger than the bills. If we could ever get both of these individuals talking together, your question

would probably be unnecessary. Believe it or not, in most cases the envelopes and bills are designed and procured by the same person.

In the latter case, then, we hope that the "talking together" will not be out loud.

Is there any hope to end this crisis? The popularity of window envelopes is forcing forms analysts to size the bills properly; if they don't, the address won't show through the window. Otherwise, the only answer is education. One of our contacts, the Business Forms Management Association, Inc., provides continuing education on these types of subjects; its executive director, Andy Palatka, wrote us:

> The Business Forms Management Association, the international society for forms professionals, has existed since 1958 to provide the training, networking, and information needed to improve productivity in the workplace through forms-systems integration.

We have no idea what forms-systems integration means, but it sure sounds important, and although it is not our policy to endorse associations and their educational programs, we hope that every company that sends out bills (and, judging from our mail, there are a lot of them) hires folks with Ph.D.s in forms-systems integration. After all, it must take incredible savvy to design a stub small enough to fit into an actual envelope. Ain't this a wonderful world?

Submitted by Bert Garwood of Grand Forks, North Dakota.
Thanks also to Dorothy Kiddie of Nashua, New Hampshire;
Sharon Sherriff of Alameda, California; John Hevlow of Idaho
Falls, Idaho; John Beton of Chicago, Illinois; Rev. Ken Vogler of
Jeffersonville, Indiana; and John R. Green of Cincinnati, Ohio.

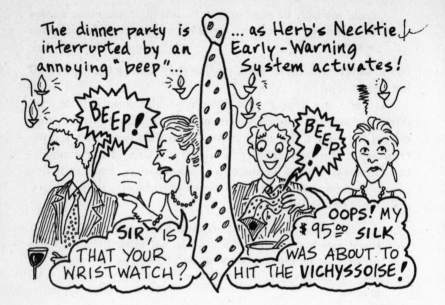

The dinner party is interrupted by an annoying "beep"... ...as Herb's Necktie Early-Warning System activates!

BEEP!

BEEP!

SIR, IS THAT YOUR WRISTWATCH?

OOPS! MY $95⁰⁰ SILK WAS ABOUT TO HIT THE VICHYSSOISE!

Why are men's neckties tapered at the bottom?

Neckties don't *have* to be tapered on the bottom. In fact, they weren't until the early twentieth century. Before then, ties were cut straight down from a piece of material. But now, the vast majority of silk ties are cut on a bias (on an angle to the floor). According to fashion writer G. Bruce Boyer, there are two main benefits to cutting on an angle: it produces a tie "more impervious to the rigors of knotting and maximizes the natural elasticity of the silk."

When the end of the necktie is finished, it is "trimmed square" (along the lines of the weave) so that the end forms a natural point. The larger point, the one presented to the outside world, is known as the "blade" or "apron" end, and the smaller, covered-up point is known as the "upper end."

Have you ever noticed that knitted ties are not tapered on

DAVID FELDMAN

the bottom? You may have figured out the reason already. Knitted ties (whether made out of yarn or silk) are cut and seamed straight across the blade end, rather than on a bias—circumstantial evidence that ties are tapered for purely functional rather than aesthetic reasons.

Submitted by Sonja Trojak of Brandon, Florida.

Why do stripes on neckties always run in the same direction? And why do American ties run in the opposite direction from English ties?

We don't mind our books being browsed and sampled in random dollops, in the bathroom or in more prestigious rooms of your castle, but if you haven't read the previous chapter, please read it. We'll wait for you.

Now that you have mastered the intricacies of tie cutting, you are ready for the simple answer. The reason why the stripes are all on the same angle is that the stripes on the bolt, before the material is cut, are in perfectly horizontal position. The angle is achieved by cutting on the bias.

Although the origin of the practice is lost in antiquity, American tiemakers traditionally cut their material face up, while the English cut it face down. We don't know whether this discrepancy has anything to do with squeamishness or prudishness on the Brits' part (a culture that gave us Johnny Rotten and Sheena Easton can't be *that* afraid of stripes) or some technical requirement of machinery. But we do know the end result: The stripe

DAVID FELDMAN

on an American tie will run from the right on top and downwards to the left, while the English will slant in the opposite direction.

The striped tie originated in England in 1890, where different stripes were used to identify particular military regiments and, later, schools and clubs. One expert recounts a theory that the English stripe stems from the left side so that it will "descend from the heart." Another source speculates that Americans consciously rebelled against English tradition. We've heard the latter theory used to explain everything from why we drive on the right side of the road to why we, unlike the British, put our fork down and switch hands when eating meat. But we think it's a tad preposterous to believe that long after the Civil War, American tiemakers were still trying to fight the revolutionary war.

Submitted by Mary Jo Hildyard of West Bend, Wisconsin. Thanks also to Jill Palmer of Leverett, Massachusetts; Ed Hawkins of Warner Robins, Georgia; and Fletcher Eddens of Wilmington, North Carolina.

What is the purpose of the oil found in the head of sperm whales?

Sperm whales lend a new dimension to the term "greasy." Their spermaceti oil is located in their "case," a trunk about five feet deep and ten to twelve feet long, and nearly the entire depth, breadth, and length of their heads. Surely, this odd anatomical arrangement must have a function. But what is it? In his 1991 book *Men and Whales*, Richard Ellis stated the problem:

> When some ancient Europeans first discovered a dead sperm whale on a beach (sperm whales are notorious stranders), they were unable to explain the clear amber liquid in its head, and guessed that it was the animal's seminal fluid. . . . Hundreds of years later we know the fluid is not the seed of the whale, but we do not know what the whale uses it for.

But this hasn't stopped aquatic researchers from theorizing over the last two centuries. Here are some of the more intriguing hypotheses:

1. *The oil provides buoyancy.* This is the "answer" found in most encyclopedias and books about whales. The lighter specific gravity of the oil allows the sperm whale to rise to the surface of the water with less effort, an obvious advantage to a mammal that must breath air. Buoyancy helps keep the whale's blow hole above the surface of the water, so that it can inhale and exhale without water constantly streaming into its respiration apparatus.

Why does a sperm whale need greater buoyancy than other whales? The main reason is that the sperm whale has a huge head, and its jaws contain the largest teeth not only of any whale but of any animal. Without the buoyancy lent by the oil, the weight of the jaws and teeth would make the whale's head "bottom-heavy."

The biggest flaw of this theory is that the very buoyancy that allows sperm whales to glide effortlessly on the surface of the water would also require them to struggle when attempting deep dives.

2. *The oil facilitates movement in the water.* The trunk that contains the oil might dispense oil to a particular section of the case to increase the specific gravity of that end. By shifting the oil to one end, the whale can change direction much more easily.

3. *The oil protects whales from the effects of nitrogen.* Nitrogen buildup creates decompression sickness in whales, and sperm whales dive deeper than any other whale. Some theorize that spermaceti oil is capable of filtering out nitrogen from the respiratory and circulatory system. In the past, hunters of sperm whales often found themselves slimed in the worst possible way: Not only did they come away full of oil, but they were beset by other, more serious calamities—severe skin irritations and even temporary blindness. Sea water and oxygen wouldn't cause such a reaction. Perhaps the oil literally carries the nitrogen out of the whale's system.

4. *The oil might be a food source.* Dr. Robert R. Rofen, of the Aquatic Research Institute, wrote *Imponderables* that many aquatic animals store their energy in the form of oil—lipids for future use when their food supply is down.

5. *The oil is used in sound production.* Humpback whales are

DAVID FELDMAN

not the only whales to produce sound. Sperm whales emit high-pitched "wails" and locate objects by sensing how and where their sounds bounce back to them. When on the prowl, there is evidence to suggest that they may incapacitate and stun their prey by producing a sound more piercing than Yoko Ono at her worst. Nobody knows for sure what role the oil may play in production of the scream.

6. *The oil allows whales to dive deeper.* Even though the added buoyancy provided by the spermaceti oil acts to make deep diving more difficult, the case that holds the oil might act as a force pump, drawing in air when necessary and, more importantly, preventing air from escaping when the whale is deep below the surface. The facilitation of oxygen flow between nostrils and lungs is crucial in allowing sperm whales to dive deeper than other whales, but the role of the oil itself in the process is unclear.

7. *The oil provides equilibrium for the whale regardless of what depth it is.* When sperm whales dive, they are hungry. Researchers note that although sperm whales plunge as deep as ten thousand feet, when they resurface, they arrive in the same spot from which they launched. The inescapable conclusion is that the whales are not cruising around but rather descending vertically to the ocean floor and resting there until a promising group of squid or other prey passes overhead.

The natural tendency of the spermaceti-laden whale is to rise to the surface, so adherents of this theory suggest that when sperm whales want to rest on the ocean floor, they fill their nasal passages with water. We are talking about *major* nasal passages here. They are capable of ingesting hundreds of thousands of pounds of water! Since the water is cooler than the sperm oil it now mixes with, it cools and condenses the oil, lowering the buoyancy. Thus, by regulating the amount of water it ingests through its nostrils, the whale can "choose" whether it wants to be buoyant (not ingest water) or to lie on the ocean floor (cram all the water in its nose it can).

All of these theories have some merit, but we must admit that the last is the most inviting, if only because it is the most inclusive.

Submitted by Dan Arick of New York, New York.

WHEN DID WILD POODLES ROAM THE EARTH?   89

Why do women put perfume on their wrists?

We've wondered the same thing. When we pass through the cosmetics counters of department stores, we see women applying perfume to their wrists and then sniffing intently. Why not on their fingers? The back of their hands? Their arms? Their underarms?

What do they know that men don't know? A cursory poll of some females indicated that most of them had no idea why they put perfume on their wrists. But it turns out that there is a method to their madness. Irene L. Malbin, of the Cosmetic, Toiletry, and Fragrance Association, explains:

> Women put perfume on their wrists because there is a pulse point there. Pulse points are located wherever the pulse of the heartbeat is closest to the surface of the skin. The heat generated by the pulse point will intensify a perfume's impact.

Malbin lists other pulse points: behind the ears, the nape of the neck, the bosom, the crook of the elbows, behind the knees, and at the ankles. Obviously, it is easier for a consumer to apply perfume to the wrist than the back of the knee, at least in a department store.

All of this makes perfect sense. But then why don't men apply cologne to *their* wrists? Or do they?

Submitted by Jesse Flores of Henrico, Virginia.

DAVID FELDMAN

Why do pretzels have their strange shape?

We don't know how every source we read or contacted dated the origin of the pretzel to Italy in A.D. 610, considering that none of them can point to the identity of the inventor or the exact location. But all agree that the pretzel was invented by a monk who used it as a reward for students who recited their catechism properly.

According to the conventional wisdom, the shape was not an accident, and it had nothing to do with expediency in baking. The Italian word for pretzel, *bracciatelli* (variously translated as "small arms" and "folded arms") is the clue: The shape of the pretzel was meant to resemble the arms of a child in prayer. Norma Conley, a self-professed pretzel historian and president of the Pretzel Museum in Philadelphia, told *Imponderables* that in medieval times, people prayed by putting their arms across their chest in a cross shape, placing each hand on the opposite shoulder.

The shape of boys' arms in prayer, and not the letter B, a

knot, or parts of the human body, are what the pretzel was designed to look like. Conley reports that pictures of pretzels can be found in early bibles, sometimes used as page borders.

This said, we would still not be surprised if the monk story was apocryphal. But it's all we have, at present.

Occasionally, rituals around the world take advantage of the unusual shape of the pretzel. A woodcut from the seventeenth century, found in a cathedral in Switzerland, shows the pretzel used as a nuptial knot—a wishbone, of sorts. The bride and groom each pulled on one side of the pretzel; whoever grabbed the larger piece had his or her dreams come true. The two linked arms and ate the pretzel, and the possessor of the short end pretended that the inevitable loss of face involved in losing this contest wouldn't ruin the marriage irreparably.

In parts of Europe, even today, the pretzel is used as a good-luck charm. In Germany, for example, many folks wear a pretzel on a loop around their necks on New Year's Eve. (Try doing that with a pretzel stick!) Supposedly, the pretzel necklace brings them good luck and a long life. If nothing else, it gives them something salty to eat to motivate them to drink more beer—another, less esoteric, German New Year's Eve custom.

Submitted by Jacob Schneider of Norwalk, Ohio.

Why do disposable lighters have two separate fluid chambers, even though the fluid can flow between the two?

One look at Bic's disposable lighter reveals the seemingly needless use of two chambers. When we queried folks at Bic and other lighter manufacturers, representatives calmly and without defensiveness denied that there were two chambers in their lighters.

Not until we heard from Linda Kwong, public relations manager at Bic, did we get the answer: Our eyes deceived us. There *aren't* two chambers, but . . .

> The wall of plastic that makes up the fuel reservoir portion of the main body has to be reinforced with a cross rib or web to assure that this containment vessel will exceed the high pressure of the fuel. This cross rib gives the *appearance* of two separate chambers.

Submitted by Joseph P. McGowan of Glenolden, Pennsylvania. Thanks also to Dori Moore of Wheelersburg, Ohio.

In *Do Penguins Have Knees?*, our readers obsessed about bubble gum, but this time around, we seem to have a new junk food obsession: Just what are they putting into those soft drinks of ours?

What ingredient in diet drinks provides the one calorie? Why do some diet drinks have one calorie and some have no calories?

Let's solve the second part of this Imponderable first. Most diet drinks, ones containing aspartame or saccharin, contain less than one calorie per twelve-ounce can but more than one half-calorie. Whether or not the drink gets promoted as "zero calories" or "one calorie," then, usually depends upon how the marketer defines a serving size. Six ounces is the most popular serving size in the soft drink industry. If a twelve-ounce can of diet soda contains .66 of a calorie, then a six-ounce serving would contain .33 of a calorie. Because all figures are rounded off on nutritional labels, this soft drink can be advertised as containing zero calories.

A few soft drinks with mostly artificial sweeteners contain some natural flavorings, such as fruit juice, that contribute a meaningful number of calories (the flavored ginger ales marketed by Canada Dry and Schweppes contain a whopping two

DAVID FELDMAN

calories per six-ounce serving). But for the most part, the contrib-
utors to any caloric content in artificially sweetened drinks
comes from trace carbohydrates and other elements in flavorings.

So don't blame the sweetener if you binge on one of those
fattening one-calorie diet drinks. NutraSweet brand, the most
popular artificial sweetener for soft drinks, is made of two amino
acids, which are, technically, protein components. So aspartame
has the same caloric count, per gram, as the protein in a T-Bone
steak—four calories per gram. Fortunately for the dieter, the
amount of aspartame in a soft drink doesn't compare to the
weight of the protein in a steak. Phyllis Rosenthal, consumer
affairs analyst for NutraSweet, explains:

> Since NutraSweet is 200 times sweeter than sugar, only a
> small amount is needed to sweeten products. Therefore, it con-
> tributes negligible calories to a product. A level teaspoon of sugar
> has 16 calories while the amount of NutraSweet with equivalent
> sweetness has 0.007 calories.
>
> One 12-ounce carbonated beverage contains approximately
> 180 mg of NutraSweet, a very small amount, which provides a
> negligible amount of calories.

Negligible yes. But sometimes enough to push a drink over the
precipice into one caloriedom. Of course, then the soft drink
company can decide that a serving size should really be three
ounces, and the product magically becomes zero calories all over
again.

Submitted by Barry Long of Alexandria, Virginia.

Why do diet colas, but not sugared colas, contain phenylalanine? Isn't phenylalanine the same substance found in chocolate?

Relax, Jon. Phenylalanine is one of those two amino acids we referred to above that are used to make aspartame (the other is aspartic acid). You can find phenylalanine in all kinds of foods, including meats, grains, dairy products, and sometimes even chocolate.

If a soda uses sugar as its sweetening agent, it won't contain phenylalanine.

Submitted by Jon. L. Carleen of Chepachet, Rhode Island.

What is brominated vegetable oil, and why is it found only in orange soda?

BVO, as it is known in the trade, is used as a stabilizing agent in beverages. Actually, it is in many other citrus drinks besides orange sodas. BVO consists of a vegetable oil base—usually soybean, but occasionally cottonseed—combined with bromine. You can't taste BVO because it is used in minute amounts.

BVO keeps the flavoring ingredients in sodas from separating from the rest of the drink. It is much less convenient to shake a bottle of carbonated orange soda than it is to shake a carton of orange juice that has been sitting in the refrigerator for a few days. At least, it's more convenient if you are the one who has to clean up the mess from shaking the soft drink.

BVO adds a side benefit, as well, for it is also a clouding agent, lending the liquid a more opaque appearance. Subliminally, the consumer might think of an orange drink as healthier

DAVID FELDMAN

because the opaqueness conjures up an image of actual food, a pulpy, fruit-based rather than a chemical- and flavorings-based beverage.

Submitted by William Rockenstire of Poestenkill, New York.

How do they put the pockets in pita bread?

Who would have ever thought that the pocket is created without human hands intervening? Bakery engineer Simon S. Jackel, director of Plymouth Technical Services, explains:

> Pita bread is placed in the oven as a thin, solid piece of dough. There is no pocket in the dough when it goes into the oven. But the oven temperature is so high, about 900 degrees Fahrenheit, that there is a rapid, explosive expansion of the water in the dough, causing the formation of a pocket by literally ripping the bottom part of the dough piece from the top dough piece. Total baking time at this high temperature is only one and one-half to two minutes.

Submitted by James Frisch of Great Neck, New York.

Why do we wear caps and gowns at graduations? Why are the caps flat and square? What does the color of gowns signify?

The first organized institutions of higher learning appeared in Paris and Bologna in the early twelfth century. In this era, virtually everyone, male and female, old and young, wore long flowing robes that didn't look too different from our graduation gowns of today. Rich people might have worn silk robes with ornamentation while the poor wore plain, coarse wool robes, but the style varied little.

Robes were in vogue until around 1600, when gowns were generally worn only by older and professional men. By the end of the seventeenth century, only legal and other officials wore gowns. But by the time robes for men had become passé, they had long been prescribed for use as academic garb, especially by English universities, and the tradition of wearing gowns at graduation had stuck.

In Roman law, a slave was freed when he was allowed to wear a cap. This symbol of emancipation might have been the inspiration for Oxford adopting the practice of placing a cap on the recipient of a Master's of Art when he graduated. The cap symbolized independence for the former bachelor.

Why was the hat square? Square hats called birettas were already in vogue at the time, but they weren't totally flat like the mortarboard that Oxford established as the standard. In her book *The Story of Caps and Gowns,* published by graduation uniform giant E. R. Moore Company, Helen Walters offers three theories:

1. The shape was derived from the master workman's mortar board.
2. The cap was meant to resemble the quadrangular shape of the English university's campus.
3. The shape symbolized the "squareness" of both the scholar and his books. In those days, we presume, squareness was a positive trait.

Early academic caps sported tufts where we now have tassels. Tassels appeared in the eighteenth century, and appear to be merely cosmetic additions.

Americans were quick to adopt English university customs in graduation garb all the way back to colonial times. Several Ivy League universities and prestigious small colleges used gowns and mortarboards from the start.

Only around 1885 did the practice extend to most colleges. In 1894, a commission was authorized to choose a standard for graduation uniforms. Its conclusions have determined our uniforms for the last hundred years:

Bachelors—wear black gowns with worsted material and long, pointed sleeves.

Masters—wear black silk or black woolen gowns with long, closed sleeves that have an arc of a circle near the bottom and a slit for the arm opening.

> Doctors—wear black silk gowns with full, round, open sleeves that are faced with velvet and have three bars of velvet on each sleeve.

> All three graduates wear a mortarboard, but only doctors' caps may be velvet, and only doctors and presidents of universities may wear gold tassels.

English universities vary clothing and color schemes from school to school. The United States is one of the only countries to have a standardized code.

In 1911, E. R. Moore introduced the Official High School Cap and Gown. It was gray to differentiate it from the university gown, its sleeves were full and round, and the matching gray cap was the typical Oxford mortarboard with a silk tassel.

Although E. R. Moore's motive might have been commercial, the popularity of caps and gowns for secondary school graduations spread quickly, not only because parents appreciated the pomp and circumstance at a momentous occasion, but for financial reasons. In the early twentieth century, students of affluent families might pay forty or fifty dollars for a graduation outfit when the caps and gowns could be rented for $1.50. The caps and gowns allowed poor students to "compete" with their richer comrades.

Of course, every school soon wanted caps and gowns. Normal schools, and later their descendants, junior colleges, chose blue for the color of their gowns. Some grammar schools even started using caps and gowns—maroon became the most popular color.

Several of the readers who posed this question also asked about the tradition of moving the tassel from left to right to signify graduation. Obviously, the tassel shift symbolizes the graduation itself, but we have been unable to trace its exact origins. We do know that this practice goes in and out of favor. While some schools retain the practice, many, if not most, universities do not, insisting that the tassel remain hanging on the left side of the mortarboard while the commencement speaker drones on and on and on.

Submitted by Andrew Kass of Staten Island, New York. Thanks also to Michael Silverson of Exeter, New Hampshire; Lisa Coates-Shrider of Cincinnati, Ohio; Linda Galvao of Tiverton, Rhode Island; Gina Guerrieri of Shawnee, Oklahoma; and Jamie Hubert of Spring Lake, Michigan.

Why aren't skyscrapers ever made out of brick?

We consulted many architects about this question, and they flooded us with reasons why bricks weren't a particularly desirable material for skyscrapers. In no particular order, here are some of the problems involved:

1. Bricks are more expensive than the alternatives. Not only are they relatively expensive to manufacture, but laying bricks is extremely labor-intensive, which is one of the reasons we see fewer bricks even in ranch style suburban homes than we used to.

2. In order to support a skyscraper, the walls at the base of the building must be extremely thick, wasting valuable space. David Bahlman, of the Society of Architects, indicated that bricks would need to be two and one-half feet deep at the base to support even a six-floor building.

3. Bricks need a substructure of steel beams to support them. According to architectural consultant Bill Stanley of Buellton, California, skyscrapers with steel frames can be covered (or "clad") with brick panels, but "brick is a poor material for cladding because of its weight, and the possibility of coming loose and falling."

4. The size of individual bricks is not large enough aesthetically to fit the scale of a skyscraper.

Notwithstanding this brick bashing, we have a confession to make. The premise of this question is incorrect. There are skyscrapers made of brick. Indeed, one of the first skyscrapers in

DAVID FELDMAN

the world, the Monadnock Building in Chicago, built in 1889, rests mainly on brick. The Monadnock Building is sixteen stories high and is often studied by urban architects.

The design problems inherent in such a tall brick building are elucidated by Lynn S. Beedle, director of the Council on Tall Buildings and Urban Habitat. The bricks make the building so heavy that the walls must be made thicker and thicker on the lower floors, so that the walls at the base are almost six feet thick. You couldn't build a brick building much higher because "there wouldn't be much space left on the ground floor for elevators."

Charles N. Farley, director of the Brick Institute of America, wants *Imponderables* readers to know that brick is being used on newer skyscrapers, too. Most laymen don't realize that the gargantuan Empire State Building contains brick because it is clad with limestone panels. Two recently built New York City skyscrapers, the fifty-three-story World Wide Plaza and the sixty-story Carnegie Hall Tower, both use brick for the exterior skin. Brick remains a feasible exterior for those who can afford it.

Submitted by Herbert Kraut of Forest Hills, New York.

THE FARQUHAR PREPARATORY
ACADEMY TESTS ANOTHER APPLICANT.

Why are nine-volt batteries rectangular?

Most of the best-selling battery configurations (e.g., AA, AAA, C, D) are 1.5 volts. Nine-volt batteries, formerly known as "transistor batteries," contain six 1.5-volt batteries. The 1.5 cells within the casing are cylindrical.

If you were to stack six cylinders in the most economical shape, wouldn't a rectangle be the most natural choice? Just try putting six cylinders into a square or cylindrical casing without wasting space.

Dan Halaburda, marketing manager for Panasonic, told us that the shape of nine-volt batteries goes back to when they were used to power communication devices in which space was at a premium. Today, the most common application for nine-volt batteries is in smoke detectors.

Submitted by Matt Garrett of Augusta, Missouri.

DAVID FELDMAN

Why do most mailboxes say "Approved by the Postmaster General" on them? How do they differ from mailboxes without the approval?

We thought these were simple and innocent questions. But as grizzled veterans of researching postal Imponderables, we should have known better. For the saga of the U.S. mailbox is a long one; in fact, the household mailbox debuted in 1891, when Postmaster General John Wanamaker launched an experiment. Until then, it was the policy of postal carriers to knock on the door of households and hand-deliver mail. Just the seconds waiting for house occupants to come to the door wasted delivery time, so mailboxes were inevitable.

We may think of a mailbox as a rather simple object, but an earlier commission appointed by the postmaster general in 1890 examined 564 prototypes of mailboxes and found them all wanting. What the commission was looking for, as the 1891 annual report of the postmaster general stated, was a device

> in which the letter carrier could deposit mail without delay and from which he could also, as he went his rounds upon the same trips, collect mail without delay. Not one of these devices exactly fitted the requirements; for the box must necessarily be inexpensive, neat, proof against the weather, proof against mischiefmakers or thieves, simple enough not to get out of order and not to require time to open, ornamental enough to please the household, big enough to receive papers, and ingenious enough to indicate the presence of mail matter to the passing collector.

The commission later examined another 1,031 designs, and found that "Not one of these was entirely acceptable."

Originally, only rural delivery mailboxes had to be approved by the postmaster general. Imagine the problems of the rural postal carrier with farflung routes. Megaera Harris, research historian at the office of the postmaster general, explains:

> Early rural carriers and the public they served were forced to create their own rules and regulations in the fledgling days of rural mail service. Farmers had been asked to put up their own mailboxes, "buggy high," and within easy reach of the mail carriers, a request with which most of them complied. The resulting mailboxes under these general guidelines were a study in individuality and creativity.

Aware that minimum standards were necessary, the post office department established rules and regulations, effective October 1, 1902, mandating the size, shape, and accessibility of the box. Fourteen manufacturers were approved to build boxes. Each box was to be stenciled with the statement "Approved by the Postmaster General."

In the following ninety years, only mailboxes served by rural carriers were required to have the postmaster's approval, but manufacturers found it a good marketing device to include the approval on all their boxes.

In 1991, the postal regulations widened. Roy Preston, operations officer of the delivery management division, told *Impon-*

DAVID FELDMAN

derables that "all new [curbside] boxes or replacement boxes must now have the 'Approved' inscription." As old, "grandfathered" mailboxes deteriorate or are replaced for cosmetic reasons, the nonapproved boxes will be a thing of the past.

Preston was kind enough to pass along the rules and regulations to which approved mailboxes must conform, and they are truly scary in their specificity. Boxes are tested for everything from salt spray resistance to flammability to color shade.

Steve Korker, a communications spokesman for the United States Postal System, says that the USPS itself tests mailboxes for manufacturers. Tests include the dreaded "door and flag" test, in which each part is attached to a machine and opened and closed a minimum of 7,500 times. Boxes are dropped on hard surfaces to test their durability, tested for leakage, and exposed to water and high humidity.

So although the postmaster general cannot personally test the flag on each household's mailbox, rest assured that if you have the "Approved by the Postmaster General" inscription, your mailbox is ready to withstand rain, sleet, snow, and the dark of night, and is less likely to complain about these weather conditions than your postal carrier.

Submitted by Scott Kovatch of Dublin, Ohio.

Why does a ball tend to veer toward the ocean when one putts on a golf course?

We were shocked when this truism of the links was denied by the golfing authorities we contacted. Typical was the response of Frank Thomas, technical director of the United States Golf Association:

> I have no evidence that this is the case or that there are any strange forces that could possibly make this happen. If the natural shape of the land is down toward the ocean and the green has a

similar grade, then the ball will tend to veer according to the slope.

We were stymied until we heard from Rand Jerris, at the USGA's museum and library. He called the premise of this Imponderable "one of those great half-truths of life," and indicated that although under certain conditions the ball does tend to veer toward the ocean, "just as often you will find a putt that breaks away from the water." Jerris, however, was our only source to explain the conditions on the golf course that might cause the ball to move in mysterious ways:

> 1. Drainage. Most greens are constructed with subtle slopes to facilitate drainage in a specific direction. Economically, it makes sense to drain toward natural bodies of water, whether that be an ocean or a lake.
>
> 2. Grain of the green. Any golfer knows that putts will tend to break with, and not against, the natural grain of the grass. Jerris notes that grass found in the western United States, such as Bermuda grass, tends to be stronger and thicker than eastern varieties. Since blades of grass tend to grow toward the setting sun to maximize photosynthetic activity, the strong grains of western grass tend to steer putts toward the ocean. Even when the weaker, thinner, bent grass in the East bends toward the West Coast, the effect is imperceptible because the grass has weak grain or no grain at all.
>
> 3. Winds. In some shore regions, the dominant winds tend to blow from land toward the sea. According to Jerris, "These winds may also add to the effects of grain, forcing the blades of grass to orient in the direction of the ocean."

So don't blame the tides for your next errant putt. Chances are, your victimizer is the grass beneath your feet, paying you back for all those divots you've dug.

Submitted by John R. Green of Cincinnati, Ohio.

Why do dishwashers have two compartments for detergent? And why does only one compartment close?

Our ever cheerful appliance expert, Whirlpool's Carolyn Verweyst, replied to this Imponderable with uncharacteristic testiness: "Consumers frequently ask these questions but never think to consult their use and care manuals supplied with the appliance." Ah, c'mon, Carolyn. Force us to hand-wash our dishes. Refuse to answer our question. But don't condemn us to actually having to read the user's manuals!

An informal survey of moderately intelligent individuals (i.e., we asked a bunch of our friends) indicates that the average dishwasher owner doesn't have the slightest idea how much detergent to put in the dispensers, nor the significance of loading one or both cups.

To save you the agony of user manual ocular bleariness and brain rot, we're here to help. Although there are differences among the dishwashers of different companies, and even among different models from the same manufacturer, a few truisms emerge. Perhaps the most important principle is that you need fill both sections of the dispenser only if you are cleaning heavily soiled dishes or pots and pans—*cycles that require two different wash periods*. The "pots and pans" cycle typically consists of these phases: light wash (using the soap in the uncovered section of the dispenser); rinse-wash (using the covered section); rinse-rinse-dry-off.

In most dishwashers, the "normal" cycle consists of rinse-wash-rinse-rinse-dry-off. Ordinarily, you need fill only one of the two sections with detergent. But make sure you put the detergent in the correct slot. Fill up the covered cup, close it, and a timer within the dishwasher will pop it open automatically at the proper time (after the first rinse cycle). If you put detergent in the uncovered section in a cycle that begins with a rinse, not only are you wasting detergent by washing away the detergent during the first rinse cycle, but you won't have any detergent left to use during the main wash.

A few dishwashers begin their normal cycles with a "light wash" rather than a rinse and do require both sections of the dispenser to be filled with detergent. The only way to be sure, and we say this with *deep* regret, is to consult your use and care manual.

Submitted by Bethany Marcus of Parma, Ohio.

DAVID FELDMAN

Is it true that horses cannot vomit?

WARNING: If you have eaten within the last hour, or contemplate eating within the next hour, we do not recommend perusal of this chapter at the current time.

Equine vomiting is highly unusual but not unheard of. Vomiting is almost impossible because of the acute angle at which a horse's esophagus enters the stomach. In most cases, what might seem to be vomiting is actually regurgitation—the coughing up of food still in the esophagus. A horse's regurgitated food is much more likely to exit through the nose than the mouth (we did warn you!) because the pharynx—the tube connecting the mouth and esophagus—works as a safety valve to prevent exit through the mouth.

Guarding the entrance from the esophagus to the stomach is a strong set of sphincter muscles that allow food to enter the stomach but prevent food from returning back into the esophagus. These muscles remain closed even after the death of a horse.

Although humans might not look forward to retching, vomiting allows us to purge substances from our body that might make us far sicker. Horses aren't so lucky. Dr. Cindy Jackson, of the Cornell University College of Veterinary Medicine's Large Animal Clinic, told *Imponderables* that horses would be better off if they could vomit. Horses commonly die from colic.

Submitted by L. Love of San Antonio, Texas.

Why does the tax stamp on a pack of cigarettes say "20 *CLASS A* CIGARETTES"?

The grade refers not to the quality of the cigarettes but to their size. Class A cigarettes are the smallest grade—those that weigh not more than three pounds per thousand—and therefore, the class with the smallest excise tax bite.

Submitted by John C. White of El Paso, Texas. Thanks also to Donald Marti, Jr., of New York, New York.

What are the small, light-colored spots on a brown cigarette filter? Do they have any function?

Those spots have one of the most important imaginable functions—to look pretty. Most American cigarettes have either white or brown filter papers. According to Mary Ann Usrey, of R. J. Reynolds, most women prefer white filters. But most men, evidently, find the brown color more macho.

Cigarette companies print the dots with nontoxic ink to simulate the look of cork (in fact, this style is known as a "cork tip"). Winston, Camel, and Marlboro are just three of the brands that feature cork tips, and include them solely because of the delicate aesthetic preferences of their customers.

Submitted by Leroy Thompson II of Leesburg, Virginia.

In movies and television dramas, what is the purpose of boiling water when babies are delivered at home?

Considering the urgency with which characters in movies bark orders to boil water as soon as it becomes evident a woman is going to give birth at home, we assumed there *was* a better reason for the command than to rustle up some tea. But we've never seen the boiled water actually being used on-screen.

Most of the medical authorities we contacted echoed the sentiments of Dr. Steven P. Shelov, professor of pediatrics at the Montefiore Medical Center:

> This is an attempt to make as sterile an environment as possible, though clearly it is far short of inducing any sterility whatsoever. There might be some ability with hotter water to allow for a cleaner, more efficient cleansing of the baby and of the mother postpartum.

Obviously, it can't hurt to sterilize equipment that comes in contact with the mother or baby, such as scissors, cord clamps,

DAVID FELDMAN

white shoelaces (used in lieu of cord clamps), syringes, and tongs (used to lift the other sterile items), or even more importantly, to sterilize other household implements commandeered to act as sterilized medical equipment.

But boiling water isn't confined to emergency deliveries. Midwives have been boiling water for years for planned home deliveries. Most attempt to boil sterile equipment for thirty minutes and then place instruments in a covered dish (syringes are usually wrapped in a sterile cloth).

Dr. William Berman, of the Society for Pediatric Research, indicated that it couldn't hurt to sterilize water for washrags used to cleanse mother and baby, whether they are washcloths or ripped-up bed sheets. Actually, it *could* hurt—if they forget to let the boiled water cool down.

Submitted by Scott Morwitz of Pittsburgh, Pennsylvania.
Thanks also to Jil McIntosh of Oshawa, Ontario; and Dr. John
Hardin of Greenfield, Indiana.

Why do frogs close their eyes when swallowing?

There is a downside to those big, beautiful frog eyes. While they may attract the admiration of their beady-eyed human counterparts, frog eyes bulge not only on the outside but on the inside of their faces. The underside of their eyeball is covered by a sheet of tissue and protrudes into the mouth cavity. Frogs literally cannot swallow unless they use their eyes to push the food down their stomach. Richard Landesman, zoologist at the University of Vermont, amplifies:

> In order for frogs to swallow, they must be able to push material in the mouth backwards into the esophagus. Humans use their tongue to accomplish this task; however, frogs use their eyes. By depressing their eyes, food can be pushed posteriorly in the

mouth. Frogs also use this same mechanism to breathe, since they lack a diaphragm.

Actually, if we ate what frogs eat, we might close our eyes when swallowing, too.

Submitted by Scott McNeff of Wells, Maine.

DAVID FELDMAN

Why do the paper bags/sacks in supermarkets have jagged edges where you open them?

Not an earth-shatteringly important Imponderable, perhaps, but we were startled by how little paper bag manufacturers knew about the subject. They couldn't even agree on what to call these edges; depending upon to whom we spoke, the edges were referred to as "serrated," "pinked," "jagged," and "chain cut."

But Brent Dixon, president of the Paper Bag Institute (and, in a naked lust for power, also the majordomo of the Paper Shipping Sack Manufacturers Association), referred us to the only person who knows the real story—George Stahl, who works in sales for Potdevin Machine Company, a large manufacturer of machines that produce paper bags, and has been in the business longer than most of our sources have been alive.

Stahl explains that sack machines are run at a high speed; they produce from four hundred to five hundred sacks per minute. The individual bags are cut from long strips of paper by an anvil-type blade. For technical reasons, if straight edges were desired for the sack's opening, two blades would be necessary, dramatically slowing down the production process.

Although serrated edges might help you open the paper sack faster and more safely, don't for a second presume that your welfare was the reason for the design. The accountants, not the designers, dictate the form of the finished product.

Submitted by Diane Cormier of Bath, Maine.

HOW and why do hotel amenities (such as turndown service and bathrobes) spread so quickly among different hotel chains?

One of the stranger aspects of our job is the "publicity tour," when we are sent to eleven different cities in eleven days, to flog unremittingly our latest tome upon an innocent public. When we are on our own dime, we tend to stay at motels where the size of the complimentary bath soap slightly exceeds the circumference of a commemorative postage stamp, and the "bath mat" has the texture and width of the paper place mat at Denny's. But for whatever reason, our esteemed publisher sends us to the type of hotels that charge as much for one night's lodging as Motel 6 does for a week's. And since we are pliant, malleable types, we don't complain about being forced to alter our bohemian lifestyle.

On these tours, we have noticed a curious fact. Every year, it seems there is a new "hot" amenity. Two years ago, for example, we noticed that virtually all the hotels we visited now had alarm clocks. In the past, you called the hotel operator if you wanted a wake-up call. We thought perhaps the hotel was saving money by having guests reduce their dependency on operator-assisted wake-up calls. But then last year, those clocks were replaced by clock radios. And when we went up to our room for the first time, the radio, invariably, was on, and tuned to classical music. If the city didn't have a classical music station, the radio played classy elevator music.

We could understand how an individual hotel, or single hotel chain, might decide that the "musical introduction" to the new guest was an elegant touch, but how did many different chains all adopt the practice so quickly? How and why did they all decide simultaneously that guests could not enter their rooms without being greeted by Chopin?

Welcome to the wonderful world of what the lodging industry calls "amenities." In the 1950s and 1960s, patrons of all but the most luxurious hotels were satisfied with a few basic amenities: free soap, a color television, ice, air conditioning, a telephone, and perhaps a swimming pool.

But in the 1980s, when lodging chains overbuilt and the economy turned sour, hotels were faced with severe overcapacity and a true dilemma: how to gain market share without dropping prices? Most decided that the answer was to increase amenities. In most cases, the price differentials among hotels within the same class are small, and business travelers, in particular, are not extremely sensitive to price. As James McCauley, executive director of the International Association of Holiday Inns, told us, the task of the smart hotelier in the 1980s was to attract loyalty among customers by offering amenities that would "impress and attract customers from competitive hotels."

In many cases, the strategy worked. Adding amenities to what were originally budget motels (e.g., Holiday Inns and Ramadas) allowed them to charge more for rooms. Hyatt became identified with their nightly turndown service (including a free mint on the pillow), and Stouffer gained fans for their complimentary coffee and newspaper with wake-up calls. These amenities came at a price to the providers. That little mint on the pillow (along with the labor costs of the turndown service) cost Hyatt more than five million dollars a year.

Still, the list of amenities now offered in hotels is mind-boggling. Some have: business centers; health clubs; two-line telephones; special concierge floors with lounges; in-room movies, VCRs, CD players, safes, coffee makers, and hair dryers; free

WHEN DID WILD POODLES ROAM THE EARTH?   119

local telephone calls, breakfast, and airport limousines; shoe polishers; voice mail; and nonsmoking rooms.

How do all these amenities spring up at the same time?

1. Amenities are often pitched to many hotels simultaneously. As Raymond Ellis, of the American Hotel & Motel Association, put it:

> the more effective sales representative is going to be presenting an amenity as the ultimate item or service for attracting the guest, without, of course, indicating that the same article or service has just been sold to three or four other competing properties within the community.

2. Richard Brooks, vice-president of room management at Stouffer Hotels & Resorts, mentioned that outside rating services often act as stimuli to add certain features.

> [AAA, Mobil, and Zagat and other rating services] freely tell us of new amenity items or services they have seen, and often tell us they believe they are appropriate for the ratings we hope to achieve.

3. Spies. The big chains can afford inspectors to scrutinize not only their own units but those of competitors.

4. Trade magazines. The American Hotel & Motel Association was kind enough to send us more information about amenities, just from trade magazines, than we ever imagined. There aren't many secrets in the hotel field.

5. Market research. The biggest hotel chains might employ focus groups or written and telephone surveys. Smaller groups might use guest comment cards (yes, they really *do* read those things) or simply chat with guests about their needs. Richard Brooks indicated that some of Stouffer's most popular amenities, such as two-line telephones, in-room movies, no charge for incoming facsimiles, and complimentary coffee and newspaper with wake-up call, all started with guest requests. Many such guest requests are inspired by seeing the same amenity provided at another hotel, another reason why amenities spread so quickly.

Market research also helps hoteliers avoid costly mistakes. Research shows that the vast majority of patrons expect a swimming pool but fewer than one in five ever use it. One chain con-

DAVID FELDMAN

templated putting color TVs in their bathrooms until research indicated that guests would much prefer a decidedly less costly offering—an ironing board and iron. Any amenity that doesn't add market share is wasteful. In fact, most surveys we perused indicate that low-cost items are among the most popular: in-room coffeemakers, TV remote control, and facial tissues were the favored amenities in one study.

Occasionally, an amenity may be turned into a profit center. The minibar is such an attempt. Contrary to popular opinion, soft drinks and snacks are consumed much more than hard liquor or beer, but the minibars still turn a profit, since they charge more for the same products than vending machines could. One of the secrets of the success of the minibar: For business travelers, the cost is added to the room charge. Coke machines in the hallway don't take company credit cards or give receipts.

Amenity creep is so pervasive that budget hotels have tried to create a backlash. Days Inn based an advertising campaign around the slogan, "We don't have it because you don't want it." At one time, Motel 6 forced you to pump in quarters if you wanted light to emit from the television in your room. The truth is—most patrons "want it," but only if they don't think they are paying for it.

Of course, amenities can also foster goodwill. On our last tour, we encountered our all-time favorite amenity at Chicago's Ambassador East Hotel. As we entered our beautiful room, there above the fireplace, on the mantel, was a spanking new copy of *Do Penguins Have Knees?*, with a request for an autograph from the manager. Guess where we are staying the next time we're in Chicago?

Slash Blade Co. I Inc.
Product Development

One Razor, Two Names!

"Mr. Beard" and "Ms. Legs"

OUR ORIGINAL NAME FOR THE LADIES' RAZOR, "MS. ARMPIT," DIDN'T TEST WELL FOR SOME REASON...

Is there any difference between men's and women's razors?

Our examination of this issue, conducted with the naked eye, reveals that the main difference between men's and women's razors, at least the disposable type, is their pigment. Women's razors are usually pink; men's razors are found in more macho colors, like royal blue and yellow.

But the naked eye can deceive. Chats with representatives at Bic, Schick, and Wilkinson indicate that there are at least three significant differences:

1. The most important difference to the consumer is the "shave angle" of the two. A man's razor has a greater angle on the blade, what the razor industry calls "aggressive exposure," for two reasons. Men's beards are tougher than women's leg or underarm hair, and require more effort to be cut and, at least as important, women complain much more than men about nicks and cuts, the inevitable consequence of the aggressive exposure of the men's blades. Women don't particularly like putting hosiery over red splotches, while men seem perfectly content walking around their

DAVID FELDMAN

offices in the morning with their faces resembling pepperoni pizzas.

    2. Most women's razors have a greater arc in the head of the razor, so that they can see the skin on the leg more easily as they shave.

    3. Women don't shave as frequently as men, especially in the winter, when most wear pants and long-sleeved blouses. Schick offers a "Personal Touch" razor line for women that features guard bars that contain combs, so that longer hair is set up at the proper angle for shaving.

As far as we can ascertain, all the major manufacturers use the same metallurgy in men's and women's razors.

After enumerating the design features that his company incorporates to differentiate men's and women's razors, Fred Wexler, director of research at Schick, offered a rueful parting observation: Despite all of their design efforts, Schick's research reveals that a solid majority of women use razors designed for men.

Submitted by Kim MacIntosh of Chinacum, Washington.

What are the numbers on the bottom right of my canceled checks? Why aren't those numbers there before the check is canceled?

You are probably vaguely aware of the preprinted numbers running along the bottom left of your personalized checks. The numbers on the far left identify your bank. The numbers to their immediate right are your bank account number. The right half of the bottom of the check is blank.

But when the check is returned with your statement, a mysterious ten-digit number appears. If you look carefully, it doesn't take a rocket scientist to figure out to what the numbers refer— they indicate exactly how much your check is for—down to the penny. Any amount up to $99,999,999.99 can be expressed with these numbers. The fact that most folks are not H. Ross Perot explains why most of these codes start with a bunch of zeros.

You didn't think that banks clerks pore over every check individually and add or subtract from your account with a calculator, did you? These funny numbers on the bottom of your checks are called "MICR" (magnetic ink coding) numbers. Brian Smith, executive vice-president of the United States League of Savings Institutions, explains how the amounts of your check are encoded, as well as a personal Imponderable of ours—does anyone ever read the part of the check where we have to write out in words the dollar value of the check?:

> MICR numbers are keyed in very fast, by clerks reading the items and typing them in via special keyboards on the machine that first processes each check. Writing the dollar amount clearly in numbers at the upper right is vital since nobody ever reads the amount in words, beginning in the middle left, though, legally, that is supposedly the controlling description of the amount of the check. All processing is done by the MICR process after the initial coding.

Why do banks sometimes attach a white piece of paper to the bottom of canceled checks?

The white strip is affixed to the bottom of a check when the MICR process misfires. Sometimes, a scanner can't read the MICR numbers. More often, a clerk mistypes the amount of the check.

John Hall, of the American Banking Association, told *Imponderables* that there is no way for a clerk to erase or overstrike a typing error on a check. Instead, the MICR numbers are encoded on a plain piece of paper, which is placed on the bottom

of the check and is read by the same scanners that decode checks
without the white appendage.

Submitted by Douglas Watkins, Jr. of Hayward, California.
Thanks also to Joseph P. McGowan of Glenolden, Pennsylvania.

Why do the clearest days seem to follow storms?

Our correspondent wondered whether this phenomenon was an
illusion. Perhaps we are so happy to see the storm flee that the
next day, without battering winds, threatening clouds, and endless precipitation, seems beautiful in contrast.

No, it isn't an illusion. Meteorologists call this phenomenon
"scavenging." The rainwater that soaks your shoes also cleans
away haze and pollutants from the atmosphere and sends it to
the ground. At the same time, the wind that wrecks your um-
brella during the storm diffuses the irritants that are left in the
atmosphere, so that neighbors in surrounding areas aren't subjected to those endless days of boring, pollution-free environments.

Of course, where the pollutants end up depends upon the
direction of the prevailing winds. If you are living in a commu-
nity with generally bad air quality, the wind is your friend anyway. Chances are, the wind is carrying in air from a region with
superior air quality.

Submitted by Jack Schwager of Goldens Bridge, New York.

Why are paper and plastic drinking cups wider at the top than the bottom?

A reader, Chuck Lyons, writes:

> I have never been able to understand why paper and plastic drinking cups are designed with the wide end at the top. That makes them top-heavy and much easier to tip over. Making them with the wide end on the bottom would make the cups more stable and less likely to tip over, with no disadvantage at all that I can see.

Come to think of it, Chuck's suggestion has been used for eons in the design of bottles. We certainly never found it difficult drinking from a "bottom-heavy" beer bottle. Most glass bottles and many glass or ceramic drinking cups don't taper at the bottom, so why should disposable cups? What are we missing?

Plenty, it turns out, according to every cup producer we spoke to. John S. Carlson, marketing director of James River, put it succinctly:

> The cups are wider at the top so that they can be "nested" in a stack during shipping, storage on the grocery store shelf, and in your cupboard at home. If they weren't tapered slightly, they'd stack like empty soup cans. The current configuration saves space and spills, and is more efficient and cost effective.

In retailing, not only time but *space* is money. Better to get more of your product on the shelf and live with the consequences of an extra customer or two tipping over a cupful of Kool-Aid.

Submitted by Chuck Lyons of Palmyra, New York.

DAVID FELDMAN

Why do steak houses always serve such huge baked potatoes?

The poser of this Imponderable, Gene McBride, advances his own theory to explain the prodigious potatoes we encounter in steak houses. He feels that no home cook would ever buy these elephantine spuds for personal use, so farmers are forced to unload them at bargain basement prices to restaurants, "which is better than using the potatoes for hog feed."

We spoke to restaurateurs, meat marketers, and potato marketers to help confirm Gene's theory, and found only the potato folk eager to speak on the record. Everyone disagreed with our reader, saying that restaurants pay a pretty penny for portly potatoes.

But that doesn't mean that economics don't enter into the equation. Several restaurateurs indicated that a big baked potato adds to the perceived value of a meal, for steak houses, with their macho image, unlike nouvelle cuisine outposts, always would rather send a customer home stuffed to the gills and reaching for the Pepto-Bismol than starving to death and looking for the nearest McDonald's.

Don Odiorne, vice-president of food service at the Idaho Potato Commission, gave us a history of the potato's role in the U.S. steak house and his own theory about the reason for using the huge potatoes:

> Steak houses typically started out serving enormous portions of steaks, bread, and potatoes—steaks so large they wouldn't fit on the plate. Sometimes to accomplish this claim, the plates an operator ordered were smaller in diameter (the standard 12 to 14 inch plate went down to 9 to 11 inches), but it was generally accepted that the cowboy-size western steak was huge and hard to finish eating in one sitting.
>
> This quest for "value" evolved over the years as the cost of food, which had been relatively stable for quite some time, began to rise. Food cost pressures reduced portion sizes or increased the selling prices. Both had negative effects on customer counts. As steaks got smaller, the side dishes, such as potatoes, got larger.
>
> Generally, it is much less expensive to up the size of a potato than to up the size of the meat portion. For example, if an operator serves a 90 count potato (about 9 ounces), and a carton of potatoes cost the restaurant $15.00, the individual serving cost of the potato, not including condiments, would be less than 17 cents. Go up to a 50 count potato (one pound), and the individual cost is 30 cents. Now try and find a cut of steak for 30 cents a pound—it's impossible.

As several restaurateurs told us off the record, the baked potato thus becomes one of the cheapest ways to stuff the customer without increasing costs—but not because the restaurant is paying less per pound for the big potato than the small one. Note that the "bargain" chain steak houses, such as Ponderosa and Bonanza, who don't sell such huge steaks, also downsize their baked potatoes, because their "value" is in their price, not the quantity (or quality) of food.

Still, not all our sources were willing to lay the tradition of the immense Idaho solely on economic preoccupations. To some, the size of the potato is a matter of aesthetics, of poetry, as it were. For example, Meredith Hughes, managing director of the Potato Museum, in Great Falls, Virginia, weighs in with an explanation that is deeper than anything we ever heard on *Kung Fu*:

> You would think that habitués of meat and potato palaces would already know the answer to the question you pose. They enter the gates for the biggest piece of dead animal flesh they can get, and by gum, they get a baker to lie parallel to it in perfect symmetry. Symmetry must be the answer. Balance, the harmony of equals, the yin and yang of it all.

Linda McCashion, director of advertising and public relations for the Potato Board, while acknowledging the perceived "value" added by the hefty potato, also spoke of the "balance to the plate" provided by the vast vegetable. And big potatoes help reinforce the macho image of the steak house. As McCashion puts it, "Real studs eat real spuds."

Submitted by Gene McBride of Winston-Salem, North Carolina.

Since computer paper is longer than it is wide, why are computer monitors wider than they are long?

As Robert Probasco, professor of Computer Sciences at the University of Idaho, puts it, the short answer is: "Monitors (video display tubes) and paper sizes evolved at different times for unrelated technologies, so their recent marriage has been a marriage of convenience." Our personal computer monitors evolved from the round screens of early television; Probasco reminds us that radar screens still retain this efficient shape.

Many of the early microcomputers were designed so that the user could employ a television as the monitor. Early micros had such poor resolution that only forty legible characters per line could be displayed on the screen; now the number has doubled. Still, the monitors aren't long enough to display a whole printed page. The average screen displays about twenty-five lines, whereas a printed single-spaced paper holds about fifty-five lines—hence the need for scrolling up and down when drafting a document on-screen.

But the personal computer configuration is hardly universal in the computer world. For example:

- Newspapers require huge screens capable of displaying an entire page of newsprint. They use monitors that do duplicate the shape of the paper.
- Large work stations often use squarish screens that can display a full page, or more, of information.
- "Page-format" monitors are available for some microcomputers. David Maier, professor in the department of Computer Science and Engineering at the Oregon Graduate Institute of Science & Technology, reports that some monitors alternate between page and standard orientation.
- Many computer printers, especially in business applications, can handle many different sizes and shapes of paper. Many of these papers are wider than they are long—not just mailing labels but wide papers used to print out spread sheets or plans drawn by engineers and architects.

The idea of customizing monitor proportions to specific applications is impractical and could be downright silly. As computer programmer Larry Whitish put it, "Imagine the size of monitor you would need to view a spread sheet that was over six feet long when printed in landscape mode on your printer."

Microcomputer designers found it simpler and less expensive to adapt the monitor to existing technologies. So they appropriated the tubes and circuitry from older VDTs. They used 8½ × 11-inch paper as the standard size so that the paper transport and printing hardware in their printers were compatible with counterparts found in electric typewriters and teletypes. Maier mentions that laser printers borrow much of their optics, hardware, and electronics from small copy machines. They even use the same cartridges, which are made for 8½ × 11-inch paper. This lessens the price of newer technology for both the supplier and the consumer.

DAVID FELDMAN

As we finished this chapter, we hear a question forming on the lips of an *Imponderables* reader: Why don't monitors have the same format as printers? To forestall the inevitable question, we also found out why these two components couldn't be aligned.

Well, they could, but David Maier explains why they are unlikely to be changed in our lifetimes:

> That would mean making the screen maybe 70 columns wide by 65 lines long to match a page printed in 12 pt. font. Turning a standard PC monitor 90 degrees would give about the right ratio of width to height. However, you would have to shrink the size of characters on the screen and increase the electronic circuitry to handle the greater number of characters. The standard monitor has 80 × 24, or 1920, characters, whereas the page monitor would need 70 × 65, or 4550, characters. It could get hard to read.
>
> However, if all the PC users in the country decided they were only going to buy page-format monitors from now on, the PC manufacturers could provide them in volume at a cost not much greater than what standard monitors cost now. Except.
>
> Except there are now thousands of PC programs that assume a monitor screen has the standard format and whose developers might not be real happy at having to recode them to work with page format.

Submitted by Henry J. Stark of Montgomery, New York.

Why are all calico cats female?

Not quite all. According to Judith Lindley, founder of the Calico Cat Registry International, approximately one male calico is born for every 3,000 females.

The occurrence of male calico cats is theoretically impossible. Ordinarily, male cats have XY sex chromosomes, while females have XX. The X chromosomes carry the genes for coat colors. Therefore, female cats inherit their coat color from both their queens (XX) and their toms (XY). To create a calico (or tortoise-shell) pattern, one of the X chromosomes must carry the black gene and the other the orange gene. If a black male and an orange female mate, the result will be a half-black and half-orange female offspring, a calico. A black female and an orange male will also produce a calico female.

Usually, the male kitten inherits its coat color from the queen alone, since the Y chromosome determines its sex but has nothing to do with its coat color. A male black cat mating with an orange female will produce an orange male; a male orange cat and black female will produce a black male kitten.

Geneticists have discovered that only one of the two X chromosomes in females is functional, which explains why you usually can make a blanket prediction that any male offspring will be the color of the queen. But occasionally, chromosomes misdivide, and a male calico is born with an extra chromosome— two X chromosomes and one Y chromosome. If one of the X chromosomes carries the orange gene and the other the non-orange, a calico will result.

Note that the presence of the extra X chromosome doesn't in itself create the calico. If both chromosomes are coded for orange or black, the offspring will be that color rather than a combination.

Abnormal chromosome counts are unusual but not rare. Most cat cells contain nineteen pairs of chromosomes, but sometimes a mutation will yield one extra chromosome or double or triple the normal number.

Although male calicoes are oddities, the cat experts we consulted indicated that they are normally healthy and have excellent life expectancies. But, unlike their female counterparts, male calicoes do tend to have a common problem—their sexual organs are often malformed, so they are usually sterile.

Submitted by Stacey Shore of West Lafayette, Indiana.

DAVID FELDMAN

Why do ditto masters come in purple rather than blue ink?

Instant copiers may have supplanted spirit process duplicators (also known as mimeograph duplicators—"Ditto" is actually a trade name of a brand of spirit duplicators) in businesses, but many a handout in schools today is still flecked with the same aromatic purple streaks that we older folks knew and loved as children. For those of you who never made it to the teachers' lounge, a short description of how mimeos are made will help explain why the stains on teachers' hands usually are purple rather than blue or black.

To make copies on a mimeo, one must type, write, or draw on a sheet of white master paper hard enough to make an impression on a sheet of purple backing carbon paper. A negative carbon image is created on the back of the master paper. The master paper is then separated from the carbon and placed on the drum of the duplicating machine. Each time the drum rotates, the machine automatically coats the paper with a small amount of spirit fluid. According to Bill Heyer, the third-generation owner of Chicago's Heyer Company, the spirit fluid dissolves a minute amount of aniline dye found on the carbon sheet and transfers it to the copy sheet each time the drum is rotated, producing a positive image. Heyer reports that this dye is extremely powerful. One thimbleful can turn an entire room blue.

The aniline dye used in spirit duplicators is derived from coal. Don Byczynski of Colonial Carbon Co. of Des Plaines, Illinois, told *Imponderables* that duplicating companies buy the dye in powdered form and mix it with vegetable oils and waxes to arrive at carbon ink.

So why did purple become the industry standard? Carbon companies, of course, wanted the cheapest possible dyes to make their product economical. Although many other solvents were available, alcohol was and still is the cheapest available, so the industry sought to use dyes with the best alcohol solubility. According to Byczynski, the cheapest dye available was crystal violet dye, the lowest-cost color dye with alcohol solubility.

As we learned in *Why Do Dogs Have Wet Noses?*, cash register receipts are purple because the ink lasts longer than other colors. Bill Heyer indicated that the same is true for carbon inks. Other colored dyes (e.g., blue, green, red, and black) are available, but they cost more and would produce fewer copies.

Heyer answered another question we wondered about. Is the carbon in ordinary carbon paper identical to the carbon used in spirit carbons? Surprisingly, the answer is no. The oils and waxes used are identical in both, but carbon paper uses pigments rather than dyes. Carbon paper wouldn't work on duplicating machines because it doesn't have alcohol solubility.

For those of you who worry about kids getting hold of alcohol-laden carbon products—relax. The alcohol is denatured by chemicals so that it is undrinkable.

Submitted by Diana Berliner of Eureka, California.

Why are the interior walls of tunnels usually finished with ceramic tiles? Are they tiled for practical or aesthetic reasons?

Come on. Do you really think tunnel-makers are obsessed with aesthetics? Tiles may look nifty, but they also have many practical advantages.

We heard from officials of the International Bridge, Tunnel & Turnpike Association, the Port Authority of New York and New Jersey, and the chief of the bridge division of the Federal Highway Administration. All hailed ceramic tiles for having two big advantages over other surfaces:

1. Tiles are easy to clean. Tunnel walls collect dirt the way Madonna collects boys. Walls are subject to fumes, dust, tire particles, exhaust, and, in some locations, salt. Tiles can be cleaned by many means, including detergents, brushes, and high-pressure water jets.

2. Tiles are durable. As Stanley Gordon, the aforementioned

FHA official, put it, "Finish systems must be resistant to deterioration caused by various kinds of dirt and grime, vehicle emissions, washing, water leakage, temperature changes, sunlight, artificial light, vibration and acids produced by combinations of vehicle emissions and moisture." Tiles perform admirably in this regard.

Gordon mentioned several other qualities that make tiles both practical and economic:

3. Reflectance. The more reflective the wall surface, the less money is spent on lighting.

4. Adaptability. "The finish [of the wall surface] must accommodate various special conditions at openings, recesses, corners, and sloping grades [of the tunnel], as well as service components such as lights and signs."

5. Fire Resistance. Tiles are noncombustible and are likely not to be damaged by small fires.

6. Weather Resistance. Fired clay products, tunnel tiles are, for example, frost-resistant.

7. Repairability. Nothing is easier to replace, if damaged, than one or more matching tiles.

8. Inspectability. It is easy to see if tiles are deteriorating and in need of repair.

What are the alternatives? Gordon elucidates:

Although many other products, such as porcelain enameled metal, epoxy coated steel, polymer concrete and painted concrete, have been investigated as possible tunnel finishes, the selection of tunnel tile prevails in most cases.

All in all, tunnel tiles are an unqualified success. Unless, perhaps, you are the person responsible for taking care of grout problems.

Submitted by Ann Albano of Ravena, New York. Thanks also to Anthony Masters of San Rafael, California.

Why does heat make us sleepy in the afternoon when we're trying to work but restless when we're trying to sleep at night?

Fewer experiences are more physically draining than sitting in an overheated library in the winter (why *are* all libraries overheated in the winter?) trying to work. You can be reading the most fascinating book in the world, (e.g., one of ours), and yet you would kill for a spot on a vacant cot rather than remaining on your hardback chair. So you trudge home, eventually, to your overheated house and try to get a good night's sleep. Yet the very heat that sent your body into a mortal craving for lassitude now turns you into a twisting and turning repository of frustration. You can't fall asleep. Why?

There is no doubt that heat saps us of energy. Many Latin, Asian, and Mediterranean cultures routinely allow their work force to take siestas during the hottest portions of the day, aware both that productivity would slacken during the early P.M. hours without a siesta and that workers are refreshed after an hour or so of sleep.

Yet all of the sleep experts we consulted agreed with the declaration of the Better Sleep Council's Caroline Jones: "Heat is not what makes us sleepy in the afternoon. Researchers have documented a universal dip in energy levels that occurs in the P.M. regardless of the temperature." These daily fluctuations of sleepiness within our body are known as "circadian rhythms." David L. Hopper, president of the American Academy of Somnology, told *Imponderables* that late evening and early afternoon are the "two periods during the twenty-four-hour cycle when sleep is possible or likely to occur under normal conditions."

Some sleep specialists believe that circadian rhythms indicate humans have an inborn predisposition to nap. But somnologists seem to agree that the natural sleepiness most of us feel in the afternoon, when it happens to be hottest outside, has little or nothing to do with the other very real enervating effects heat has upon us.

Environmental temperatures *do* affect our sleep patterns, though. Most people sleep better in cool environments, which explains why many of us are restless when trying to sleep in hot rooms even when we are exhausted at night. And if the temperature should shift while we are asleep, it can cause us to awaken, as Hopper explains:

> Our body temperature is lowest in the early morning hours and highest in the evening. During deep NREM and REM sleep, we lose our ability to effectively regulate body temperature, so if the outside temperature is too warm or too cold, we must arouse somewhat in order to regulate our body temperature more effectively. During sleep we are not unconscious, so signals are able to get through to arouse us when needed, much as when we awaken from sleep when we need to go to the bathroom.

Submitted by Mark Gilbey of Palo Alto, California. Thanks also to Neal Riemer of Oakland, California.

Why do we feel drowsy after a big meal?

Eating, unlike heat, does directly affect our sleepiness quotient. After we eat a big meal, the blood supply concentrates around the digestive organs and intestinal system, reducing the blood supply for other activities. We tend to slow down metabolically and in our ambitions. ("Sure, why not have a fourteenth cup of coffee? They won't miss us at the office.")

Equally important, during digestion, foods are broken down into many chemicals, including amino acids such as l-tryptophan, which help induce sleep. Serotonins, which constrict the blood vessels, also make us drowsy. Alcohol, too, often produces sleepiness—which may be another reason why so many business lunches end up with fourteen cups of caffeine-loaded coffee.

Submitted by David O'Connor of Willoughby, Ohio. Thanks also to Chaundra L. Carroll of Hialeah, Florida.

"Workshop 2-A: Choosing the processing method that's right for you"

What's the difference between jams, jellies, preserves, marmalades, and conserves?

All of these products started as a way to preserve fresh fruit (although they are now used primarily to provide a semblance of flavor on tasteless bread). The preparation of each involves adding sugar or other sweeteners (including other fruit juices) to the fruit to insure flavor preservation, and the removal of water to increase the intensity of taste. And most include additional ingredients found naturally in fruit: citric acid, to impart tartness; and pectin, a natural jelling agent.

The main difference among these foods is texture. Jellies are prepared from strained fruit juices and have a smooth consistency. Jams are made from crushed fruit (conserves, a type of jam, are made from two or more fruits, and often include nuts or raisins). Preserves use whole fruit or pieces of whole fruit. Marmalades use citrus fruit only and include pieces of the peel.

Fruit syrups and toppings, the type used in ice cream parlors, are prepared with the same cooking methods as other preserves. They are usually made from juices or purees of fruit and often contain corn syrup as well as sugar, to provide the runny consistency that insures the topping will topple off even a flat-top ice cream scoop.

Submitted by Pamela Gibson of Kendall Park, New Jersey. Thanks also to Dana Pillsbury, parts unknown (please write with new address); Rich DeWitt of Erie, Pennsylvania; Jeffrey Bradford of Berkeley, California; and Elmo Jones of Burbank, California.

Why don't trees on a slope grow perpendicular to the ground as they do on a level surface?

Trees don't give a darn if they're planted on a steep hill in San Francisco or a level field in Kansas. Either way, they'll still try to reach up toward the sky and seek as much light as possible.
Botanist Bruce Kershner told *Imponderables* that

this strong growth preference is based on the most important of motivations: survival. Scientifically, this is called "phototropism," or the growth of living cells toward the greatest source of light. Light provides trees with the energy and food that enable them to grow in the first place.

There is also another tropism (involuntary movement toward or away from a stimulus) at work—*geotropism*—the movement away from the pull of gravity (roots, unlike the rest of the tree, grow *toward* the gravitational pull). Even on a hill slope, the pull of gravity is directly down, and the greatest source of average light is directly up. In a forest, the source of light is only up.

There are cases where a tree might not grow directly up. First, there are some trees whose trunks grow outward naturally, but whose tops still tend to point upward. Second, trees growing against an overhanging cliff will grow outward on an angle toward the greatest concentration of light (much like a house plant grows toward the window). Third, it is reported that in a few places on earth with natural geomagnetic distortions (e.g., Oregon Vortex, Gold Hill, Oregon), the trees grow in a contorted fashion. The gravitational force is abnormal but the light source is the same.

John A. Pitcher, of the Hardwood Research Council, adds that trees have developed adaptive mechanisms to react to the sometimes conflicting demands of phototropism and geotropism:

> Trees compensate for the pull of gravity and the slope of the ground by forming a special kind of reaction wood. On a slope, conifer trees grow faster on the downhill side, producing compression wood, so named because the wood is pushing the trunk bole uphill to keep it straight. Hardwoods grow faster on the uphill side, forming tension wood that pulls the trunk uphill to keep it straight.
>
> Why softwoods develop compression wood and hardwoods develop tension wood is one of the unsolved mysteries of the plant world.

We'll leave that unsolved mystery to Robert Stack.

Submitted by Marvin Shapiro of Teaneck, New Jersey. Thanks also to Herbert Kraut of Forest Hills, New York; and Gregory Laugle of Huber Heights, Ohio.

On nutrition labels, why does the total number of grams of fat often far exceed the sum of saturated and polyunsaturated fats?

Foraging through our kitchen cabinet, we lit upon a box of Nabisco Wheat Thins. A consultation with the nutritional panel yielded the following information about the fat content of a half-ounce serving:

DAVID FELDMAN

Fat:	3 grams
Polyunsaturated	*
Saturated	*
* contains less than one gram	

And a look at the label on a Stouffer's Lean Cuisine Oriental Beef with Vegetables and Rice Entree wasn't much more enlightening:

Fat:	9 grams
Polyunsaturated	*
Saturated	2 grams
* contains less than one gram	

We may not have been math whizzes, but even we know that two plus less than one does not equal nine.

What's going on? Sally Jones, food technologist at the USDA's food labeling division, told us that our arithmetic was impeccable but our nutritional IQ was in the dumper. We forgot that there is a third type of fat, monounsaturated, which can often, such as in the case of the Lean Cuisine entree, constitute more than half of a product's fat.

Current labeling laws make it optional whether manufacturers list the grams of monounsaturated fat, often affectionately known as the "good fat." The government doesn't insist on listing monounsaturated levels, since there is some evidence that monos are actually good for us, fighting to raise our levels of HDLs, the "good cholesterol."

When the giant upheaval of American food labels takes place, supposedly in 1993, but presumably later, food manufacturers will only be required to list their products' percentage of saturated fat (i.e., the "bad fat"), the culprit that most consumers are trying to find out about when they consult the nutritional panel in the first place.

Submitted by Solomon Marmor of Portland, Oregon.

Why do ambulances have the emblem of a snake wrapped around a pole painted on them?

For as long as there have been ambulances, manufacturers have sought a symbol so that citizens could recognize the vehicle as an ambulance, even without the wail of the siren. As far back as the nineteenth century, the cross was the most frequently used symbol on ambulances around the world, but it never proved satisfactory, for two reasons. The cross was on the national flags of many countries, causing needless confusion, and the Red Cross Society screamed, pardon the pun, bloody murder whenever the cross was used on anything but military or Red Cross vehicles.

When the National Highway Traffic Safety Administration and the General Services Administration developed new federal specifications for ambulances in 1974, they decided that a new symbol specifically designating an ambulance was needed. The result: two new symbols were affixed to the exteriors of ambu-

DAVID FELDMAN

lances—a six-barred cross and the emblem in question, the "staff of Aesculapius." Aesculapius was the son of Apollo and, in both Roman and Greek mythology, the god of medicine and healing; the snake was Aesculapius's seal.

According to W. J. Buck Benison, national accounts manager for Southern Ambulance Builders, the staff of Aesculapius is a registered trademark of the NHTSA, designated for use only by and for ambulances and emergency medical personnel. But individual ambulance companies are free not to emblazon their vehicles with the staff of Aesculapius if they choose—if they want to risk incurring the wrath of the gods, that is.

Submitted by Gabe Miller of Ann Arbor, Michigan.

What's the difference between "super" and ordinary glues?

The main difference between "super" glues and merely mortal ones is that Super and Krazy glues are fabricated from a man-made polymer called "cyanoacrylate," while most other glues are a combination of natural resins in a solvent solution.

The different ingredients create a different bonding process, too, as Rich Palin, technical adviser to Loctite Corporation, reveals:

> Most adhesives rely on mechanical fastening, meaning they penetrate into the tiny holes and irregularities of the substrate and harden there. Super Glue, on the other hand, creates a polar bond. The adhesive and substrate are attracted to one another like two magnets. Mechanical fastening also occurs with Super Glue, increasing the bond strength.

Borden Glue's John Anderson adds that because super glues don't rely solely on mechanical fastening, they are such better at bonding dissimilar surfaces than conventional glues. Thus, with super glues, the consumer is now able to accomplish many everyday tasks for which regular glue is frustratingly inadequate, such as applying glue to the top of a hardhat so that one can stick to steel girders without any other means of support.

Submitted by Tiffany Wilson (in Mary Helen Freeman's Millbrook Elementary School class) of Aiken, South Carolina.

In what direction are our eyes facing when we are asleep?

Upward, usually. Our eye muscles relax when we are asleep, and the natural tendency, known as Bell's Phenomenon, is for the eyes to roll back above their usual position. Of course, when we experience rapid eye movements during sleep, our eyes dart back and forth.

Submitted by Nadine Sheppard of Fairfield, California.

Why do weather thermometers use red chemical instead of the silver mercury found in medical thermometers?

The liquid found in weather thermometers is usually alcohol with red coloring. The main reason why alcohol is preferred over mercury for weather thermometers is that it is much, much cheaper. And alcohol is superior to water because alcohol is far hardier—it won't freeze even at temperatures well below −40 degrees Fahrenheit.

Why the red additive in weather thermometers? So that you can read it more easily. If weather thermometers used a liquid the color of mercury, you'd have to take the thermometer off the wall to be able to read it.

Since the advantages of alcohol are so apparent, why don't medical thermometers, notoriously difficult to read, contain red-colored alcohol instead of dingy mercury? Despite its greater cost, mercury is prized for its greater expansion coefficient—that is, it expands much more than alcohol or water when subjected to small increases in temperature. A weather thermometer might measure temperatures between −30 degrees and 120 degrees

Fahrenheit, a span of 150 degrees, while a medical thermometer might cover only a ten- to twelve-degree range. A doctor might want to know your temperature to the nearest tenth of a degree; if a liquid with a small expansion coefficient were used, you would need a thermometer the length of a baseball bat to attain the proper degree of sensitivity. We don't know about you, but we'll stick with the stick thermometer.

Couldn't the medical thermometer manufacturers color mercury, then? Actually, they could, but don't, for reasons that Michael A. DiBiasi, of Becton Dickinson Consumer Products, explains:

> When you produce medical instruments, the rule of the road states that the fewer additives that you incorporate into any device or component material, the better off you are in gaining approval to market the device, and in avoiding product recalls that may be tied in to those additives. So fever thermometers use mercury in its natural silver-white color, and the glass tube is usually silk-screened with a background color to make it easier to see the mercury level.

Submitted by Herbert Kraut of Forest Hills, New York.

How do they measure the vitamin content of foods?

Some vitamins are present in such small concentrations in food that there are only a few micrograms (millionths of a gram) of the vitamin per hundred grams of food, while other vitamins might constitute ten milligrams per hundred grams of food. The techniques that work to measure the abundant vitamin often won't work to evaluate the presence of the other.

Jacob Exler, nutritionist for the Nutrient Data Research Branch of the Human Nutrition Information Service, told *Im-*

ponderables that there are two types of analytical procedures to measure the vitamin content of foods, chemical and microbiological:

> The chemical procedures measure the actual amount of a vitamin or a derivative of the vitamin, and the microbiological procedures measure the biological activity of the vitamin on some selected organism.

Today, chemical procedures are in vogue. In the past, microbiological studies were more common, and researchers tested not only on bacteria but on live rats. In fact, as late as the 1970s, the FDA used approximately twenty thousand rats a year just to test foods for vitamin D content! Roger E. Coleman, of the National Food Processors Association, explains the theory behind microbiological studies:

> An older, but still very acceptable method for vitamin assay is to measure the amount of microbiological growth a food supports. There are certain bacteria that require an outside source of one or more vitamins to grow. The growth of these bacteria is proportional to the amount of the required vitamin in the food.

But microbiological work is extremely sensitive. If conditions are not perfect, results can be skewed. As an example, an article in *FDA Papers* states that "the organism used for measuring vitamin B12 activity will show a measurable response when dosed with less than one ten-billionth of a gram of the vitamin." Microbiological assays work more effectively than chemical methods for measuring B12 levels (and some other vitamins, such as biotin, B6) because chemical analysis isn't sensitive enough to respond to the minute amounts of the vitamin contained in food.

In a chemical analysis, each vitamin in a given food must be measured separately. There are many chemical procedures to choose from, with catchy names like "gas-liquid chromatography" and "infra-red spectroscopy." Coleman explains a few different types of chemical analysis that are a little more comprehensible:

Each measuring technique is based on a property of the vitamin. For example, riboflavin fluoresces [produces light when exposed to radiant energy] and is measured by a fluorometer or fluorescence detector. Vitamin C combines with a certain purple dye and makes it colorless. By measuring the amount of this dye that is changed from purple to colorless, we can calculate the amount of vitamin C present.

Despite the high-tech names, chemical analysis tends not to be as sensitive as old-fashioned microbiological methods, but it is cheaper and faster—and doesn't necessitate twenty thousand rats a year sacrificing their life for vitamin D.

Submitted by Violet Wright of Hobbes, New Mexico. Thanks also to Todd Grooten of Kalamazoo, Michigan.

Why doesn't the water in fire hydrants freeze during the winter?

It would . . . if the wrong type of fire hydrant were used. In areas that experience cold weather, fire departments use "dry barrel hydrants," with operating valves located below the freezing level of the ground. The fire hydrant itself does not contain any water until the valve is opened.

In temperate climates, "wet barrel hydrants" are often utilized. These hydrants do contain water above ground level. What are the advantages of the wet barrel hydrant that help compensate for the risk of water in the hydrant freezing? We got the answer from the president of fire hydrant maker Hydra-Shield Manufacturing, Henry J. Stehling: "With wet barrel hydrants, each outlet has an operating valve. The wet barrel hydrant will have two or three outlets, each with its own operating valve, providing greater control."

Submitted by Todd Sanders of Holmdel, New Jersey.

DAVID FELDMAN

Why do baked goods straight from the oven often taste (sickeningly) richer than after they are cooled?

When you ponder this Imponderable for a while, you realize there are only two approaches to the answer: one, the baked item really is different straight from the oven than it is ten or twenty minutes later, or two, that for some reason, the taster perceives the same item differently depending upon when it is consumed. Turns out there are experts who subscribe to each explanation.

Bakery engineer Simon S. Jackel assures us that items really do change in structure after being cooled because of a process called "starch retrogradation." In raw flour, starch exists in a coiled, closed structure. When flour is baked into bread or cakes, the starch uncoils and opens up when exposed to the water in the dough and the high temperature of the oven.

When the product comes out of the oven, it starts to cool down, and the starch begins to revert or "retrograde" to a partially coiled structure. Most importantly for our purposes, when the starch retrogrades, it absorbs some of the flavors and locks them up in the coiled starch so that the taste buds cannot process them. In other words, less flavor is available to the consumer as the product cools. Jackel states that retrogradation continues until the product is stale.

Two other baking experts lay the "blame" for the noxiousness of just-baked products on our noses. Joe Andrews, publicity coordinator for Pillsbury Brands, explains:

> A great deal of taste perception is determined not only by the taste buds, but also by the olfactory senses. . . . When a food is hot, it releases many volatiles that the nose may perceive as sweet. Thus a cake may seem sweeter when it is warm than when it is cold.

> The volatiles are perceived by the nose, both by sniffing through the nostrils and by the aromatics released in the mouth

that make their way to the nose via a hole in the back of the mouth, the nasopharynx. We say we "taste" these, but in actuality we are smelling them.

Andrews believes that the "richness" our correspondent complains about may actually be sweetness.

Tom Lehmann, of the American Institute of Baking, also emphasizes the importance of volatiles in taste perception. Many aromatics, including spices, are simply too powerful when hot. Lehmann blames egg whites as particular culprits in making hot bakery items smell vile and taste noxious. Angel food cake, a dessert with a high concentration of egg whites, is particularly lousy hot, Lehmann says, because egg whites are volatiles that are released in heat and have to cool completely in order to avoid producing an unpleasant smell.

Of course, there is nothing mutually exclusive about the retrogradation and volatiles theories. Unlike arguments about genetic versus environmental factors in deviant behavior, or creationism versus evolution, the theories can coexist peacefully and respectfully. After all, bakers are engaged in an important and soul-lifting pursuit; it's hard to get bitter and angry when your life revolves around a task as noble as trying to concoct the perfect doughnut.

Submitted by Connie Kuhn of Beaumont, Texas.

DAVID FELDMAN

Why is gravel often placed on flat roofs?

We were taken aback when Scott Shuler, director of research at the Asphalt Institute, referred to this Imponderable as "oft-asked." But he didn't seem to be kidding, for he had a quick comeback: "Obviously, because it rolls off pitched roofs and there needs to be a place to put all that small gravel."

Shuler put aside his burgeoning stand-up comedy routine long enough to inform us that flat roofs usually consist of aggregate ("there are generally two sources for this stuff: gravel from rivers and stone from quarries are both such materials") embedded in the asphalt mopping. With this technology, often referred to as "built-up roofing," alternating piles of roofing felt and asphalt are placed on the roof to provide a surface. According to Richard A. Boon, director of the Roofing Industry Educational Institute, the gravel is set in a "flood coat" of hot bitumen and is about the size of peas.

What function does the gravel serve?

1. According to William A. Good, executive vice-president of the National Roofing Contractors Association, the gravel helps to protect the roof membrane ("a combination of waterproofing and reinforcing materials" located just above the insulation and below the gravel) from puncture or tear by foot traffic from construction workers, dropped tools, hailstones, or stray meteorites.

2. Gravel provides a lighter, more reflective, color than black asphalt, making the roof more energy-efficient. A side benefit: Gravel lessens the ultraviolet degradation of the roof membrane that would exist if the membrane were exposed directly to the sun.

3. The gravel acts as ballast. In windy conditions, the membrane, which is, in essence, tar paper, can actually lift up and even fly off if left exposed.

4. The gravel provides more secure, less sticky, footing for anyone walking on the roof, increasing the safety not only of maintenance workers but of civilians. (Remember, frisbees and baseballs have a much better chance of landing on a flat roof than a pitched roof.)

5. The gravel acts as a fire retardant.

But gravel's status as the ballast of choice is in jeopardy, according to Boon:

Today, newer technology has allowed for single-layer roofing systems. Larger, ¾"–1½"-diameter stone is used . . . to hold the roofing system in place. The larger stones provide the same protection from sun, traffic, and fire, and the larger size reduces the potential for wind blow-off.

Submitted by Howard Livingston of Arlington, Texas.

There are many miniature dogs. Why aren't there any miniature house cats?

Our correspondent, Elizabeth Frenchman, quite rightly points out that there are legitimate breeds of dogs that resemble rodents more than canines. If poodles can be so easily downsized, why can't Siamese or Oriental cats? If dogs can range in size between the pygmyesque Pekingese or a sausage-like Dachshund to a nearly three-foot-high Borzoi or a lineman-shaped Saint Bernard, why is the size variation so small in cats?

According to Enid Bergstrom, editor of *Dog World*, the answer is in the genes. Bergstrom says that dogs are the most genetically variable mammals, the easiest to breed for desired characteristics. The genes of cats, on the other hand, are much less plastic. If you try to mix two different breeds of cats, the tendency is for the offspring to look like an Oriental tabby. Of course, as dog breeder Fred Lanting points out, domestic breeds are miniature cats of sorts, the descendants of the big cats found in zoos.

Helen Cherry, of the Cat Fanciers Federation, told *Imponderables* that felines could be reduced somewhat in size by interbreeding small cats, but she, as well as all of the cat experts we spoke to, insisted that they had never heard of any interest expressed in trying to miniaturize cats. A representative of the American Cat Association remarked that a cat is small enough already.

Cat associations and federations are conservative by nature. Helen Cherry predicted that miniature cats would not be allowed to register or show or be "acknowledged in any way." It isn't easy being small.

Submitted by Elizabeth Frenchman of New York, New York.

What is the meaning of the numbers inside the arrows of the triangle on recyclable plastics? And what do the letters below the triangle mean?

Both the numbers and the letters signify the composition of the plastic used in bottles and other containers. Imagine the problems at recycling centers if workers were forced to judge, by eye, whether a bottle was made out of polypropylene or polyethylene terephthalate, to mention merely two of the hardest to spell plastics.

So the Society of the Plastics Industry, Inc., developed a voluntary coding system for manufacturers to classify plastic containers according to their resin composition. The most common plastics received the lowest numbers. The letters are abbreviations of the dominant resin from which the container is made. If containers are made from more than one material, they are coded by the primary material:

> 1 = PET, or polyethylene terephthalate, used in plastic soda bottles
> 2 = HDPE, or high-density polyethylene, used in plastic milk and juice jugs
> 3 = V, or vinyl
> 4 = LDPE, or low-density polyethylene
> 5 = PP, or polypropylene
> 6 = PS, or polystyrene
> 7 = Other

The use of the plastic container coding system is voluntary, and the manufacturer does not in any way guarantee that the product will be recyclable or that the resins in the container will be compatible with other containers that have the same code number.

This disclaimer is necessary for several reasons. Virgin materials are manufactured for specific applications; not all polypropylene products, for example, can be blended successfully. In some cases, the intended application for the recycled product might be more demanding than its original use. And plastic, like any other material, can be contaminated by the contents of the container during its original use. We know we have a strong preference not to have the plastic containers recycled at some of the fast food joints where we have eaten.

Submitted by Dave Hanlon of Aurora, Illinois.

DAVID FELDMAN

Why are there no public bathrooms in most supermarkets?

After trying about ten different supermarket chains, we got one on-the-record response—from giant Kroger. Off the record, we got the same response from other stores as we received from Kroger's customer relations representative, Ginger Rawe: "Restrooms have always been available for customers' and employees' use, while not always visible to the public."

What incentive do supermarkets have to make restrooms noticeable or to encourage their use? Shelf space is at a premium, and supermarkets already suffer from very low profit margins. And stores have no desire to encourage noncustomers off the street to use restrooms. Department stores have long made it a policy to locate their bathrooms in the most obscure nooks of their space. You may have to walk past some unopened cartons or some unpackaged meat, but you'll find every supermarket has bathrooms. The next time nature calls, just ask a clerk—assuming you can find one. He or she will know how and where to find relief.

Incidentally, supermarket bathrooms are coming out of the closet, so to speak. With the advent of food superstores and warehouse supermarkets, many chains are trying to keep customers inside the store as long as possible, and floor space isn't quite as tight as in "regular" supermarkets. Some chains are making their bathrooms user-friendly by posting signs so that customers can actually find them. Now if they would just stock the bathrooms with paper towels instead of those infernal hand driers, we'd be content.

Submitted by Michael Reuzenaar of Colorado Springs, Colorado. Thanks also to Jadon Welke of Hebron, Indiana.

Why do babies blink less often than adults?

Babies blink a lot less than adults—many babies blink only once or twice a minute. The purpose of blinking is to spread tears over the surface of the eyes. Adults vary widely in their blink frequency, and such exigencies and circumstances as corneal touching, irritation, drying, foreign matter entering the eye, and emotional distress or excitement can all cause the blinking rate to rise dramatically.

Ophthalmologists we contacted are full of theories but not a definitive answer. James P. McCulley, of the Association of University Professors of Ophthalmology, points out that the nerve structure of the infant's eye is much less well developed than its adult counterpart. Babies don't even manufacture tears during their first month of birth, so they clearly seem immune to the pain of dry eyes that would afflict adults who don't blink more often.

Ophthalmologist Samuel Salamon, of the Cataract Eye Center of Cleveland, Ohio, muses over other possible explanations:

> It is puzzling to us as to why babies' eyes don't simply dry out. Of course, they don't spend that much time with their eyes open and the tiny bit of mucus that the eyes manufacture is usually enough to keep the front surface of the eye, the cornea, moistened sufficiently.
>
> Babies probably do not need to blink as often as adults because their fissures are much smaller. That is, much less of their front eye surface is exposed to the environment both because of the shape of their skulls and because their eyelid openings are very small. Thus, the eyes dry out much more slowly, and need lubrication much less often.

Some ophthalmologists we contacted also speculated that babies' blinking rates may not be caused as much by emotional

DAVID FELDMAN

components as adults' are. Perhaps, but any parent who has had a baby cry for hours for totally unexplained reasons may hesitate to believe that stress isn't a major part of the infant's ecosystem.

Submitted by Julie Ann Jimenez of Houston, Texas.

Why do your eyes hurt when you are tired?

Why do couch potatoes have such a bad reputation? While lying on the sofa perusing an Archie comic book or studying the impact of television violence on children by viewing Bugs Bunny cartoons, they are actually exercising what ophthalmologist James P. McCulley, of the University of Texas Medical School, calls "among the most active muscles in the body."

Actually, your eyes contain three sets of muscle groups:

- Each eye has six *extraocular muscles* attached to the outside of the eyeball, which turn the eyes in all directions. The extraocular muscles must coordinate their movements so that both eyes look in the same direction at the same time.
- The *sphincter and dilatory muscles* open or close the pupils, defining how much light is allowed into the eye.
- The *ciliary muscles* attach to the lens inside the eye. When these muscles contract or relax, they change the shape of the lens, altering its focus.

Concentrated reading or close work provides a workout for these muscle groups strenuous enough to make Richard Simmons proud. Unfortunately, as in all aerobic programs, the saying "no pain, no gain" applies, as Winnipeg, Manitoba optometrist Steven Mintz explains:

> The human eye is designed so that, if perfectly formed, it will form a clear image on the retina (at the back of the eye) of any distant object without having to use any of the muscles. In order to see closer objects clearly, however, each set of muscles has to

work. The extraocular muscles must turn each eye inward; the sphincter muscles must work to make the pupil smaller; and the ciliary muscles must contract to allow the lens to change to a shape that will produce a clearer image.

This minimal muscular effort is significant in itself. However, no human eye is perfectly formed and these imperfections will increase the amount of effort required. For instance, people who are farsighted must exert more than the normal amount of effort on the part of the ciliary muscles. Many people have extraocular muscle imbalances that force them to work harder. Virtually every person, as [he or she] approaches or passes the age of forty, suffers from a stiffening of the lens inside the eye, which forces those ciliary muscles to work even harder. Reading under poor light (either too much or too little) will cause the sphincter and dilatory muscles to work excessively.

Just like doing 100 pushups can cause the arm muscles to become pain[ed], so can the muscular effort . . . described above cause sore eyes. Add to this that after several hours of close work, all of your body's muscles are going to be more fatigued, your level of tolerance or your pain threshold for sore eyes will be less than when you are fresh.

Ophthalmologists we consulted speculated that much of the eye strain attributed to tiredness is in reality caused by dryness. Dr. Ronald Schachar, of the association for the Advancement of Ophthalmology, notes that when one is tired, the blink rate slows down and the eyes are not properly lubricated. Close work also slows down the blink rate. Eye specialists are finding that workers at computer visual display terminals experience decreased blinking. This is one reason most consultants recommend stepping away from VDTs at least once an hour. While most of us are more than happy to rest our muscles after doing a few pushups, we expose our eyes to a marathon just about every day.

Submitted by Martin Nearl of Monsey, New York.

DAVID FELDMAN

Why does after-shave lotion have to sting? What causes the sting, and could it be replaced by a nonsting ingredient?

What's the stinging culprit? Demon alcohol. John Corbett, vice-president of technology at Clairol, elaborates:

> The reason that most after-shave lotions sting is that they contain a relatively high percentage of ethyl alcohol, which, coupled with the fact that the facial skin has been subject to abrasion by the process of shaving, sets up an ideal situation for eliciting the sensation of stinging. The importance of the abrasion contribution can be readily tested by applying after-shave lotion some hours after shaving—no stinging sensation will be observed.

Corbett mentioned that there are nonstinging after-shave balms on the market, but "none have achieved significant popularity." So why do men crave a little pain in the morning? Corbett offers a few possibilities: "Presumably men find the sting of after-shave products an aid to waking up and proof that something is happening—or, maybe, men are masochists at heart."

Irene L. Malbin, vice-president of public affairs at the Cosmetic, Toiletry, and Fragrance Association, told *Imponderables* that after-shave lotions are not merely repackaged colognes or perfumes. Some lotions contain cooling astringent ingredients to heal small nicks and cuts; others moisturize and smooth the skin. Unlike perfumes, the scent is formulated to "perform for a short time."

The alcohol in after-shave lotion that stings you also protects you—it acts as an antiseptic. Cosmetics companies won't brag about this fact in ads, for if they do, the lotion will be classified as a drug. Cosmetics companies avoid the drug classification so that the product will not fall under the regulatory and marketing constraints for pharmaceuticals, which are far more rigorous than for cosmetics.

Submitted by Dr. John Hardin of Greenfield, Indiana.

Why do you often see tires on top of mobile homes in trailer parks?

Our initial research wasn't encouraging. Augie, at Sunset Trailer Park, in San Jose, California, insisted that someone was pulling our leg. He had never heard of putting tires on a trailer and thought it would be a bad idea—if the tire dented the roof, rust, and eventually a hole, would create a major repair job.

We were disappointed when Jane Owens, at Western Trailer Park in San Jose, agreed with Augie that she hadn't seen tires on the roofs of trailers in northern California. But, she added, "They put tires on the roof in Nevada, where it gets windy."

"Oh, no," we thought, "don't tell us that the tires are used to weigh down the trailers to keep them from blowing away during tornadoes?" We were assured not. Kay McKeown, who runs a trailer park in Battle Mountain, Nevada, explained that most mobile homes have tie-downs to keep the trailers in place during severe wind.

The purpose of the tires on the roof, Kay and Jane agreed, is to kill the noise of wind and rain hitting the surface of the aluminum or tin roof. The tires deflect the pinging sound of rain; even better, the weight of the tires keeps the wind from making the roof pop in and out, the most annoying and sleep-destroying sound since the invention of the leaky faucet. One layer of tires does the job effectively, and the tires needn't have new treads or high biases. Of course, some trailers boast shingled roofs—these don't pop in and out, and don't need tires atop them, but they tend to cost more.

We never would have thought of the "prevent the roof popping" answer to this Imponderable, but as ignorant as we were, we still couldn't resist challenging the trailer park mavens about why tires were chosen to kill the sound of falling rain or hail. Surely, the owners could have found a better tool for the purpose —a tire, after all, is almost as much hole as substance. While Jane Owens acknowledged that tires can't cover the whole surface of the roof and are much more successful at solving the popping roof problem, they greatly soften the noise. And, she adds, some people place a tarp or plywood directly over the roof and then place the tires on top. The additional covering not only kills the sound but helps prevent corrosion of the metal roof.

Submitted by Lynne Lichtenstein of Hickory, North Carolina.

Why do cows stick their tongues up their nostrils?

We were tempted to say, "Because they can!" But in our relentless quest for truth we asked several cattle experts about this unsightly habit. Our serious guess was that the tongue was the easiest way to lubricate the dreaded "dry nose" condition that we assumed plagued our bovine friends. Wrong. Cows stick their tongues up their nostrils for two distinct reasons.

Cows have nasolabial glands located in the dermis (just under the epidermis of the skin) that produce a watery secretion that helps keep their noises moist. Cows and other ruminants use these secretions to digest their food, as Michael T. Smith, of the National Cattlemen's Association, explains:

> They frequently thrust their muzzles into the feed and, during rumination, run their tongues into the nostril and over the muzzle, thus bringing the secretion into the mouth. The chemical properties of nasolabial secretions are similar to saliva and aid in the digestive process (e.g., swallowing, enzymatic activity, buffering of the rumen [the cow's first stomach]).

Smith adds that buffalo exhibit the same behavior as their bovine cousins.

Cows frequently endure respiratory infections that involve involuntary nasal discharges, sometimes quite heavy. Dr. Harold Amstutz, of the American Association of Bovine Practitioners, told *Imponderables* that these discharges are quite irritating and need to be expelled. But "cows don't have handkerchiefs or fingers." So they use their tongues to remove the irritant instead.

Submitted by Gena Stephenson of Bloomington, Illinois. Thanks also to Irvin Lush of Louisville, Kentucky.

Why don't banks return canceled checks in numerical order?

They could, but it would take one additional step that would ultimately cost the consumer, as well as the banks, more money. Ann Walk, executive director of the National Independent Bank Equipment & Systems Association, explains:

> The average account has only twenty-eight checks per month, and the banks feel that the customer can sort these and save the banks time. If you will notice on your monthly statement, the checks are listed in numerical order for your convenience. This is done automatically by machine and not by hand, as sorting checks would be.

Are the checks placed in your statements in random order? Not really. Banks send bank checks with your statement in the order *they* received them.

Submitted by R. A. Pickett of Danville, Illinois.

What makes cotton shrink more when washed than wool when cleaned?

If we had known how complicated this subject was, we might have tried tackling an easier problem, perhaps solving the unresolved issues in quantum physics or conducting an exhaustive search to find either a scintilla of humor or a decent female role in an Oliver Stone movie.

Trade groups in both the wool and cotton industry sent us literature full of equations and formulas, the likes of which we hadn't seen since we glanced at the textbook for that math class in college that we decided not to take because it was too difficult or, rather, not relevant to solving the social ills of our country. But since we are stuck with the issue at hand, please believe us when we tell you we are *simplifying* our answer.

All the processes that turn cotton into a finished garment (e.g., spinning, weaving or knitting, dyeing, finishing) strain and contract the fabric. Cotton shrinks when this strain is relaxed. Although many factors can contribute to shrinkage, by far the biggest factor is swelling of the yarn when exposed to water.

One might think that swollen yarn would increase the size of the garment, but what happens is that a greater length of yarn, known as warp yarn, is required to interweave the greater diameter of the swollen filling threads if the fibers are to remain in position. But the knitting process doesn't allow enough extra yarn to interweave, so the filling threads are drawn together. This results in a relaxation of the internal strain and shrinkage in length. This shrinkage can occur in the clothes dryer as well

DAVID FELDMAN

as in the washing machine, as anyone who has ever seen an extra-large T-shirt turn into a medium after a prolonged spin can attest. Chemical processes, such as Sanforizing, can eliminate all but about 1 percent of this shrinkage, but the treatment affects the feel and wear characteristics of the cotton.

Despite wool's reputation as a relatively shrink-free material, it is susceptible to the same relaxation of strains problems as cotton, and one more as well: felting shrinkage. Felting shrinkage is why you can't put most wool garments in the washing machine, as the American Wool Council explains:

> Felting shrinkage occurs when wool is subjected to heat, moisture, and friction, the kind of friction that takes place in washing agitation. The microscopic scale-like structures of the wool fiber interlock; the fabric becomes thicker and smaller; it shrinks or felts. This kind of shrinkage is irreversible.

So why doesn't wool shrink when exposed to the heat in dry cleaning? Because as part of the finishing process of making a wool garment, the wool is preshrunk in a process called "fulling" or "milling." Heat, moisture, and friction are applied to the fabric so that it shrinks a specified amount in length and width. Fulling tightens the weave and helps provide the softer texture desired of wool garments. Many chemical processes have been invented to allow treated wool garments to be machine washed and dried.

One advantage of wool over cotton is that shrinkage caused by relaxation of fiber strains can often be reversed. We have been testing this hypothesis by bravely, and without regard to our own welfare, gaining weight over the years. We can conclusively state that our old cotton T-shirts, which once fit perfectly, are not capable of expanding to fit our now ampler frame.

Submitted by John Clark of Pittsburgh, Pennsylvania.

Why are powdered laundry detergents sold in such odd weights?

Call it rigid and boring, but there is something comforting about the sizing of liquid detergents. Most brands, such as the largest-selling liquid detergent in the United States, Tide, manufacture 32-ounce, 64-ounce, 96-ounce, 128-ounce, and 156-ounce sizes. But compare these nice, even sizes (which make sense both as even pound equivalents and as units of quarts and gallons) to Tide's "regular" and "Ultra" powdered detergents. According to Procter & Gamble spokesperson Joe Mastrullo, the company now produces only two sizes of "regular" detergent—in two rather strange sizes: 39 ounces and 136 ounces.

What gives? According to Edna Leurck, of P&G's consumer services,

> When detergents were first introduced, the weight selected was chosen to make the products compatible with those laundry soaps that were in general use. Over the years, increased detergent technology led to changes in the products, which have caused the standard weights to jump around a bit.

The sizes selected are not arbitrary, though. Sheryl B. Zapcic, of Lever Brothers Company, explains that powdered detergents are sold to provide consumers with

> an approximate number of standard dry measured uses. For instance, if a detergent is packaged to provide the consumer with 20 uses and each use measures ½ cup of detergent, the weight of the package is calculated by multiplying 20 times the weight of each ½-cup use. Therefore, the consumer gets an "even" number of washing uses, rather than an "even" number of ounces.

This explains the odd sizes of regular Tide packages we mentioned. The 39-ounce size is meant to clean thirteen loads; the 136-ounce size should handle forty-six loads.

We thought that when concentrated detergents swept the supermarket aisles, their weights might be rounded off like their liquid counterparts, but alas, the tradition of the weird sizing

DAVID FELDMAN

continues. Ultra Tide, the best-selling concentrated powdered detergent, is marketed in five configurations: 23 ounces (ten loads); 42 ounces (eighteen loads); 70 ounces (thirty loads); 98 ounces (forty-two loads); and 198 ounces (eighty-five loads).

If you calculate the weight per load, you will see that the definition of a "load" isn't absolutely precise. But then how many of us are meticulous in measuring the amount of detergent we toss into the washing machine, anyway?

Submitted by Chris Allingham of Sacramento, California.

What are we smelling when it "smells like rain is coming"?

This isn't the type of question that meteorologists study in graduate school or that receives learned exegeses in scholarly journals, but we got several experts to speculate for us. They came down into two camps.

1. *It ain't the rain, it's the humidity.* Biophysicist Joe Doyle blames the humidity, which rises before rainfall. Of course, humidity itself doesn't smell, but it accentuates the smells of all the objects around it. Everything from garbage to grass smells stronger when it gets damp. Doyle believes that the heightened smell of the flora and fauna around us tips us off subliminally to the feeling that it is going to rain. Richard Anthes, of the National Center for Atmospheric Research, points out that many gaseous pollutants also are picked up more by our smell receptors when it is humid.

DAVID FELDMAN

2. *The ozone did it.* Dr. Keith Seitter, assistant to the executive director of the American Meteorology Association, reminds us that before a thunderstorm, lightning produces ozone, a gas with a distinctive smell. He reports that people who are near lightning recognize the ozone smell (as do those who work with electrical motors, which emit ozone).

Kelly Redmond, meteorologist at the Western Regional Climate Center, in Reno, Nevada, also subscribes to the ozone theory, with one proviso. Ozone emissions are common during thunderstorms in the summer, but not from the rains from stratiform clouds during the cold season. So if it's "smelling like rain" during the winter in Alaska, chances are you are not smelling the ozone at all but the soil, plants, and vegetation you see around you, enhanced by the humidity.

Submitted by Dr. Thomas H. Rich of Melbourne, Victoria, Australia. Thanks also to George Gudz of Prescott, Arizona; Anne Thrall of Pocatello, Idaho; Dr. Allan Wilke of Toledo, Ohio; Matthew Whitfield of Hurdle Mills, North Carolina; Philip Fultz of Twentynine Palms, California; and William Lee of Melville, New York.

Why do unopened jars of mayonnaise, salad dressing, fruit, and many other foods stay fresh indefinitely on the shelf but require refrigeration after being opened?

The three main enemies of freshness in perishable foods are air, heat, and low acidity. Foods such as mayonnaise, salad dressing, and canned fruit all undergo processing to eliminate these hazards. Burton Kallman, director of science and technology for the National Nutritional Foods Association, explains:

Unopened jars of perishable foods can remain at room temperature because they are sealed with low oxygen levels (sometimes under vacuum), are often sterilized or at least pasteurized, and may contain preservatives which help maintain their freshness.

All three of these foods contain *natural* ingredients that act as preservatives. Roger E. Coleman, senior vice-president of public communications for the National Food Processors Association, differentiates between foods that must be refrigerated immediately and those that can remain unopened on the shelf:

> Products such as marinated vegetables, salad dressings, and fruits, which contain adequate amounts of added acid ingredients such as vinegar and/or lemon juice, will not support the growth of hazardous microorganisms and only need to be refrigerated after opening to prevent them from spoiling. Other products, such as canned meats and vegetables, do not contain acidic ingredients and, thus, can support the growth of hazardous microorganisms. These products must be refrigerated, not only to retard spoilage but to keep them safe to eat after opening.

This last point is particularly important, for many foods that state "Refrigerate after opening" are perfectly safe to store back on the shelf after they are opened. So why the warning? Barbara Preston, executive director of the Association for Dressings and Sauces, writes:

> Most commercial dressings (with the exception of those bought from a refrigerated display case) are perfectly safe stored at room temperature. The words 'Refrigerate After Opening' on the label are intended only to help preserve their taste, aroma, and appearance. They do not relate to spoilage. If an already opened jar of salad dressing is accidentally left out for several hours, don't throw it away. There is no danger of spoiling . . . it just may not taste as fresh.

Submitted by Nancy Schmidt of West New York, New Jersey.

DAVID FELDMAN

Why are matchbooks assembled so that the sharp side of the staple is on the striking side, risking injury to the fingers?

What piece of legislation in 1978 has affected and changed American life most profoundly? Some would argue it was the Senate's vote to turn the Panama Canal over to the Panamanians. Or Jimmy Carter's signing the Humphrey-Hawkins bill, which attempted to ensure full employment while keeping inflation in check. But some, with great sincerity, will point to the federal regulations enacted requiring the striking strip to be moved to the back of the matchbook.

We all know that the federal bureaucracy gets blamed for imposing too many regulations, but this one actually made some sense. Although matchbooks before 1978 were clearly marked "Close Cover Before Striking," macho types or those in the throes of a nicotine fit often struck the matches without closing the cover; with the striking strip on the front, the exposed matches often came in contact with the heat, or even the flame, of the match, causing burns.

Manufacturers were required to move the strip to the back of the book. Couldn't they simply reverse the staple position on the new books, lessening the chances of staple cuts?

The problem is that the matchbook industry would have had to retrofit all of their existing machinery. So instead of changing the position of the staple, today a machine clinches the staple to ensure it is properly closed. Furthermore, the striker is placed high enough above the staple so that even shaky smokers can avoid hitting the staple. The staple should not penetrate the striking strip at all.

We asked Iain Walton, customer service representative for match manufacturer D.D. Bean & Sons, if they have encountered problems with the staples in post-1978 matchbooks. He replied that there weren't problems with staple cuts, but . . .

> Some people do complain that the staple was responsible for causing flying heads from the matches. In all cases, if the match is struck correctly, the staple is in no way responsible. In fact, the reason this happens is that the match was not struck along the length of the striking strip, as is intended. Instead, it is struck across the width of the striking surface and into the staple.

We have often wondered about this Imponderable ourselves. But we still find it amusing that *staple cuts* are the health hazard smokers worry about.

Submitted by Pete Johnson of Fargo, North Dakota.

Why are paper (book) matches dark on one side and light on the other?

If 1992 seemed like an especially exciting year to you, and you didn't quite understand why, may we suggest the reason. Even if you didn't know it consciously, you were celebrating the hundredth anniversary of the book match. Certainly Iain K. Watson was excited about the August centennial celebration in Jaffrey,

DAVID FELDMAN

New Hampshire. Even so, he took a little time out to provide us with a precise answer to this Imponderable.

We may take for granted the design of a match book, but manufacturers don't. Who would have thought that the reason for the different colors of matches was . . . aesthetics?

> If you look at a book of matches, you will notice that one side is brown, or "kraft" [the type of strong wrapping paper used in paper shopping bags], while the other is either blue or white. Match stems are manufactured from recycled paper stock, which in its finished form is the ugly brown color of the match backs.
>
> In order to enhance its appearance, in the final stages that this brown paper pulp is being pressed, additional processes are added. In the case of the blue color of the front of the stem stock, blue dye is added to the paper. When this dye is added, the blue coloring only goes partway through the stock. Hence the brown remains the color of the back.
>
> In the case of the white-fronted match sticks, during the final pressing processes of the recycled paper stock, cleaner, whiter recycled paper pulp is added, giving the final layers a whiter appearance than the bulk of the brown recycled board. Generally, the whiter recycled stock is comprised of papers such as white envelopes and white bond papers, whereas the majority of the match stem stock is composed of a mishmash of recycled papers.

We don't know of anyone who ever selected, or for that matter refused, to use book matches (which, after all, are usually given out for free) based on the color of the matches themselves. But match manufacturers hardly want to test the hypothesis. For there are other alternatives, like lighters, lurking around for consumers to use.

Submitted by Rory Sellers of Carmel, California.

HOW can the blades of electric can openers be sharp enough to cut through metal yet not sharp enough to cut our fingers when touched?

The blade of a can opener is far from dull, but it need not be as sharp as a scalpel to open cans. As Marilyn Myers, of Norelco Consumer Products, put it, "The metal in the opener is made of sturdier stuff than the can it opens."

Just as important, the blade has a lot of help in opening the can. Liz Wentland, of Sunbeam-Oster, explains that pressure is exerted on the blade by the can opener lever to drive it into the can. Once the drive wheel of the can opener pushes the blade through the lid so that the seal is broken, a razor-sharp blade isn't necessary. On an electric can opener, the drive wheel obtains its power from the motor; on hand models, the crank (and human hands) provides the power.

DAVID FELDMAN

Myers adds that can opener blades do occasionally need replacement. Why? "Mainly because they get clogged with goo."

Submitted by Patti Willis of Endicott, New York.

Why do most retail establishments with double doors usually lock one of the two leaves?

In every *Imponderables* book, one chapter becomes an obsession. This time around, we were fixated on solving the double door dilemma, mainly because we face this predicament on a daily basis.

We approach a store. We see double doors in front of us with both leaves closed. Which leaf is locked? Should we try the left or the right? And should we pull? Or should we push? Four possible combinations. Invariably, we succeed. On the fourth try.

We spoke to or received letters from dozens of sources about this Imponderable over the last five years. We heard no consensus and not much sense, either. In despair, we asked trusty researcher Sherry Spitzer to speak to store managers, architects, door manufacturers, and safety inspectors to see if she could make sense out of a confusing assemblage of responses. After many person-hours of work by both of us, all we can report is that while there are many theories to explain why proprietors might lock one leaf of a double door, few of the people who actually *do* lock them could provide a reasonable explanation for their behavior.

Still, we'll share what we've come up with, and pray that an empathic reader will help relieve the pounding sensation in our brain.

First of all, why do stores have double doors in the first place? Local fire codes mandate the minimum width of doors used as exits in public buildings. Double doors are lighter and more practical than single doors to cover a wide area. Electric sliding doors, one possibility, are extremely expensive, while one wide door would sweep over a tremendous area within and outside of the store, posing the threat of accidents and occupying valuable store space. Double doors also allow for easier movement in and out of the store, particularly if customers are trying to enter while others are trying to exit. Double doors also make it possible to move in furniture or other wide objects if the service entrance is impassable.

What explanations did we hear for closing one of the leaves? Here are the most plausible:

1. *Saves energy costs. By opening only one side, stores can retain heat in the winter and air conditioning in the summer.* True, but the savings are minimal, indeed. An individual will not open both sides at once. If a group of people, leaving and/or entering, can't open both leaves at once, they will keep one open much longer than if they were using both to make their transition. Approximately the same amount of heat/air conditioning would be lost.

2. *The wind can kick up when both leaves are open.* Again, not untrue. A good architect can assure that doors will not buckle with gusts, but wind problems are one of the reasons why double doors are often supplied with deadbolts for one leaf. Vestibules also absorb most of the wind tunnel effect that occasionally occurs.

3. *Prevents shoplifting.* Several store managers claimed that this was the main purpose for locking one leaf. But Jack Schultz, of the National Retail Federation, claimed that this argument is ridiculous on its face. The thief has already entered the store—he or she knows full well which door(s) will be open on the way out.

4. *Crowd control/traffic flow.* You must be kidding. Closing leaves causes congestion at the doorways. Control? Maybe. Flow? No. (Besides, we've seen leaves locked in many stores and office buildings without any security or crowd control efforts whatsoever.)

5. *Astragals.* Between 10 and 20 percent of the double doors installed include astragals: metal, rubber, or felt material that cov-

ers the gap between the two leaves of the double door. Astragals help keep the elements, notably dirt, smoke, wind, and precipitation, from entering the store, and help preserve conditioned air inside. Astragals also keep potential criminals from sticking a coat hanger or other wedge in between the doors to force entry.

Obviously, a metal astragal is a far more effective deterrent to thieves than softer materials, but it makes life more difficult for the shopkeeper. According to architect David B. Eagan, of Eagan Associates, the astragal is usually placed on the active door. Why? The door with the astragal has to close last so that the two leaves will close appropriately. (If the leaf with the astragal is closed first, the other leaf won't close all the way.)

If both doors are activated, "coordinating hardware," usually placed at the top of the door, is necessary to make the leaves close harmoniously. But coordinating hardware is very expensive. The path of least resistance (and least strain on the pocketbook) is to lock one leaf and activate the second leaf only when necessary.

While we are always ready to accept any explanation that hinges on saving money or hard work, most stores don't have doors with metal astragals (soft astragals don't require expensive coordinating hardware or one particular leaf to be designated as the active one), so theory number 5 can't explain this universal condition.

Still, we argue that laziness is the dominant motivator in The Case of the Locked Doorleaf. It is easier for store employees to contend with one door than two. Rose Smouse, executive assistant of the National Retail Federation, concurs:

There is no standard as to why this second double door is locked. It is, best as we can tell, pure convenience. This second door usually has [flush-bolt] locks that go into the top part of the doorjamb and another one that goes into the floor. Some doors have special locks that open them. These second doors are not convenient or easy to open and, therefore, remain locked.

A few off-the-record remarks from store managers and their underlings indicated that the laziness theory has much to commend it.

Judging from our mailbag, most folks wish door policies were more convenient for them, rather than the storekeepers.

National Retail Federation's Jack Schultz, who once operated-department store giant Bloomingdale's, calls closing any of the doors to a retail establishment "the most customer-insulting activity a retail establishment can engage in."

May we include one more, not insignificant point? Closing one leaf may be illegal. Local fire codes ordain the width required of any "means of egress" from an establishment open to the public. If an exit must be six feet wide, can it be counted at that width if one of the two leaves is closed, and the doorway is effectively only three feet wide?

We spoke to Bruce W. Hisley, program chair of the Fire Prevention Technical Program Series at the National Fire Academy, who informed us that although there is no single national standard for such matters, virtually all localities require that doors identified as exits must be open when the building is occupied. The question remains: Does that mean both leaves of the door or only one?

In practice, many stores meet fire codes by installing double doors that the fire department assumes will stay open during business hours. They are committing a code violation by closing one leaf. But until localities hire many more inspectors, we'll all have to play the "guess which door" game a little longer.

> *Submitted by Paul Dunn of Morton, Illinois. Thanks also to Douglas Watkins, Jr., of Hayward, California; Jean Harmon of Silver Spring, Maryland; John V. Dixon of Wilmette, Illinois; Thomas Schoeck of Slingerlands, New York; Nancy Stairs of Revelstoke, British Columbia; Frank P. Burger of Nashville, Tennessee; Nelson T. Sparks of Louisa, Kentucky; and Ralph Kaden of New Haven, Connecticut.*

In large enclosed shopping malls, why is the last door on both sides of the main entrance often closed?

The answer once again is, of course, laziness. Mark Weitzman posed this Imponderable in 1987, and ever since we've sought the solution, we have met with obfuscation worthy of politicians and beauty pageant contestants.

Fire codes mandate wide exits for malls. We've seen many with eight sets of double doors side by side. Barring an emergency, the main entrance/exit is rarely congested. Too often, security personnel at malls find it more convenient to not unlock some doors (usually the doors on the far left and right), so as not to have to lock them up again later. Some mall employees have tried to convince us that outer doors are closed to conserve energy or for security reasons, but the explanations ring hollow for the same reasons as they did in the last entry.

Our friend at the National Fire Academy, Bruce Hisley, told *Imponderables* that when he was a fire marshall, he often found that all but one set of a local mall's doors were locked shortly before closing time, in clear violation of fire codes. A little investigation yielded the discovery that this was the employees' less than subtle method of deterring customers from going into the mall at the last minute. Anyone who has ever entered a restaurant five minutes before the stated closing time and received less than stellar service will comprehend the operative mentality.

Submitted by Mark Weitzman of Boulder, Colorado.

Why are there two red stripes around the thinnest part of bowling pins?

Their sole purpose, according to Al Vanderneck, of the American Bowling Congress, is to look pretty. Part of Vanderneck's job is to check the specifications of bowling equipment, and he reports that without the stripes, the pins "just look funny." The area where the stripes are placed is known as the "neck," and evidently a naked neck on a bowling pin stands out as much as a tieless neck on a tuxedo wearer.

Actually, we almost blew the answer to this Imponderable.

We've thrown a few turkeys in our time, and we always identified the red stripes with AMF pins; the other major manufacturer of bowling pins, Brunswick, used a red crown as an identification mark on its pins. So we assumed that the red stripes were a trademark of AMF's.

AMF's product manager Ron Pominville quickly disabused us of our theory. Brunswick's pins have always had stripes, too, and Brunswick has eliminated the red crown in their current line of pins. A third and growing presence in pindom, Vulcan, also includes stripes on their products.

We haven't been able to confirm two items: Who started the practice of striping the necks of bowling pins? And exactly what is so aesthetically pleasing about these two thin strips of crimson applied to battered, ivory-colored pins?

Submitted by Michael Alden of Rochester Hills, Michigan.
Thanks also to Ken Shafer of Traverse City, Michigan.

DAVID FELDMAN

Does catnip "work" on big cats like lions and tigers?

Catnip (or *Nepeta cataria*, as scientists so eloquently call it) is a perennial herb that drives many house cats wild with delight. It was probably first noticed as an attractant when big cats swarmed around withered or bruised plants growing in the wild.

A full response to catnip involves four separate actions, usually in this order:

1. Sniffing
2. Licking and chewing with head shaking
3. Chin and cheek rubbing
4. Head-over rolling and body rubbing

The full cycle usually lasts under fifteen minutes. Some cats will also vocalize after the head-over rolling, presumably a response to hallucinations. Although the cats exposed to catnip mimic their behavior when in heat, catnip does not increase sexual interest or activity and doesn't seem to affect cats in heat more perceptibly.

Scientists know quite a bit about how domestic cats react to catnip. Most cats do not begin responding to the plant until they are six to eight weeks of age, and some may not respond until they are three months of age. All of the research provided by the Cornell Feline Health Center indicates that cats' reaction to catnip is independent of sex or neutering status. Susceptibility is inherited as an autosomal dominant trait—about a third of domestic cats have no reaction to catnip.

Two-legged mammals have not been immune to the charms of catnip. Veterinarian Jeff Grognet cites the historical use of catnip by humans; the versatile herb was used to make tea, juice, tincture, poultice, and infusions. Catnip was also smoked and chewed for its reputed therapeutic, hallucinogenic, or euphoria-inducing properties.

Scientists, like our reader, have also been curious about the effect of catnip on other cats, and other types of animals. In the largest study of catnip's effect on a wide range of animals, Dr. N. B. Todd's conclusion was clear: Although a few individual animals of almost every type reacted in some way to catnip, cats responded most often and most intensely.

Out of sixteen lions tested, fourteen had full household cat-type responses. Almost half of twenty-three tigers tested had no response at all, but many had incomplete responses: Some sniffed; fewer licked; only a couple chin-rubbed; and none exhibited head-over rolling. But young tigers had violently strong reactions to catnip. Most leopards, jaguars, and snow leopards had strong, full-cycle reactions to catnip. We know that bobcats and lynx love catnip, for the herb is sold commercially to lure these cats for trapping purposes.

Noncats, such as civets and mongooses, were mostly indifferent to catnip, although a few exhibited sniffing reactions. An

DAVID FELDMAN

earlier study that predates Todd's concluded that dogs, rabbits, mice, rats, guinea pigs, and fowls were indifferent to a powdered form of catnip that seduced domestic cats. Yet many dog owners report that their pets respond to catnip.

For some anecdotal evidence, we contacted several of the largest American zoos to see if they exposed their big cats to catnip. We found cat keepers almost as curious about catnip as the cats themselves.

We spoke to one cat keeper who fed jaguars catnip directly. "They like it," he said. "They get goofy." But the same keeper reported that a snow leopard wasn't interested. Another keeper reported that tigers responded "to some extent."

Rick Barongi, director of the Children's Zoo at the San Diego Zoo, reports that although most pet owners usually spray catnip scent on a favorite toy of their cat, zoo keepers cannot. A jaguar or lion will simply rip apart and then eat the toy, so instead they spray a piece of wood or a log that a big cat can claw or scratch. Barongi shares the belief that all cats respond to catnip to some extent but that younger cats respond more than older cats, and that all cats react more on first exposure to catnip than in subsequent encounters.

After a thrill or two with catnip, the San Diego Zoo keepers have found that big cats are more entertained in the long run by scratch posts, boomer balls, larger cages, or—most expensive, but most satisfying of all—the pleasure of the company of a cage mate.

Submitted by Dave Williams of Ithaca, New York.

Why are there no purple Christmas lights?

We have read marketing studies indicating that purple is one of the least popular colors among consumers. But judging from all the purple stationery we receive from readers, purple is a popular color among women, especially among young women and girls. So it is probably no coincidence that the two correspondents who posed this Imponderable were of the female persuasion.

Some Christmas sets do include magenta lights, but you will never see deep purple lights. The absence is not a matter of taste but of high school physics. Carla M. Fischer, public relations representative of General Electric, explains:

> The reason there are no deep purple lights is because purple light has the shortest wavelength and is not visible to the human eye.
>
> For instance, when you see a red light, it is a result of the transparent material filtering all wavelengths of light except the red. The same is true for the other colors of the spectrum (remember ROY G BIV?) [a mnemonic for the length of wavelengths, representing red, orange, yellow, green, blue, indigo, and violet].
>
> . . . However, when the transparent material is purple, it filters out all other wavelengths of light except purple; since purple light is not visible to the human eye, you would only see black light.

Bill Middlebrook, a lighting applications specialist for Philips Lighting, concurred that purple bulbs emit a dim glow, indeed, while also making other low-output colors, such as green, look washed-out. Middlebrook added that even blue doesn't really do its share of the illumination load and would probably be omitted from Christmas sets if it weren't for its popularity. Philips has found that consumers prefer "the classics": red, green, blue, and yellow. Of these colors, red and yellow provide by far the most illumination.

We asked Middlebrook if Philips conducted research to determine how to arrange the colors in the Christmas set. The answer: They are randomly arranged.

Submitted by Laurie Muscheid of Rocky Point, New York.
Thanks also to Janice Flinn of Kemptville, Ontario.

Why do pet rodents drink water out of bottles instead of dishes or bowls?

Because we offer them bottles. Rats or guinea pigs would be more than happy to drink out of bowls or dishes as well. After all, in the wild, rodents have to fend for themselves, gathering water from lakes or ponds if they have easy access. More likely, their search for water will be more labor-intensive, involving extracting moisture from succulent plants or dew drops on greenery, or stumbling upon opportunistic puddles (the natural equivalent of a water dish).

Veterinarian David Moore, of Virginia Tech's Office of Animal Resources, says that the practice of installing water bottles with sipper tubes was developed by researchers to promote the health of laboratory animals. When a rodent soiled the water in a bowl, bacteria grew and caused illness. On the other hand, it is anatomically impossible for a rat to defecate or urinate into a water bottle with a sipper tube.

Rodent owners have adopted the practice not only to safeguard their pets but to avoid the less than pleasant chore of cleaning soiled water bowls. Although dogs occasionally treat the toilet like a water bowl, luckily both dogs and cats can both be trained not to treat their water bowls like a toilet.

Submitted by Karyn Marchegiano of Newark, Delaware.

Why are there holes on the bottom of two- and three-liter soda bottles?

Technically, the holes are not on the bottle but on the bottom of the base cup. (The base cup's function is to keep the bottle from tipping over.) The purpose of the holes is to allow the water that accumulates in the base cup (during the rinsing process at the assembly line) to drain out.

Steve Del Priore, plant manager of the Pepsi-Cola Bottling Company of New York, told *Imponderables* that soda, when first entering the bottle, is at approximately 40 degrees Fahrenheit. The bottle is then placed in a container of warm water so that the soda rises to about 60 degrees Fahrenheit, causing condensation on the bottle, another way for water to seep into the base cup. If no drainage outlet were permitted, foul water might seep out of the base cup every time a consumer poured a drink.

Actually, we may not have holes in base cups to kick around too much longer. Margie Spurlock, manager of consumer affairs for Royal Crown Cola, told us that: "In the near future, base cups may be eliminated from these bottles as technology is in place to produce a one-piece bottle which has a base rigid enough to afford the necessary stability for the tall container."

The main impetus for removing the base cups is environmental. The material used for base cups is not the same as that for the bottle itself, necessitating separating the two plastics at recycling centers, slowing down the process considerably.

Submitted by Carrie Schultz of Hinsdale, Illinois.

Why do drivers wire cardboard to their automobile grills during cold weather?

No, it isn't to keep bugs from slipping under the hood. The cardboard is there to try to keep cold air from entering the engine.

When you drive, some kind of cooling fluid is needed to prevent burning fuel from overheating the car. The fluid is pumped through the engine and then the radiator, where the liquid is cooled by passing outside air over the radiator. The fluid then returns to the engine to remove more heat.

DAVID FELDMAN

To gain efficiency in winter, some of the engine's excess heat is used to warm the interior of the car, by routing some of the engine coolant through the heater's coils and blowing inside air over the warm coils. Two experts we spoke to, one a Federal Highway Administration official who wishes to remain anonymous, and the other, automotive historian Keith Marvin, speculate that the cardboard is probably a makeshift attempt to compensate for the inability of the coolant to get warm enough to operate the heater effectively.

By putting the cardboard over their grills, drivers are blocking air flow to the radiator to decrease the ambient air's cooling effect on the coolant. The theory: If the temperature of the fluid is raised, the heater can better withstand the demands of subzero weather.

Why wire and cardboard? Presumably because they are light, cheap, and easily available materials. But aluminum and twine would do the job, too, or any materials that will shield the grill and can withstand the elements.

Submitted by Mason Jardine of Russell, Manitoba, definitely cardboard-on-the-grill country.

Judges! Try the "Voluminous" COURTROOM ROBE and NEVER be caught unprepared again!

HOLDS FOUR LAW BOOKS!

TRICK MOTION
FAMOUS TRIALS
TOP 10 TORTS
FUN LAWS

Velcro straps!

Outside: Dignity on the bench

Inside: "Not so fast, counselor!"

Why do judges wear black robes?

American law is derived from English common law. English judges have always worn robes, so it follows logically that American judges would, too. But the road from English garb to American robes has been bumpier than you might expect.

Actually, there wasn't such a profession as judge in England until the last half of the thirteenth century. Until then, high-level clergymen, robe-wearers all, arbitrated disputes and expounded law. But the church eventually forbade its clergy from the practice, and a new job category was born. From the very start, judges, like most important people, wore robes.

Not too long after the first judge donned his robe, Parliament enacted several laws (between 1337 and 1570) dictating just who could wear what kind of robe. Judges' gowns were often elaborate affairs, usually made of silk and fur. (High judges wore ermine; sergeants, lambskin.)

DAVID FELDMAN

Green was the most popular color for judges' robes at first; later, scarlet gowns and, to a lesser extent, violet gowns, predominated. Black robes did not appear until 1694, when all judges attended the Westminster Abbey funeral of Queen Mary II dressed in black, as a sign of respect for the queen. The mourning period went on for years, and some, but by no means all, lawyers and judges wore black gowns into the next century.

Our founding fathers actually argued over whether our justices of the Supreme Court should wear robes at all. Thomas Jefferson railed against "any needless official apparel," but Alexander Hamilton and Aaron Burr favored them and won the argument. At the first session of the court, Chief Justice Jay wore a robe of black silk with salmon-colored facing. By the early nineteenth century, Supreme Court judges donned black robes of the style worn today.

The solemn costumes of the Supreme Court were not necessarily mimicked by lower courts. Some colonial court judges in the eighteenth century, such as those in Massachusetts, wore gowns and powdered wigs. But in reaction to the Revolutionary War, most trappings of English aristocracy were banished. In fact, the wearing of robes was discontinued in Massachusetts until 1901.

Judges in the West and South tended to be a little less formal. In his book *The Rise of the Legal Profession in America*, Anton-Hermann Chroust described one of the first judges in Indiana as having a judicial costume consisting of "a hunting shirt, leather pantaloons, and a fox skin cap." Most legal scholars believe that the majority of judges in colonial and pre–Civil War times did not wear robes at all.

One reason why so little is known about the dress of judges in early America is that few laws or regulations govern what judges wear. Only Michigan prescribes a dress code ("When acting in his or her official capacity in the courtroom, a judge shall wear a black robe"), and nothing can stop judges from wearing a chartreuse robe if they desire, or none at all.

Still, the vast majority of judges do wear black robes today.

The only reason they aren't wearing more colorful attire is because Queen Mary II died three hundred years ago.

Submitted by Susie T. Kowalski of Middlefield, Ohio. Thanks also to Karen Riddick of Dresden, Tennessee.

Why does the whitewall of a new tire usually have a bluish or greenish tinge?

Isn't there any truth in advertising anymore? Our correspondent wonders why manufacturers don't call them "bluewalls" or "greenwalls."

Ironically, the blue-green stuff on new tires is paint. And it is put there to make sure the whitewall stays white.

Huh? We never said tackling Imponderables was going to be easy, did we? Actually, all will become clear in due time. We heard from General Tire and Goodyear about this subject, but the most complete explanation came from a retired Firestone executive, K. L. Campbell, who wrote a veritable treatise on the subject:

> If black rubber is allowed to be in contact with white sidewall rubber for a few days, the white rubber begins to absorb some of the oils and antioxidant chemicals from the black rubber compound and the result is a permanent brown stain. The longer the black rubber is in contact, the darker the stain. The white rubber compound must be made without any of these oils or antioxidants in order to stay white. Furthermore, it must be protected by barriers so that when it is assembled into a tire, the ordinary black rubber compounds in the rest of the tire are not in contact with it.

Before World War II, manufacturers separated the two by wrapping the white sidewalls with paper at the factory. During the war, whitewalls were not allowed to be manufactured. Once the restriction was lifted, whitewalls became a fad, and tire man-

DAVID FELDMAN

ufacturers looked for a way to eliminate the expensive paper and concomitant labor expense of unwrapping it.

The answer? The blue or green coating you see on tires now. This paint protects the white rubber from contact with the chemicals in the black rubber. According to Campbell, this paint was always intended to be completely washed off *before* the purchaser took possession of the tires. Bright colors were probably chosen to make it obvious that the paint should be removed to expose the white-as-the-driven-snow rubber underneath.

How do tire dealers (or you) remove the protective paint? Jean Bailey, of General Tire, recommends a good dose of soap and water. Campbell says that even a scrubbing with a stiff brush will usually do the trick. But the way that dealerships solve the problem is by utilizing a steam jet, the type you see at the beginning of most car washes.

Submitted by Lori Videla of Berkeley, Illinois.

Why does inflating tires to the proper pressure help gasoline mileage?

Do you remember, as a child, how hard it was to ride a bicycle with a flat or seriously soft tire? It was harder than trying to pedal a Stairmaster for an hour now, wasn't it?

When you drive an automobile, the same principle applies. The mission of tires is to soften the bumps and bruises you would otherwise experience while negotiating roadways, but a tire that bends too much, whether from underinflation or overloading, is going to take a lot of extra energy to push. Tire pressure can actually affect your gasoline mileage. K. L. Campbell explains:

> About 80% of the energy in the gasoline you buy is used up within your car engine. Of the 20% that is available to move the

car, a small percentage goes into friction losses in the various rotating and moving parts outside the engine. Most of the available energy goes into overcoming wind resistance and in rotating the tires, or in climbing grades.

In order for tires to perform their function of softening the ride of the vehicle, they must deflect under the load of the vehicle and the irregularities encountered on the road. When they deflect, there is internal movement throughout the tire that absorbs energy. The greater the deflection, the more energy the tire consumes as it is rolling.

Tire deflection is increased either by putting more load on the tires (filling up your trunk for a vacation trip or piling a few passengers in the rear seat) or by reducing the pressure in the tires.

When you inflate the tires to the proper pressure, you reduce the rolling resistance. In other words, as Jean Bailey puts it, "It requires much more force or energy to rotate a tire that is underinflated than it does to rotate a tire that is inflated to the proper pressure."

Campbell estimates that by decreasing a typical radial tire pressure of 32 psi (pounds per square inch) to 24 psi, a car traveling at 55 miles per hour would increase fuel consumption by about 2 percent. Perhaps 2 percent does not sound earth-shattering, but to put the matter in perspective, the Department of Energy estimates that if all Americans kept all of their vehicle tires inflated to the manufacturers' recommended pressures, four million gallons of gasoline could be saved *every day*.

One of the reasons why modern radial tires perform much better than their bias-ply predecessors is that radials distribute the deflection around most of the tire, whereas bias plies concentrated the deflection near the road surface. Unfortunately, the byproduct of this technological improvement is that it is difficult to see with the naked eye when a radial is underinflated. A pressure gauge is a necessity.

Don't think that you can get even better mileage if you over-inflate your tires. Once you get above 35 psi, a diminishing effect occurs. Not only do you not increase fuel efficiency, but you will be rewarded with a harsh and potentially wild ride.

Submitted by Linda Seefeldt of Clark, South Dakota.

What do coffee companies do with the caffeine left over from making decaffeinated coffee?

You wouldn't want them to throw away the caffeine, do you? If they flushed caffeine down the drain, it could end up in the ocean, and we wouldn't want to see the effect of a caffeine jolt upon killer sharks. It might be enough to turn a blowfish into a slayfish. If they discarded caffeine in the trash, could the caffeine wake up organic garbage in landfills?

We'll never have to worry about these contingencies, for the decaffeination process used in coffee yields pure caffeine, a marketable commodity. Coffee companies sell caffeine to soft drink companies (who need a little less now that many of them are selling caffeine-free sodas) and pharmaceutical companies.

When coffee companies justify the higher cost of decaf by citing processing costs, they rarely add the information that *they* get reimbursed on the back end for the caffeine they "eliminate."

Submitted by Glenn Eisenstein of New York, New York.

How do they get rid of the remains of dead elephants in zoos?

When an elephant in a zoo dies, a necropsy must be performed. In most cases, the necropsy is conducted by a licensed veterinarian or veterinary pathologist from tissue and blood samples extracted from the carcass.

Most zoos we contacted remove selected organs from the dead elephant, pack them in ice or Formalin, and ship them to various research institutions for reproductive or physiological studies. Typical is the response of San Francisco Zoo's Diane Demee-Benoit. She reports that her zoo has a binder full of requests from universities, zoos, and museums for various animal parts. Forensic labs might need DNA to help identify other creatures. A natural history museum might want skulls or a particular set of bones to perform comparative studies. Zoos make sure that all animal parts are used for research and educational purposes only and are not permitted to sell or donate parts to private individuals.

After organs and other body parts are removed, the least pleasant task is performed—cutting the elephants into smaller pieces, for even elephant *parts* are heavy. The parts are carried by forklifts and cranes and placed on flatbed trailers, dump trucks, or whatever vehicles are available.

Where do the trucks take the remains? That depends upon the zoo. The preference is always for burying animals on the premises. Alan Rooscroft, manager of animals at the San Diego Wild Animal Park, said that out of respect for the animals, their elephants are buried on the grounds of the zoo. But not all zoos have room enough for this "luxury."

Many zoos, such as the San Francisco Zoo, incinerate or cremate elephants. Ed Hansen, president of the American Association of Zoo Keepers, indicated that in areas where such disposal is legal, some elephants are buried in licensed landfills.

Some elephants, particularly those from circuses, meet a more ignoble fate—they are sent to rendering plants. Mark

DAVID FELDMAN

Grunwald, of the Philadelphia Zoo, told *Imponderables* that such boiled elephants end up as an ingredient in soap.

Submitted by Claudia Short of Bowling Green, Ohio. Thanks also to Richard Sassaman of Bar Harbor, Maine; and David Koelle of North Branford, Connecticut.

Why do modern gas pump nozzles have rubber sleeves around them? And what are those red, blue, and green things near the nozzle?

Newfangled gas pumps sport nozzles considerably "pumped up" compared to the puny nozzles of yore. Why is it that as soon as most gas stations became self-service, the pumps became five times as bulky?

The rubber bellows are not there for show. The new nozzles, known as Stage II nozzles, help protect us from harmful fumes emitted by the gas going into our automobiles' tanks. J. Donald Turk, of Mobil Oil's public affairs department, explains:

> These nozzles are part of the vapor recovery system at the service station. The rubber sleeves create a seal between the delivery hose and the car's gas tank so that gasoline vapors are returned to the underground storage tank. From there, the vapors are returned to a gasoline terminal so that no [polluting hydrocarbon] vapors are released to the atmosphere.

And what about those colored doohickeys around the nozzle? According to Mobil Oil's Jim Amanna, those are scuff guards used to protect the car from being scratched by the nozzle.

Submitted by David Kroffe of Los Alamitos, California.

Why do "sea" gulls congregate in parking lots of shopping centers where there is little food or water?

The reason why "sea" is in quotation marks above is that there are many different species of gull, and quite a few of them spend little time near the sea. Several species live inland and survive quite easily.

Nancy Martin, naturalist at the Vermont Institute of Natural Science, told *Imponderables* that ring-billed gulls, the most common inland species, display great affection for fast-food restaurant dumpsters as a feeding site. Ring-billed gulls are happy to leave wide-open landfills to the more aggressive herring and great black-backed gulls.

But even gulls who normally feed at the shore might have reason to visit the local mall parking lot. Little-used areas of parking lots are safe and warm. And don't assume there is nothing to eat or drink there. Humans, whether the intentional bread crumb tossers or the unintentional litterers, leave a veritable smorgasbord for the birds, and gulls can take advantage of pud-

DAVID FELDMAN

dles on the surface of the pavement to take a drink or a quick bath. Martin adds that near the ocean, "hard pavement is good for dropping clams or mussels onto to break them open, although gulls will usually choose an area away from other gulls to carry on this activity."

Tim Dillon, researcher at the Cornell Laboratory of Ornithology, speculates that the open space of a parking lot provides "sea" gulls a terrain "similar to a sandbar or beach where they naturally congregate in large numbers." Just as we may occasionally go to the beach as a break from the dull routine of parking lots and shopping, so might gulls take a spiritual retreat to the natural glories of the shopping center parking lot.

> *Submitted by Marilyn Chigi of Clarkstown, Michigan. Thanks also to Doc Swan of Palmyra, New Jersey; Annie Bianchetti of East Brunswick, New Jersey; Melanie Jongsma of Lansing, Illinois; and Tim Poirier of Silver Spring, Maryland.*

How do they keep air out of light bulbs when they are manufactured? Is a vacuum important for a bulb to function?

As we learned in fire prevention class, oxygen is fire's best friend. If oxygen were inside a light bulb while it operated, the filament would melt as soon as electricity was applied. So at the last stage of manufacture, the air is pumped from the incandescent bulb through a glass exhaust tube that is part of the filament support assembly. Richard Dowhan, GTE's manager of public affairs, told *Imponderables* that the exhaust tube is shortened and sealed so that air cannot reenter and so that the screw base can be installed. Any air that remains is removed with a chemical called a "getter."

An old friend of *Imponderables*, GE Lighting's J. Robert Moody, surprised us by saying that not all bulbs do have a vacuum inside the glass bulb:

The vacuum is not necessary for the operation of the lamp. In fact, if the lamp is 40 or more watts, a fill gas, usually a mixture of nitrogen and argon, is added after the air is pumped out.

Inert gases allow the filament to operate efficiently at higher temperatures, and simultaneously lessen the rate at which the tiny pieces of tungsten evaporate from the filament, yielding a longer bulb life.

Submitted by Mitchell Zimmerman of Palo Alto, California.

Why can't you find English muffins in England?

Probably for the same reason you can't find French dressing in France or Russian dressing in Russia. Or why you're more likely to encounter a New York steak in Kansas City than in New York City. Locales mentioned in food names are more often marketing tools than descriptions of the origins of the product.

At least Samuel Thomas, the inventor of the English muffin, was actually born in England. Thomas emigrated to the United States in 1875 and opened his own bake shop in New York City in 1880. According to Kari Anne Maino, of Best Foods Baking Group, the division of CPC International that markets Thomas' English Muffins, Thomas was probably inspired by the crumpets, scones, and cakelike muffins that were popular in England when he left the country. And he was smart enough to realize that the word "English" would lend his product a certain panache in the United States.

Maino says that her company knows of no "English muffins" that are marketed in England today, but "We have learned that a product very similar to our Thomas' English Muffins did exist in England until about 1920." Why an item would fade in popularity in England while gaining popularity in the United States is anybody's guess. An explanation of the gustatory preferences of the English—a culture that deems baked beans on white toast a splendid meal—would require an exegesis far beyond our mortal powers.

Submitted by Rosemary Bosco of Bronx, New York.

What are those beanbaglike packs found inside electronics boxes that warn, "DO NOT EAT"?

We've always thought that instead of having "DO NOT EAT" plastered on them, a little self-disclosure would help. Why not identify what is inside? (Come to think of it, what is inside regular beanbags?) Most of us don't go around eating beanbags, after all.

It didn't take much digging around to find out that inside those packets is silica gel. Silica is the dioxide of silicon. (Did you know that there is more silicon in nature than any other element except oxygen? You do now.) The "gel" part of the equation is a little more puzzling, since the stuff inside the bag is actually in the form of crystals, but heck, we're not purists.

The sole purpose of the silica gel packet is to absorb moisture (silica gel's most common industrial use is as a drying agent in air conditioning equipment) and help keep your electronic gear in top shape. So that it can fall apart, dependably, the day after your warranty runs out.

Randy Acorcey, of Diversified Electronics Corporation, told *Imponderables* that silica gel isn't used much by American manufacturers. Most often, you will find them inside boxes of goods manufactured in the Far East, because the merchandise is shipped by boat, where it can be exposed to high humidity (and in some cases, water) for weeks.

Submitted by Megan Baynes of Richmond, Virginia. Thanks also to Mary Warneka of Perry, Ohio.

What is the purpose of the sign "THIS DOOR TO REMAIN UNLOCKED DURING BUSINESS HOURS" found atop many doors in retail establishments?

This sign, long present on the West Coast, is spreading throughout the United States. Surprisingly, most of the retail trade associations and architects we consulted didn't understand its purpose. The signs never made much sense to us, since they are often placed aside clearly marked EXIT signs.

The key phrase in the sign, for our purposes, is "business hours." Fire codes specify how many exits are required for each business during operating hours. The required number of exits, and the width of those exits, are based upon the hypothetical stress created by an emergency when the place of business is at maximum occupancy.

But what about when the business is closed and a few employees are working inside? Does a K Mart store have to open every fire exit while a skeleton crew is conducting inventory? Absolutely not. Bruce Hisley, of the National Fire Academy, said that in many localities, doors that are ordinarily used as exits can be locked when only employees are present if the door is marked with these signs. The sign serves as a reminder to store owners and managers to unlock the doors when the store opens.

Mike Fisher, vice-president of sales and marketing at door manufacturer Besam, Inc., told *Imponderables* that these signs are also a reminder to the public to remember their rights. If a door sporting this sign is closed when you are in the store, blow the whistle—unless you are an employee doing inventory, of course.

Submitted by Bryan J. Cooper of Ontario, Oregon. Thanks also to Derek King of Huntington Beach, California.

DAVID FELDMAN

What causes the clicking sound inside a car when you put your turn signal on? Why don't some turn signals make that clicking noise?

The mechanics of the turn signal are simple. Frederick Heiler, public relations manager for Mercedes-Benz of North America, explains the technology:

> The electrical current to make turn signals blink usually comes from a relay—a small box enclosing an electromagnetic switch. Whenever the electromagnet is energized, it mechanically pulls together a pair of contacts, sending a pulse of current to the signal lights and, at the same time, making a clicking sound.

Why do some cars not have clicking turn signals? It's all up to the manufacturer. Most car makers choose to make the clicking noise loud and obvious just in case the driver leaves the turn signal on unintentionally.

What's the big deal if the turn signal is left on too long? If a pedestrian is thinking of jaywalking and sees an oncoming car signaling for a right turn, the pedestrian is lulled into a false sense of security. Oncoming cars and pedestrians often make their decisions about when to proceed based on turn signals, and a little gratuitous clicking is a small price to pay for added safety.

Submitted by Michele Al-Khal of Allentown, Pennsylvania.

Why is there a white paper band around the envelopes in a box of greeting or Christmas cards and not the cards themselves?

Would you be shaken to your core to find out that the band exists for the manufacturer's benefit, not yours? We got this less than startling response from Hallmark spokesperson Barbara Meyer:

The white paper bands are put around our envelopes to speed up the packaging process. It is much more efficient to work with one bundle of envelopes instead of 20 or 21 single ones. The reason a band is not put around the cards is because damage to the cards could occur in this process of banding.

Gibson Greetings doesn't use a band around their envelopes, but Sherry Enzweiler, manager of their Fall Seasons division, says that

many card companies buy envelopes from outside vendors already counted out and banded. They are then placed in the box, precounted and banded, by an assembly line worker.

Submitted by Rev. Ken Vogler of Jeffersonville, Indiana.

Where do computer files and programs go when they are erased?

Not to heaven. Not to hell. Not to Silicon Valley. Not even to Dubuque. For the sad story is that deleted files go nowhere at all. David Maier, professor at the Oregon Graduate Institute of Science & Technology's department of computer science and engineering, elucidates:

> The bits and bytes representing the programs and files on the computer disk are generally unchanged immediately after an erase (or delete) command. What changes is the *directory* on the disk. The directory is a list of the names of all the files and programs on the disk, plus a pointer to the portion of the disk where the contents of the file or program are actually stored. When you issue an erase command, all it generally does is to remove the file or program name from the directory and to record elsewhere that

the storage space on the disk formerly used for the file or program is now "free"—that is, available for reuse.

The mechanism for changing the directory is amazingly simple. Although the deleted files remain on the disk, programmer Larry Whitish told *Imponderables* that the first letter of the file name is deleted and replaced with a symbol that looks like "σ," (ASCII character number 229):

> This signals the computer that the disk space the files occupied is available for use by new files and programs and simply ignores their existence . . .
>
> When new files are copied to or created on a disk, they seek the first available space not being used to begin writing their data. If this space is occupied by a file that has been erased, then kiss your old file goodbye! The old file will be overwritten by the new file.
>
> Erased files and programs can be recovered easily *if they have not been overwritten*. A program like the Norton Utilities can restore these files simply by replacing the symbol "σ" in their name with any letter of the alphabet.

So the "deleted" files are no more erased than the music on an audiotape or television program on videotape that hasn't been recorded over.

Submitted by an anonymous caller on the Jim Eason Show, KGO-AM, San Francisco, California.

DAVID FELDMAN

When did wild poodles roam the earth?

The thought of wild poodles contending with the forbidding elements of nature makes us shudder. It's hard to imagine a toy poodle surviving torrential rainstorms or blistering droughts in the desert, or slaughtering prey for its dinner (unless its prey was canned dog food). Or even getting its haircut messed up.

For that matter, what animals would make a toy poodle its prey in the wild? We have our doubts that it would be a status symbol for one lion to approach another predator and boast, "Guess what? I bagged myself a poodle today."

If something seems wrong with this picture of poodles in the wild, you're on the right track. We posed our Imponderable to the biology department of UCLA, and received the following response from Nancy Purtill, administrative assistant:

> The general feeling is that, while there is no such thing as a stupid question, this one comes very close. Poodles never did live in the wild, any more than did packs of roving Chihuahuas. The

present breeds of dogs were derived from selective breeding of dogs descended from the original wild dogs.

Sally Kinne, corresponding secretary of the Poodle Club of America, inc., was a little less testy:

> I don't think poodles ever did live in the wild! They evolved long after dogs were domesticated. Although their exact beginnings are unknown, they are in European paintings from the fifteenth century [the works of German artist Albrecht Dürer] on to modern times. It has been a long, LONG time since poodles evolved from dogs that evolved from the wolf.

Bas-reliefs indicate that poodles might date from the time of Christ, but most researchers believe that they were originally bred to be water retrievers much later in Germany. (Their name is a derivation of the German word *pudel* or *pudelin,* meaning "drenched" or "dripping wet." German soldiers probably brought the dogs to France, where they have traditionally been treated more kindly than *Homo sapiens.* Poodles were also used to hunt for truffles, often in tandem with dachshunds. Poodles would locate the truffles and then the low-set dachshunds would dig out the overpriced fungus.

Dog experts agree that all domestic dogs are descendants of wolves, with whom they can and do still mate. One of the reasons it is difficult to trace the history of wild dogs is that it is hard to discriminate, from fossils alone, between dogs and wolves. Most of the sources we contacted believe that domesticated dogs existed over much of Europe and the Middle East by the Mesolithic period of the Stone Age, but estimates have ranged widely—from 10,000 to 25,000 B.C.

Long before there were any "manmade" breeds, wild dogs did roam the earth. How did these dogs, who may date back millions of years, become domesticated? In her book, *The Life, History and Magic of the Dog,* Fernand Mery speculates that when hunting and fishing tribes became sedentary during the Neolithic Age (around 5000 B.C.), the exteriors of inhabited caves were like landfills from hell—full of garbage, animal bones, mollusk and crustacean shells and other debris. But what seemed

DAVID FELDMAN

like waste to humans was an all-you-can-eat buffet table to wild dogs.

Humans, with abundant alternatives, didn't consider dogs as a source of food. Once dogs realized that humans were not going to kill them, they could coexist as friends. Indeed, dogs could even help humans, and not just as companions—their barking signaled danger to their two-legged patrons inside the cave.

This natural interdependence, born first of convenience and later affection, may be unique in the animal kingdom. Mery claims our relationship to dogs is fundamentally different from that of any other pet—all other animals that have been domesticated have, at first, been captured and taken by force:

> The prehistoric dog followed man from afar, just as the domesticated dog has always followed armies on the march. It became accustomed to living nearer and nearer to this being who did not hunt it. Finding with him security and stability, and being able to feed off the remains of man's prey, for a long time it stayed near his dwellings, whether they were caves or huts. One day the dog crossed the threshold. Man did not chase him out. The treaty of alliance had been signed.

Once dogs were allowed "in the house," it became natural to breed dogs to share in other human tasks, such as hunting, fighting, and farming. It's hard to imagine a poofy poodle as a retriever, capturing dead ducks in its mouth, but not nearly as hard as imagining poodles contending with the dinosaurs and pterodactyls on our cover, or fighting marauding packs of roving Chihuahuas.

Submitted by Audrey Randall of Chicago, Illinois.

What does the "Q" in "Q-tips" stand for?

Most users of Q-tips don't realize it, but the "Q" is short for "Qatar." Who would have thought a lone inventor on this tiny peninsula on the Persian Gulf could have invented a product found in virtually every medicine cabinet in the Western world?

Just kidding, folks. But you must admit, "Qatar" is a lot sexier than "Quality"—the word the "Q" in "Q-tips" actually stands for.

Q-tips were invented by a Polish-born American, Leo Gerstenzang, in the 1920s. Gerstenzang noticed that when his wife was giving their baby a bath, she would take a toothpick to spear a wad of cotton. She then used the jerry-built instrument as an applicator to clean the baby. He decided that a readymade cotton swab might be attractive to parents, and he launched the Leo Gerstenzang Infant Novelty Co. to manufacture this and other accessories for baby care.

Although a Q-tip may seem like a simple product, Gerstenzang took several years to eliminate potential problems. He was concerned that the wood not splinter, that an equal amount of cotton was attached to each end, and that the cotton not fall off the applicator.

The unique sliding tray packaging was no accident, either —it insured that an addled parent could open the box and detach a single swab while using only one hand. The boxes were sterilized and sealed with glassine (later cellophane). The entire process was done by machine, so the phrase "untouched by human hands" became a marketing tool to indicate the safety of using Q-tips on sensitive parts of the body.

Gerstenzang wrestled over what he should name his new product, and after years of soul searching, came up with a name that, at the time, probably struck him as inevitable but, in retrospect, wasn't: "Baby Gays." A few years later, in 1926, the name changed to "Q-Tips Baby Gays." Eventually, greater minds decided that perhaps the last two words in the brand name could be discarded.

DAVID FELDMAN

Ironically, although we may laugh about the dated use of the word "Gays," the elimination of the "Baby" was at least as important. Gerstenzang envisioned the many uses Q-tips could serve for parents—for cleaning not just babies' ears but their nose and mouth, and as an applicator for baby oils and lotions. But the inventor never foresaw Q-tips' use as a glue applicator or as a swab for cleaning tools, fishing poles, furniture, or metal.

Even though Chesebrough-Ponds, which now controls the Q-tips trademark, does nothing to trumpet what the "Q" stands for, the consumer somehow equates the "Q" with "Quality" nonetheless. For despite the best attempts from other brands and generic rivals, Q-tips tramples its competition in the cotton swab market.

Submitted by Dave and Mary Farrokh of Cranford, New Jersey. Thanks also to Douglas Watkins, Jr., of Hayward, California; Patricia Martinez of San Diego, California; Christopher Valeri of East Northport, New York; and Sharon Yeh of Fairborn, Ohio.

Why do deer stand transfixed by the headlights of oncoming cars? Do they have a death wish?

Although no zoologist has ever interviewed a deer, particularly a squashed one, we can assume that no animal has a death wish. In fact, instinct drives all animals to survive. We asked quite a few animal experts about this Imponderable, and we received three different theories, none of which directly contradicts the others.

 1. *The behavior is a fear response.* University of Vermont zoologist Richard Landesman's position was typical:

> Many mammals, including humans, demonstrate a fear response, which initially results in their remaining perfectly still for a few seconds after being frightened. During this time, the hormones of the fear response take over and the

DAVID FELDMAN

animal or person then decides whether to fight or run away. Unfortunately, many animals remain in place too long and the car hits them.

The self-defeating mechanism of the fear response is perpetuated because, as Landesman puts it, "these animals don't know that they are going to die as a result of standing still and there is no mechanism for them to teach other deer about that fact."

2. *Standing still isn't so much a fear response as a reaction to being blinded.* Deer are more likely to be blinded than other, smaller animals, such as dogs and cats, because they are much taller and vulnerable to the angle of the headlight beams. If you were blinded and heard the rumble of a car approaching at high speed, would you necessarily think it was safer to run than to stand still?

3. *The freeze behavior is an extension of deer's natural response to any danger.* We were bothered by the first two theories insofar as they failed to explain why deer, out of all disproportion to animals of their size, tend to be felled by cars. So we prevailed upon our favorite naturalist, Larry Prussin, who has worked in Yosemite National Park for more than a decade. He reports that deer and squirrels are killed by cars far more than any other animals, and he has a theory to explain why.

What do these two animals have in common? In the wild, they are prey rather than predators. The natural response of prey animals is to freeze when confronted with danger. Ill-equipped to fight with their stalkers, they freeze in order to avoid detection by the predator; they will run away only when they are confident that the predator has sighted them and there is no alternative. Defenseless fawns won't even run when being attacked by cougars or other predators.

The prey's strategy forces the predator to flush them out, while the prey attempts to fade into its natural environment. Hunters similarly need to rouse rabbits, deer, and many birds with noises or sudden movements before the prey will reveal themselves.

Prussin notes that in the last twelve years, to his knowledge only one of the plentiful coyotes in Yosemite National Park has been killed by an automobile, while countless deer have been mowed down. When confronted by automobile headlights, coyotes will also freeze but then, like other predators and scavengers, dart away.

Although deer may not be genetically programmed to respond to react one way or the other to oncoming headlights, their natural predisposition dooms them from the start.

Submitted by Michael Wille of Springhill, Florida. Thanks also to Konstantin Othmer of San Jose, California; and Meghan Walsh of Sherborn, Massachusetts.

Frustables
The 10 Most Wanted OR Imponderables

If we have heretofore dazzled you with our erudition, it's time to confess our frustrations: ten, to be exact. These are the ten Imponderables we most wanted to answer for this book but could not. Either we couldn't find experts qualified to answer them or we found many experts who couldn't agree on an explanation.

Can you help? We offer a complimentary, autographed copy of the next volume of *Imponderables* to the reader who supplies the best answer, or the first reader who leads to the proof that supplies the answer. And, of course, your efforts will be duly acknowledged and displayed in the book.

We're trying something a little different this time. The first five Frustables deal with the always Imponderable world of gender differences, Frustables many more of you than usual should have an opinion about. We often get questions from men about female psychology, and from women wondering what makes men tick. In this case, you are as expert as any psychologist. Help stamp out Frustability!

FRUSTABLE 1: *Why do women often go to the restroom together? And what are they doing in there for so long?*

It doesn't occur to the average male to turn nature's call into a social occasion. And why do women usually spend so much time once they are in a public bathroom? Are there saunas or video games in women's rooms?

FRUSTABLE 2: *Why do men tend to hog remote controls and switch channels on television sets and radios much more than women?*

Research indicates that women often decide which television show is watched in the home. Yet, give a man a remote control and it is likely you won't be watching any one show for more than fifteen seconds at a time. Why?

FRUSTABLE 3: *Why do some women kick up their legs when kissing?*

And why don't men do it?

FRUSTABLE 4: *Women generally possess more body fat than men. So why do women tend to feel colder than men in the same environment?*

Why do men usually want to open a window before they go to bed while women want to throw on another blanket and turn on the heat?

FRUSTABLE 5: *Why is the average woman a much better dancer than the average man?*

We're not talking about professional dancers, or even serious nightclub amateurs. At any school dance, wedding, or office party, the ineptitude of most males is on display. What accounts for the prancing gender gap?

FRUSTABLE 6: *Why do so many people put their hands up to their chins in portrait photographs?*

We've noticed this pose in author photographs, yearbook pictures, actors' publicity stills, and other types of head shots. Any explanation?

FRUSTABLE 7: *Why do very few restaurants serve celery with mixed green salads?*

Of course, celery is a staple in egg, tuna, and chicken salad. But while celery is a common ingredient in home salads, one rarely encounters celery in restaurant mixed green salads. Celery is cheaper than, say, tomatoes, so why the reluctance of restaurants to use celery?

FRUSTABLE 8: *In English spelling, why does "i" come before "e" except after "c"?*

Where does this arcane rule come from?

FRUSTABLE 9: *What in the world are grocery store managers looking for when they approve personal checks?*

We have been most dissatisfied with the answers we've received from supermarket chains on this topic, so we're hoping that some grocery store checkers, managers, or perspicacious customers can help us with this Frustable. To us, it seems that the manager simply peeks at the check, glances at the customer, and approves the check without really looking for anything in particular. In fact, we've never seen a check rejected.

FRUSTABLE 10: *Why do so many policemen wear mustaches?*

Several policemen have recently sued their department over a regulation that would ban facial hair. The complainants didn't mind a prohibition on beards. But "Don't take away my mustaches!" they insisted. What explains the persistent love affair between cops and upper-lip hair?

Frustables Update

Our Readers Respond to the Frustables First Posed in Do Penguins Have Knees?

Rx

Dr. N. Decipherable
Dr. L. Legible

SPECIALISTS IN EYESTRAIN
and
MANUAL MOTOR-SKILLS DISORDERS

We write prescriptions
like this because
what we prescribe
for patients is
none of their business!!

N Decypherd✓ L Legible

FRUSTABLE 1: *Why do doctors have bad penmanship?*

We were inundated with response to this Frustable. No one disputed the problem. In fact, you were full of anecdotes highlighting the predicament of the poor patient or pharmacist required to read physician chicken scrawlings. Marilyn Brown of Utica, New York, says that she was once given a prescription that three separate pharmacists couldn't read, so she had to traipse back to the doctor:

He eyed it for a short while and inquired, "Who is the patient?" and "What's wrong with her?" With that clue he was able to read the prescription, rewrite it, and call a pharmacy to tell them what it said.

If physicians can't read their own handwriting, we definitely have a problem, one that pharmacists have had to contend with for eons. In fact, Helene Ainspan, the wife of a pharmacist, told us that one of his professional journals had a monthly quiz: Copies of six actual prescriptions were printed; the pharmacists had to decipher them.

Readers were remarkably sympathetic to the plight of doctors. From time to time, we receive queries from readers about why they have to wait so long for doctors to fulfill appointments. Once you get past the waiting room and into an examining room, it seems you have the attention of the doctor for only a short time.

Maybe, our readers infer, doctors really are busy folks. And rushed writing leads to poor handwriting. Brian J. McGrory, a resident in orthopaedic surgery at the prestigious Mayo Clinic, sent us a neatly typed letter. But his signature was illegible; he's going to make a fine doctor:

> Have you ever seen a training surgeon on hospital rounds as he or she tries to keep up with the attending surgeon? Have you ever not had to wait for a doctor during his or her office hours? From medical school to the day of retirement, many doctors are very busy and even harried at times. So even the neatest scribe will become less than perfect when the pressure is on.

Many readers tried to pinpoint the exact time when doctors' penmanship goes bad. A lot of you think it happens during those formative years, medical school. We heard from a retired medical librarian, Aileen Tannenbaum of Irvington, New Jersey:

> Many years ago, I posed this same question to an intern at our hospital. He responded that medical students scribble notes so rapidly in classes that their once legible handwriting deteriorates into an illegible scribble (only decipherable by themselves) . . .

Carrie Schulz, the daughter of a physician, who calls her father's

DAVID FELDMAN

handwriting "despicable," says that he and his doctor friends rationalize their scribbles in the same way.

Another popular theory was that doctors' penmanship is poor because they are constantly writing (e.g., notes on charts, preparation for insurance claims, prescriptions). Cathy Calabrese of Lebanon, Pennsylvania, notes that when she was a bank teller, she often gave customers as many as a hundred traveler's checks to sign at one time: "No matter how carefully the signature was written on the first check, it was a scribbled mess by check number 50 or so." Cathy believes that not only doctors but "a goodly number of executives and other extremely busy people suffer from the illegibility syndrome." As Dr. William Voelker put it:

> It seems from medical school on, there is never enough time to get everything done, and 90 percent plus physicians are constantly rushed and in a hurry. Fast writing is usually illegible writing.

Barth Richards of Naperville, Illinois, and several other readers, pointed to not just the time pressure of physicians but the physical constraints under which they must write: "Doctors are often writing on a clipboard or on a folder held in their hands, instead of at a desk or on a table. These are far from ideal writing conditions."

Several readers noted the repetitive nature of what doctors have to scribble. Dr. Rosanne A. Derango, a dentist in Bartlett, Illinois, argues that since the same medications are prescribed many times a day, the prescriptions become the equivalent of the signature written by a harried executive faced with scores of letters to sign.

The prescriptions of a given doctor might be poorly written, but they are distinctive. Several pharmacists confirmed this. Although a particular physician's writing may be horrible, a pharmacist familiar with that doctor can always decipher it, just as a secretary can usual decode the scribbling of his or her boss.

Don Fallick of Davenport, Washington, hit home with the same point. He points out that anyone, "even authors," will develop bad writing habits if forced to repeat the same thing over and over again. We plead guilty. At autograph sessions, not only does our penmanship deteriorate, but after the fiftieth book or so, we have been known to misspell our own name.

Some readers refuse to concede that doctors' poor penmanship is directly tied to their profession. Three such theories predominated. The most popular, by far, was a sexist (but probably true) syllogism: Most physicians are men. Most men have bad penmanship. Therefore, most physicians have bad penmanship.

The two other theories were a little more bizarre. Our friend Marilyn Brown insists that the higher one's IQ, the worse the penmanship. Since doctors tend to be intelligent, they have poor handwriting. Thanks, Marilyn, for the best-ever alibi for our execrable handwriting.

Dan Butler of Los Alamitos, California, an engineer at a large organization, insists that "the higher you go in an organization, the worse the penmanship. You should see my boss's boss's handwriting."

Rosanne Derango points out that the only physician's writing that most patients ever see is on a prescription. A few readers argued that prescriptions seem illegible not because the penmanship is necessarily poor but because patients cannot interpret the symbols properly. After a few cheap shots ("Hey, if you could make $30 for a five-minute office visit, you wouldn't waste time with trivial things like writing!"), Bill and Mary Ellen Jelen of Akron, Ohio, make a convincing argument:

> Generally, when adults read, they do not focus in at the individual letter level. Rather than sounding words out, our brain recognizes the word and then we "read" the entire word at once.
>
> If you were trying to read handwriting where 20% of the words were in code, it would tend to throw you off. Medical people use lingo that is truly unique. When trying to read a prescription, the patient is facing a whole series of "foreign" words. Besides the drug name, there are all types of codes for when and how to take the drug (e.g., c [with], p [after], prn [as needed]).
>
> Mary Ellen is a nurse. When she was in nursing school, I used to type her papers. I tried to look for spelling and grammati-

cal errors, but it was impossible with those medical papers. There were times that I typed a series of words and I had no clue if it was a sentence or not. I couldn't pick out nouns, verbs, anything.

Dentist Rosanne Derango even admitted that occasionally a doctor will intentionally make a prescription hard to read, such as when the medication is a placebo. ("Sometimes we like to keep a little bit of mystery in what we do!")

Obviously, there isn't one single answer to the Frustable at hand, and we're proud of how well our readers coped with the topic. But will we ever solve the problem? Probably not.

Maybe there is a glimmer of hope. Reader Jim Vibber, who has been in the medical device industry for over fifteen years, reports that the American Medical Association is offering a penmanship improvement course for doctors, "with some kind of incentive to take it." What kind of incentives could actually lure physicians to take a continuing education class in what all would concede is a less than fascinating subject? Jim answers:

> I've seen physicians do many things for little premiums, including sitting for an hour filling out a survey. They respond to free pens, golf balls, ice cream—the same sort of "junk" that anybody else might.

Submitted by Allen Kahn of New York, New York. Thanks also to Carmel Nelson of West Henrietta, New York.

A complimentary book goes to Bill and Mary Ellen Jelen, of Akron, Ohio, who were the first to propose the "demand-side" theory of physician indecipherability.

FRUSTABLE 2: *Why are salt and pepper the standard condiments on home and restaurant tables? When and where did this custom start?*

Readers didn't get much farther than we did on this subject. Much is known about the history of salt and pepper. Sumerians ate salt-cured meats more than 5,000 years ago. Pepper didn't spread widely into Western cultures until the sixteenth century; indeed, the search for black pepper was one of the prizes that drove explorers such as Columbus around the world.

WHEN DID WILD POODLES ROAM THE EARTH?   225

Salt has become a dominant condiment in almost every culture, not only for its taste but for its preservative qualities. But pepper had to displace other, more popular spices, such as clove and cinnamon, before it became salt's main rival as a condiment.

In her fascinating book *The Rituals of Dinner,* Margaret Visser details the elaborate respect with which costly salt was treated by medieval diners. Separate salt "cellars," often made of precious silver, were placed in front of the lord and

> perhaps each of the highest ranking diners, as an "object of prestige" an indication of status. When the lord sat at what we call the "head" or the host's short end of the table, it became customary to place a standing salt [cellar] as a marker, dividing the lord's intimates grouped at his end of the table from those who were not quite accepted into his inner circle and who sat "below the salt."

We have come a long way from expensive salt dispensers to today's plastic or glass salt and pepper shakers. Visser remarks that even today, the salt shaker is disdained in many formal dining situations.

Matched salt and pepper shakers did not appear until the nineteenth century. Reader Bill Gerk of Burlingame, California, who attacks Frustables with a ferocity that is somewhere between commendable and obsessive-compulsive, believes that the "custom of having salt and pepper as condiments at our home and restaurant tables began no later than the matched salt and pepper sets that first appeared in the nineteenth century." He argues that the need for salt is clear, since saltiness is, along with sweetness, bitterness, and sourness, one of the four basic tastes. Pepper just seems to be the appropriate antidote/complementary spice to saltiness. Not a smoking gun answer, perhaps, but the best we can do for now.

Submitted by Sara VanderFliet of Cedar Grove, New Jersey.
Thanks also to John G. Clark of Pittsburgh, Pennsylvania; and Joel Myerson of Helsinki, Finland.
   A complimentary book goes to Bill Gerk of Burlingame, California.

FRUSTABLE 3: *Why don't people wear hats as much as they used to?*

Just as the popularity of the undershirt plummeted when Clark Gable took off his dress shirt in *It Happened One Night* to reveal a bare chest, several readers, as well as many popular press accounts we have encountered, credit Jack Kennedy's bareheaded appearances with dooming the hat. Steve Campion of Tacoma, Washington, makes this point:

> When Lincoln sported a beard, nearly every success-minded politician for fifty years grew whiskers. The president created a fashion. Likewise, when the young, thick-haired Kennedy took office, he rarely donned a hat as all his predecessors had done. His topless style killed the hat fashion.

Clearly, Kennedy intensified the trend, but the hat was already in decline by 1960.

Most of our readers' hypotheses fell in two general camps: those that attributed the fall of the hat to changes in fashion and those that traced the demise of the hat to lifestyle changes.

Fashion Theories

1. *Hairstyles.* Most readers felt that modern hairstyles aren't conducive to wearing hats, and haven't been since the 1950s. Imagine wearing a hat over a beehive. Or Angela Davis wearing a hat over her Afro. Nancy Branson of Safety Harbor, Florida, offers her personal testimony:

> Hairstyles today are not as *flat* as before. I wear fluffier bangs that I don't care to have matted down after I blow-dried them just perfectly. When my hair was all one length, years ago, I *lived* in hats!

Several male readers confessed that when they wore hats, their hair was left with "that helmet look" when they took the hat off. Barbara Zygiel of Alexandria, Virginia, notes that the advent of hairspray also enabled women to "keep a hairdo tidy without confining it under a hat."

Kent State University at Tuscarawas professor Dan Fuller

goes so far as to blame the blow dryer, along with longer hairstyles spearheaded by the Beatles, for hurting hat sales. Fuller points out that although we tend to associate long hair on men with the counterculture, mainstream popular culture figures like Johnny Carson, by the 1970s, were sporting long hair:

> To realize the abrupt shift in attitudes, go back and read how Joe Pepitone was ridiculed in the press for being the first professional athlete to bring a blow dryer into the locker room. It was my wife, however, who first articulated for me the truth that no one who has spent twenty bucks for a hairstyle and has spent many minutes spraying and blowing it dry wants to crush it down and create what she calls "hathead."

2. *Unisex-androgynous fashion.* Our ever-persistent Bill Gerk argues that many fashionable women today have a "tomboy" look, while many trendy men sport an appearance that once would have been called feminine. Gerk believes that both men and women today want to show off their hair, and that traditional hats, which are clearly demarcated as men's or women's apparel, would ruin the androgynous effect.

3. *Informality.* Emil Magovac of Sacramento, California, makes the important point that baseball caps are almost as popular now as fedoras used to be, so we haven't rejected hats *per se*. Magovac mentions watching old films from baseball games in the first half of this century, "where it seemed as if every male in the crowd was in a suit and tie and wearing a fedora." Of course, today neither men nor women usually wear hats for formal occasions, even Easter.

4. *Sunglasses.* We never would have thought of this imaginative suggestion from Vicky Peterson of San Jose, California:

> Prior to the invention of sunglasses, there were very few solutions to the problem of protecting tender eyes and face from the intense glare of the sun. Hats or bonnets with brims were the more practical answer. We now have sunglasses, which do a better job, don't get blown off as often, and don't mess up our hair.

DAVID FELDMAN

Lifestyle Theories

We have more sympathy with lifestyle theories.

1. *We are now an indoors culture.* Typical of the many readers who emphasized this point was this letter from Judy R. Reis of Bisbee, Arizona:

> There no longer is much reason to wear a hat. In the good old days, people didn't step out of their centrally heated homes into their heated cars and drive to their heated places of work. They lived in poorly heated houses and worked in poorly (or unheated) buildings or outside. And when they traveled, they walked, rode horses, or rode in unheated carriages. Since the head is one of the body's points of greatest heat transfer, wearing a hat made some sense—indoors and out in the winter, to keep the heat in; outdoors in summer to keep the heat out. Hats once had a practical function, although our unceasing efforts to differentiate between the haves and have-nots eventually turned them into fashion statements as well.

Anyone who doubts the practical advantages of hats is advised to visit Chicago in the dead of winter. Somehow, the Windy City's denizens are able to brush off fashion constraints and cover their heads when the wind kicks up.

2. *More women in the workplace.* Catherine Clay, who works for the State of Florida Department of Citrus and has been a valuable source for us in the past, relates a personal story that indicates that hats may not be welcome at work sites for the ever-increasing number of employed women:

> Hats draw attention to the person wearing them, making them stand out in a crowd. Since I like being unique, wearing hats seems only natural. About five years ago, however, my (male) boss told me that I should not wear hats if I wanted to be "accepted" in the South. He said people react negatively to the image of a woman in a hat.
>
> I don't really buy that concept, but I've abided by his

request during the workday. Perhaps hats don't really go well in the work place, and more women work today than ever before.

Once the critical mass of opinion goes against a fashion, it takes true courage to keep it up. Let's be honest: How would we react to a coworker who wears a Nehru jacket to work? Or a polyester pants suit? At most jobs, conformity, rather than fashion statements, is rewarded.

3. *Today's baseball cap, unlike the traditional hat, has become a means of self-expression rather than a signal of one's occupation or status.* Dan Fuller argues that at one time, a working man's hat signaled his occupation and was designed for function rather than aesthetics:

> Newspaper pressmen wore brimless hats made of newspaper to keep ink and lead out of their hair; mechanics wore brimless cloth caps to protect their hair (they worked out of the sun so they needed no brim); truck drivers, service station attendants, and policemen wore the short billed "officer's cap," either with or without the support of internal "points"; cowboys are obvious, but farmers traditionally wore a straw with a medium brim or simply an old dress hat instead of the very wide brim of the Western hat. And so on and on.

Dan is currently working on a long, scholarly article about this very Frustable and has interviewed several hundred farmers, construction workers, and outdoorsmen, and his conclusion is that, unlike most of the hats mentioned above, the cap has distinct advantages:

> The cap is a clear choice over the hat because it doesn't come off in the wind. It can be pulled down tightly, and whether on a tractor, a drill rig, or a golf course, you don't have to worry about chasing down your hat.

Plus, the logos on caps are now a way of projecting an individual identity rather than just one's profession.

4. *The automobile.* As Judy Reis mentioned, the average worker in America used to toil outdoors or take public transportation to reach his or her job. In either case, the worker would be exposed to the elements. Today, the majority of American workers

drive to the job site. Many readers·pointed to the automobile as sounding the death knell for hats. Automobiles shielded commuters from the cold, but presented a new problem—a low roof. As Catherine Clay puts it, "Who wants to keep taking a hat on and off?"

You may argue that automobiles were around long before the demise of the hat. True, but they were built differently, as William Debuvitz of Bernardsville, New Jersey, observes:

> The modern car has too low a roof to accommodate a hat. But if you look at old photos of earlier cars with drivers (or look at the movie *Bugsy*), you will see that men wore hats when they drove because the car roofs were high enough.

We don't think there is *an* answer to this Frustable, but we think we've pretty much covered all the bases.

> *Submitted by Kent Hall of Louisville, Kentucky. Thanks also to Douglas Stangler of Redmond, Washington.*
>
> *A complimentary copy goes to Dan Fuller of New Philadelphia, Ohio, in hope that his own article will plumb new depths in the area of disappearing-hat research.*

FRUSTABLE 4: *How and why were the letters B-I-N-G-O selected for the game of the same name?*

As you know, all Frustables start as Imponderables that we research—unsuccessfully. Although we rarely try to answer Imponderables with information gleaned from books, we couldn't find live human beings who could help us solve this problem. We ended up finding many written citations about the origins of Bingo, but they seemed dubious to us.

Several readers found the same books we did, and it points out the problem with "believing everything you read." If Writer A publishes false information, the mistruth is perpetuated if Writer B thinks of Writer A's "facts" as sacrosanct. For this reason, we're always suspicious of the stories of origins of products or enterprises that seem too neat and colorful.

In this case, written sources seem to agree that in December 1929, Edwin Lowe, described as either a toy salesman or a just-laid-off toy salesman, was traveling in Jacksonville, Florida, or Jacksonville, Georgia, or outside Atlanta, Georgia, and stopped at a carnival, where he saw a game called Beano being played. The game was the same as the Bingo we know now but used dried beans for markers. When a winner was called, he or she yelled out "BEANO."

Supposedly, Lowe was observing the game (depending upon the account, either at the carnival or after he tried out the game at home) and heard a young girl, excited at her victory, stutter "B-B-B-I-N-G-O" (depending upon the account, there are three to seven "B's" in her "BINGO"), and a light bulb flashed above Lowe's head. He rechristened the game Bingo and marketed the game within months.

We also know that Lowe consciously marketed the game as a church fund-raiser from its inception, and that he faced an early obstacle when a priest from Wilkes-Barre, Pennsylvania, complained that with the twenty-four-card sets that Lowe initially marketed, one game often produced too many winners to turn a profit for the church. So Lowe employed Carl Lefler, a mathematician at Columbia University, to compose 6,000 different Bingo cards with nonrepeating number groups.

Having suffered through many other shaggy dog stories to explain origins of names, our guess is that Lowe actually changed the name from Beano to Bingo to avoid lawsuits from the gentleman running the carnival game, whose rules he borrowed. Actually, Beano had its roots in similar European games, such as the original Lotto, that date from the sixteenth century. But we'll probably never know the truth for sure, certainly not if half our written sources say that Bingo was born in Florida and the other half in Georgia.

One other little bit of trivia about Edwin Lowe. Several years after his Bingo success, he marketed another game with a nonsense name that would earn him additional millions—Yahtzee. But once again, Lowe did not invent the game. A married couple created the game, which they called "Yacht Game," and asked Lowe to print up a few as gifts. According to Milton Bradley, which acquired the E. S. Lowe Company in 1973,

Lowe liked the game so much he offered to buy all rights. The couple was not interested in receiving royalties, and they readily signed away their rights in exchange for a few copies of the game. Lowe went on to make a huge profit from the game whose name he changed to "Yahtzee," but was never able to remember his benefactors' last name.

Is there any better recipe for success than knowing what products the public will buy but (conveniently) forgetting to acknowledge their inventors?

Submitted by Daniel J. Harkavy of Buffalo, New York.
A complimentary book goes to Ken Giesbers of Seattle, Washington (the first reader to send book excerpts). Thanks also to Richard Miranda of Renton, Washington; and Bill Gerk of Burlingame, California.

FRUSTABLE 5: *Why do they always play Dixieland music at American political rallies when Dixieland isn't particularly burning up the hit parade at the moment?*

We were first asked this question by Jeff Charles, the first radio host who ever interviewed us for an *Imponderables* book. In the last six years, we have spoken to the Republican and Democratic parties, numerous jazz scholars, the New Orleans Jazz Club, and many other sources. No luck.

So we threw out the gauntlet to our readers. While there is no simple answer, you are brimming with ideas.

One point that just about everybody made, including Bruce Walker of San Pedro, California, is that Dixieland is upbeat, happy, American music:

> The music has to be peppy, since they want to fire up the faithful to go out and slave away for Senator Foghorn, not go to sleep or go away crying. It has to be American music, since patriotism is a theme of almost all political campaigns.

Many readers noted that Dixieland has become a tradition at political rallies, and caters to the ever-present nostalgic cravings of Americans.

DAVID FELDMAN

A television programming executive named Paul Klein developed the "least objectionable program" (LOP) theory, which posits that the prudent programmer puts on shows that offend the fewest number of people. Once glued to the set, only an "objectionable" show will drive viewers to change channels. Many *Imponderables* readers believe that the answer to this Frustable lies in LOM—that is, Dixieland is the "least objectionable music." We enjoyed this discussion by Vladimir Kazhin of Towson, Maryland:

> Much music carries with it certain intellectual and emotional baggage, and politics in America today is an attempt to be inoffensive above all else. For example: Classical music is considered too "highbrow," too "arty"; jazz is considered too "earthy," too sensual, as of course, is rock (still the devil's music to some people); country is too "white"; soul too "black"; and new wave music is too "harsh," etc.
>
> I am not saying that there is any truth to these stereotypes, only that they exist, which is enough for most politicians. Dixieland doesn't really have a big following: No one really likes it [on this we'll have to disagree before the hate mail rolls in], but no one dislikes it either. In short, it is a nice, inoffensive, basically pleasant background music.

We received a fascinating letter from Russell Shaw, a journalist from Marietta, Georgia, who has a unique perspective—he covers both political campaigns and the music industry. Russell made all of the points discussed above but also offers a unique argument—that the popularity of Dixieland music at political rallies, despite its lack of radio airplay, might have a partly economic basis. Most music radio stations today employ niche programming, directing music at a particular age and/or demographic group:

> When something is totally noncontroversial, it is likely to be warm and bland—the same frailties that if not present, would foster listener demand and a niche for a musical form like Dixieland on radio.
>
> Yet even this inability to inspire passion has its assets. One of the ways consumers express passion in the entertainment market-

place is to buy records, and attend concerts and clubs featuring their favorite kind of music. Since Dixieland rates low in the passion/demand continuum, there are few full-time opportunities for Dixieland musicians. They, like most of us, are more concerned about the eagle flying than the saints marching.

Hence, Dixieland attracts practitioners who perform almost as a hobby. Not being full-time musicians, they likely will not be union members, and thus come more cheaply than, say, a large orchestra. Dixieland also requires fewer musicians and less in fees. Many of the above principles also apply to the popularity of bluegrass at political events—especially here in the South.

We'd be negligent if we didn't mention that Dixieland was nonexistent during the 1992 Democratic convention in New York City. Clearly, the Clinton/Gore campaign's strategy was to emphasize the ticket's youth and theme of "change" by showcasing the candidates dancing and singing along with the original recordings of Fleetwood Mac's "Don't Stop" and Paul Simon's "You Can Call Me Al." This musical watershed did not go unnoticed. On CNN's "Capital Gang," columnist Robert Novak named the absence of "Happy Days Are Here Again" from the convention as his "Outrage of the Week."

We'd still love to know exactly when and where Dixieland first became associated with political rallies, but then we're used to being frustrated.

Submitted by Jeff Charles, formerly of Minneapolis, Minnesota. Where are you now, Jeff?

A complimentary book goes to Russell Shaw of Marietta, Georgia.

FRUSTABLE 6: *Why does eating ice cream make you thirsty?*

Nothing much new to report. All of the reader responses to this question named one or more of the following culprits as the thirst inducer:

1. Salt
2. Sugar

3. Butterfat (which is left on the tongue and in the mouth and throat after consuming ice cream). Only drinking eliminates the filmy fat coating.

The answer may lie in any one or all three of these alternatives. Yet one could name foods with greater concentrations of any of these ingredients that don't make you as thirsty. Expert after taste expert we contacted in both sensory studies and the ice cream industry denied that this phenomenon even exists, and refused to single out any or all of the nominees as definitely causing thirst. To which we reply, "Then why do most ice cream parlors, such as Baskin-Robbins, have water fountains in them?"

We were so frustrated divining the truth that a letter from A. A. Spierling of Van Nuys, California, became our favorite discussion about this topic: "Ice cream doesn't make me thirsty —riding buses does. I can consume a quart of fluids after riding two or three buses, going shopping, etc. Going by car doesn't make me thirsty." Good thing they don't let you eat ice cream on the bus. You would have to carry a canteen with you.

Submitted by Kassie Schwan of Brooklyn, New York. Thanks also to Ricky E. Arpin, current address unknown; Lisa Kodish of Albany, New York; and Phil Feldman of Los Angeles, California A complimentary book goes to A. A. Spierling of Van Nuys, California, for best evasion of this Frustable.

FRUSTABLE 7: *Why are belly dancers so zaftig?*

Our curiosity about this subject stems from our wondering why belly dancers, who spend their professional life manipulating their abdomens, don't seem to have toned abdominal muscles. Professionals we originally contacted disagreed about the reasons why, but we heard from quite a few belly dancers, and they were in unexpected agreement.

As you may have guessed, we receive a lot of unusual mail here at *Imponderables* headquarters. But the first person ever to send us an 8 × 10-inch color glossy was Stasha Rustici of Berkeley, California. By training, Rustici is a social anthropologist, whose interest in folkloric dancing drew her into practicing the ancient art herself. For the last fifteen years, she has been belly dancing professionally, traveling all over the world.

No doubt, her interest in this Frustable was piqued by the fact that although she may have other problems in life, being *zaftig* isn't one of them, as her publicity still makes abundantly clear. She has a unique perspective on the subject, and answers our Frustable in both cultural and technical terms:

> The standards of beauty differ from place to place in this world. Traditionally, in the areas where food is not plentiful, a plump woman is a sign of wealth. She can afford to eat! In these arid desert regions, this maxim holds true. I can't tell you how many times a Middle Eastern person in my audience has told me I'm too skinny. Even Cairo, today, hasn't the selection and availability [of food] that we enjoy in the West. So socioeconomically, plump is pleasing.
>
> Although the lateral oblique muscles are active in this dance form, the rest of the abdomen and the diaphragm are not. In fact, the undulating spine movements, as well as the most ancient move of all, the undulation of the stomach muscles (commonly referred to as the "belly roll") necessitate a supple, yet somewhat flaccid muscle structure. Furthermore, some additional weight reinforces the quality of this dance's earthy movements, a dance whose "center of gravity" is at the hips. As you can see by the publicity photo, I'm not the standard of Middle Eastern plumpness. I can testify that it's harder for me to achieve some movements that my more *zaftig* sisters perform easily. So physiologically, plump is pleasing.

Karen Kuzsel, publisher of *Middle Eastern Dancer*, told *Imponderables* that from the days of the sultans, heavier women were prized by men as status symbols. But another reason why we wouldn't cast Heather Locklear as a belly dancer is that in the Middle East, where dancers are prized for their expressive range, most belly dancers are not spring chickens. Belly dancing is complicated technically, and true artistry doesn't come easily. According to Karen, the most accomplished dancers are usually at least forty years old; even in the ageist United States, most belly dancers are over forty.

Honestly, this Frustable was not an attempt to make fun of belly dancers. We've been known to be a little *zaftig* ourselves. And *we* can't execute belly rolls. Yet a few of our belly dancer correspondents were a tad defensive. For example, lapsed belly dancing student Beth Eastman of Richfield, Minnesota, was inspired to deliver a passionate defense of belly dancer physiognomy:

> If belly dancers looked like Arnold Schwarzenegger, their movements would make their skins appear to be lined with live snakes! Yecch! Also, while retaining cuddlability, the strengthening and toning of the muscles beneath and the increased flexibility of the body gives a real boost to the sex life of the dancer. Go for it, girls!

A complimentary book goes to Stasha Rustici of Berkeley, California.

FRUSTABLE 8: *How was hail measured before golf balls were invented?*

This started out as one of those comedian-inspired Imponderables that we detest. Any stand-up comic can get a laugh out of "Why do we drive on parkways and park on driveways?" But we have to answer these rhetorical questions/jokes everyone from Gallagher to Andy Rooney muses about and then discards without pursuing.

Pardon our self-pitying whining—we feel better now—and forgive us for thrusting this very difficult Frustable on our generous readership. But, truth be told, most of our correspondents didn't come up with anything more concrete than we did. Most of you counterpunched with jokes of your own about hail. (Our favorite: Mark Buesing of Peoria, Illinois, reminded us that David Letterman, when he was a weatherman in Indianapolis, once referred to falling hail as "the size of canned hams.")

But two enterprising readers lurched, as John McLaughlin would say, "uncontrollably into the truth." Brad Tucker of Syracuse, New York, happened to be reading *Commerce of the Prai-*

ries, a book by frontiersman Josiah Gregg, who joined a wagon train in 1831. Gregg refers to seeing "hail-stones larger than hen's eggs . . ."

But Dallas Brozik of Huntington, West Virginia, was so inspired by this Frustable that he conducted quite a bit of original research. He found two different citations that manage to avoid what every weathercaster in the world seems to find inevitable —comparing the size of hail to a golf ball:

> The 1880 edition of the *Library of Universal Knowledge* . . . describes hailstones ". . . which may have any size from that of a pea to that of a walnut, or even an orange . . ." The entry goes on to mention an incident when hailstones the size of half a brick were found . . .
>
> The 1940 edition of *Nelson's Encyclopedia* . . . shows a photo of "Hailstones Larger Than Eggs" [of course, golf balls were invented before 1940]. I checked a number of other sources during this period, and most of them refer to the size of hailstones as "one-half to three inches in diameter" or some other measure in inches.
>
> So there is at least part of your answer. If you do not play golf, consider fruits, vegetables, and Euclidian geometry.

Submitted by Donald E. Ullrich of Burlington, Iowa. Thanks also to Edward Hirschfield of Portage, Michigan; and R. W. Stanley of Bossier City, Iowa.

A complimentary book goes to Dallas Brozik of Huntington, West Virginia.

FRUSTABLE 9: *Why did 1930s and 1940s movie actors talk so much faster than actors do today?*

For some reason, this Frustable didn't inspire a great number of responses from readers, but radio talk-show hosts were fond of the topic, and many callers across the country contributed their theories.

Some ascribed the change in speed to technical advances in sound recording. This may explain why early 1930s films often sound fast to our ears. Irv Hyatt, a film buff and collector from Woodbridge, New Jersey, wrote *Imponderables* that many early 1930s movies were recorded with sound on disc rather than on film, which resulted in a higher pitch in the finished recordings:

> These discs were later converted to sound on film, and oft-times to synchronize these it was necessary to adjust these recordings as the negative was being made. Some late 1920s and early 1930s films had scenes that were still shot silent, and some even with hand-cranked cameras left over from the silent era.

But we were referring more to the machine-gun delivery of stars like Humphrey Bogart, Katharine Hepburn, Rosalind Russell, and Jimmy Cagney in classic comedies and dramas. One would think that as the moviegoing audience became more sophisticated, the pace would speed up. Certainly, movies today are visually paced at a hysterical rate compared to movies sixty years ago.

Author Nat Segaloff of Cambridge, Massachusetts, who wrote a popular biography of director William Friedkin, sent us a letter full of possible explanations. He notes that superior recording devices allowed rapid-fire dialogue without hiss and distortion. These technical improvements enabled theater-trained writers to construct scripts and stage actors to perform at a pace to which they were accustomed before live audiences. The theater is a more dialogue-driven medium than film, since the numerous and seamless set and costume changes in movies are impossible to duplicate on a proscenium stage. Most writers for the stage were not trained to allow music or crosscutting to compensate for reams of dialogue.

Segaloff believes that the key to the speed regression was the rise of Method acting, spearheaded by teacher-actor-director Lee Strasberg. Actors like Marlon Brando, Montgomery Clift, Julie Harris, and Kim Hunter, who "went for feeling and truth rather than speed and artifice," changed the pace of delivery. While Marlon Brando searched for his motivation in a scene, Jimmy Cagney would have polished off a page of dialogue. Like their style or not, Method acting rendered the faster cadence of 1930s actors artificial and superficial.

Segaloff suggests that the slower pace of today's dialogue might be a suggestion that contemporary audiences are less, not more, sophisticated. Frank Capra's screwball comedies were paced so quickly because of Capra's conviction that

> people sitting together as an audience comprehend things faster than they do as individuals, and for that reason he directed his actors to speed up their delivery by as much as one-third.

Howard Hawks later introduced overlapping dialogue to increase the sensation of speed. Today, Robert Altman uses the same technique, but without the same commercial success.

Segaloff muses about whether we may return to the "amphetamine school of acting," if only for the crassest commercial reasons:

> Ironically, we may be experiencing an unheralded return to speeded-up dialogue. Some videotape manufacturers are now "compressing" (speeding up) longer movies by as much as eight percent to squeeze them onto shorter, cheaper cassettes. One of the first examples: Walt Disney's 1942 *Fantasia*, which was painstakingly and publicly restored to its original length of 124 minutes, only later to be speeded up to 120 minutes to become the best-selling title in home video history.

The same compression techniques are being used in advertising to cram more words into fifteen or thirty seconds, and in radio, where cutting five seconds from a song allows a station to insert more commercials while still claiming they play more music.

> *Submitted by Bob Hatch of Seattle, Washington.*
> *A complimentary book goes to Nat Segaloff of Cambridge, Massachusetts.*

FRUSTABLE 10: *Why does meat loaf taste the same in all institutions?*

Your response to this Frustable was as inspiring as . . . meatloaf. Not that we have anything to offer.

But don't despair. We've solved some other Frustables that eluded us the first time around. Read on.

The Frustables That Will Not Die

As you have just learned in the "Frustables Update," solving Frustables is, by definition, frustrating. Although we can't demolish every Frustable the first time around, we have just begun to fight. In this section, you'll see the reader contributions from the past year.

Please remember we do not have the space to review all the theories we've already advanced; this section is meant as a supplement, not a substitute, for our discussions in previous books.

Frustables First Posed in *Why Do Clocks Run Clockwise?* and First Discussed in *When Do Fish Sleep?*

FRUSTABLE 1: *Why do you so often see one shoe lying on the side of the road?*

In his column "The Straight Dope," our fellow savant Cecil Adams mused about our devoting seven entire pages to this topic in *When Do Fish Sleep?* Little did he seem to know that we have published more about this subject in every subsequent book. We're afraid that the mysterious appearance of roadway single shoes is one of those problems that will not stay in the closet or just go away if left unattended. To those who may scoff at the frequency of SSS (single-shoe syndrome) or the very real suffering it can inflict, please read these testimonials and see if you can keep from dabbing suddenly moist eyes.

First of all, we cannot ignore the direct correlation between SSS and soaring juvenile delinquency rates. Gabriel Raggiunto, of Lebanon, Pennsylvania, bravely allows us to share secrets from his sordid past:

> When I was in my late teens, I used to play a game with old shoes. My friends and I would go to second-hand clothing stores, yard sales, and our closets to get old worn-out shoes. After gath-

ering a dozen or two, we would go on a long drive to throw the shoes out. Score was kept by how many road signs were hit and by the size of the sign. The low scorer would end up buying the drinks. The smaller the sign, the more points were awarded.

As they say, (whoever "they" is), kids can be cruel. But juvenile deviants don't have to be old enough to drive to create SSS, as Dave Moreau of Wappingers Falls, New York, reports:

> The mean kids I knew would grab someone else's sneakers, tie them together, and throw them on to the electric lines. The sneakers would dangle above, so close and yet so far, until the laces eventually weathered (it took almost a year), broke, and the sneaker fell to the street. Of course, this doesn't explain why one sneaker subsequently disappears, but it could help to explain how they got there. This cruel act was not isolated to my neighborhood alone; traveling through adjoining areas, I noticed this same phenomenon at least three other times.

Michael Levin, professor of philosophy at New York City's CUNY, adds that drug dealers often fling tennis shoes atop power lines to mark their territories.

Just as troublesome as our crime rate is our soaring rate of divorce. We have learned from Oprah, Phil, Sally Jessy, and Geraldo that the hallmarks of all successful marriages are respect and communication. But how can one partner withstand the intrusion of SSS into an otherwise happy marriage? Cheryl Thompson of Ludlow Falls, Ohio, faced this heartrending problem:

> One day my husband and I were going fishing, so I grabbed my old, ugly, dirty tennis shoes and threw them in the truck. As we were riding along, my husband reached over and picked one up and said, "I hate these shoes," and chucked it out the window. I grabbed the other one to keep him from littering and never saw the other again.

Can this marriage be saved?

Justin Palmer of Granby, Connecticut, realizes that he who is not part of the solution is part of the problem:

While walking home from school late one evening, wearing flexible leather moccasins, I took a shortcut through a grassy field when one of my shoes slid off. I turned around and in the dark patted about only to find what I thought was a new shoe—one of the lost single shoes that everyone comes across!

After considerable time, I abandoned my search, content with my new shoe and acknowledging the loss of the other. Later, under a street lamp, I realized it was the same shoe stuffed with grass and fitting improperly. My negligence, however, could have contributed to the wealth of lost single shoes around the world!

There, there, Justin! Confession is good for the soul. Justin then relates *another* time when he recovered his own lost single shoe, but he's turning that story into a made-for-TV movie.

Justin was kind enough to pass along an entry from *Reader's Digest's* "Life in These United States," which tells the story of a man who innocently drove his slightly tipsy secretary home after an office party. That night, he and his wife were driving to a restaurant, when he noticed a high-heeled shoe lurking out below the passenger seat. Afraid his wife would misinterpret its significance, he waited until she looked away and flung the shoe out of the car. When they got to the restaurant, his wife squirmed a bit and asked, "Honey, have you seen my other shoe?"

Our guess is that the odds that this story is true are about 100 to 1 against. Still, the story is proof that SSS has achieved urban legend status.

Speaking of legends, Angel Kuo of West Nyack, New York, points out that another book claims to have the answer to SSS: *Faeries*, by Brian Froud and Alan Lee:

The Irish have their own industrious faerie, the Leprechaun (lep-re-kawn) or one-shoe-maker. He is a solitary cobbler to be found merrily working on a single shoe (never a pair) beneath a dockleaf or under a hedge.

Angel theorizes that leprechauns have emigrated around the world, making single shoes and then tossing them off the sides of the road.

Too fanciful and New Agey for you? Then how about a scientific theory from our new hero, Simonetta A. Rodriguez, of Endicott, New York, who has emerged as the philosopher king of SSS. How does Simonetta explain our phenomenon? Entropy and the second law of thermodynamics, of course. These two scientific principles argue that the universe and the systems within it tend toward greater randomness and increasing disorder over time. Take the floor, Simonetta:

> We normally encounter shoes in pairs only because human life-forms are constantly working to keep them ordered, in pairs. We do not leave the system of shoes to itself; instead, we rigorously enforce extremely artificial pair-bonding in the system. Since we are life-forms, and highly ordered life-forms at that (well, I do know people who are no more ordered than amoeba, but I want to ignore them for the sake of this discussion), we must constantly work like this to prevent disorder, which is the same thing as death for us. We do not even notice our ceaseless efforts to fight entropy. Well, we don't notice most of them—I gave up on a lot of housework I used to do when I was young and dumb, because what's the point? Why fight the universe?
>
> Once some shoes get away from us, the universe does not care about our obsessions. Entropy takes over. The details do not matter: animals, traffic, weather—anything the shoes encounter serves to increase the entropy of the system. If an entire pair of shoes gets away from us, *the very first thing that must go is the pair-bond,* because it was maintained only by extreme and very unnatural efforts . . .
>
> I would be most astonished if I saw a *pair* of shoes by the side of the road, and I never have.

Simonetta must have done *very* well on essay exams.

From this point forward, we now have theoretical, scientific underpinnings for any future foray into SSS studies.

FRUSTABLE 4: *Why do the English drive on the left and most other countries on the right?*

We heard from Stanley Ralph Ross, of Beverly Hills, California, who once had the imposing task of writing the script for the Sound and Light Show at London Bridge in England and later at Lake Havasu City, Arizona. The tremendous research available to him led to some interesting conclusions about this Frustable:

> In the 1600s, London Bridge had many buildings erected on it: homes, stores, etc. . . . Although the width of the bridge was about forty-two feet, the incursion of the buildings made it only twelve feet wide at certain points. The Bridge was the only way one could travel from the city to the country and often had as many as 75,000 people cross it in 24 hours. At that time, there were *no traffic laws whatsoever* and people just pushed past each other.
>
> In 1625, on a hot summer day, a horse drawing a wagon dropped dead of a heart attack in one of the areas only twelve feet wide. This caused the Mother Of All Traffic Jams, and nobody could get through in either direction. Upon hearing of this, the Lord Mayor of London, one John Conyers, decreed that all traffic going *into* the city be on the *upstream* side of the Thames (left) and all traffic going to the country be on the downstream side. And that was the first traffic rule, a totally arbitrary decision by Conyers.

Ross explains that Conyers's fiat was soon extended to the city of London, then to the boroughs of Westminster and Chelsea, to all of England, and then exported overseas.

FRUSTABLE 8: *Why do women in the United States shave their armpits?*

Several readers have taken us to task for not emphasizing the role of advertising in creating the "sudden desire" of women for shaving armpits around 1915. It is true that deodorants were aggressively marketed at this time (ladies' razors were soon to follow) and that women's magazines of the time, ever desirous of pleasing advertisers, chimed in with advice to shave.

But fashion came first. The Mack Sennett Bathing Beauties had an immediate impact on fashion, and many of the first ads for deodorants showed women in "his" bathing suits. Advertisers are responsible for spreading the practice, but probably not for creating it.

FRUSTABLE 9: *Why don't you ever see really tall old people?*

Dr. Daphne Hare, of Buffalo, New York, was kind enough to send us a story summarizing an Ohio study of men who died of natural causes. The conclusions were startling, indicating that each additional inch in height corresponded to a reduction of 1.2 years in life expectancy. A 5'4" man can expect to live almost ten years longer than a six-footer.

According to the *Buffalo News*, an earlier study showed "an average age of death of 82 for men less than 5 feet, 8 inches tall and 73 for those more than 6 feet tall." Is this why H. Ross Perot is always smiling?

Frustables First Posed in *When Do Fish Sleep?* and First Answered in *Why Do Dogs Have Wet Noses?*

FRUSTABLE 3: *How, when, and why did the banana peel become the universal slipping agent in vaudeville and movies?*

In *Do Penguins Have Knees?*, we mentioned that a law student told us about old tort cases involving banana peel slipping, and that Oliver Wendell Holmes actually rendered an opinion on said topic. One enterprising reader, Robert W. Donovan, of Wenham, Massachusetts, went to his attic and dug through old law books to find the cases, and he was successful.

Holmes, when he was the chief justice of the Massachusetts Supreme Judicial Court, rendered a decision in the case of *Goddard* v. *Boston & Maine R.R. Co.* in 1901. Mr. Goddard slipped on a banana peel lying on a railway platform just as he exited the train. Holmes ruled that Goddard could not collect, because the peel "may have been dropped within a minute by one of the persons who was leaving the train."

But not all banana-peel slippers are skinned by the court. Ten years later, in *Anjou* v. *Boston Elevated Railway Co.*, the pratfaller won, as Donovan explains:

The distinction turned on the color of the banana peel. In *Anjou* [the plaintiff, not the pear], the plaintiff slipped on a brown banana peel that had presumably been on the ground for quite awhile. The court ruled that the railway was negligent in failing to keep its station free of ever dangerous banana peels. In *Goddard*, the banana peel was a fresh yellow color, indicating that it had been thrown on the ground shortly before Mr. Goddard had slipped on it.

In this case, the court reasoned that although the railroad owed a duty to its passengers to keep its stations clean, it was not reasonable to expect it to assign a maintenance worker to follow around every passenger who may be inclined to eat a banana and carelessly discard its peel . . .

We will assume that Anjou was not diabolical enough to carry around a mottled banana peel with her—those were more innocent times.

But our most exciting discovery came from film buff Irv Hyatt, who was gracious enough to send us a videotape of the man who might hold the key to the whole banana peel mystery —legendary film producer Hal Roach (who produced Laurel and Hardy, Harold Lloyd, and the "Our Gang" comedies, among many others). When he was presented with his honorary Oscar in 1983, the ninety-two-year-old producer spoke of how the banana peel became the universal slipping agent in movies.

Roach recounted that when he first started working in Hollywood, in 1912, he was paid one dollar a day, plus carfare and lunch. The lunch consisted of two sandwiches and a banana. Every day, after lunch, the prop man would pick up the discarded banana peels and put them away, lest anyone trip over them.

In the famous Mack Sennett comedy shorts of the era, comics took pratfalls on cakes of soaps or puddles of oil. But Hal Roach had a brainstorm. Why not use banana peels? They were available, plentiful, recognizable on-screen, and, best of all, absolutely free for Roach.

Producer and screenwriter Jeffrey J. Silverstein, of Brooklyn, New York, sent us a letter arguing that, from a comedic standpoint, it is strategically essential for the audience to be aware of the identity of the slipping agent before the "slipee" discovers it. Silverstein, having read our chapter about the selection of colors in traffic lights, feels that the fact that yellow is the most visible color from a distance didn't hurt its acceptance among directors:

> Plus, the banana has the additional advantage of giving a natural "accidental" setup. The person eating it doesn't deliberately trip the "slipee"—it is unintentional and therefore funnier.

FRUSTABLE 8: *Why do kids tend to like meat well done (and then prefer it rarer and rarer as they get older)?*

All of the theories we discussed in *Why Do Dogs Have Wet Noses?* and *Do Penguins Have Knees?* were psychological or physiological in nature. But we received a fascinating letter from James D. Kilchenman of Toledo, Ohio, who has spent decades in the restaurant and catering businesses. He believes that the most important influences in preferences for meat doneness are socioeconomic and cultural. The higher the socioeconomic status of a group, the rarer they want their meat. In Kilchenman's catering experience, middle-class white groups invariably order prime rib medium-rare. Working-class black groups tend to order the roast medium-well or sometimes well done. But Kilchenman thinks that class is much more decisive than race: Affluent blacks tend to order meat rarer than less affluent whites.

How can we explain the socioeconomic taste disparity? Kilchenman attributes the difference to exposure to different types of meat. The better the cut of meat, the more essential it is to have it cooked rare. As Kilchenman puts it, no one walks into Wendy's and demands a rare burger. Less affluent people are used to cooking cheaper cuts of meat, cuts that often need to be cooked longer to become tender.

Kilchenman argues that like poor adults, most children have limited exposure to the best cuts of meat. When Mom and Pop take Junior to the restaurant, chances are Junior isn't going to order filet mignon for dinner. He'll usually have a hamburger. Kilchenman notes that whenever he has seen children ordering meat rare, they were always from affluent families.

Just as drinkers start with Singapore Slings and end up drinking martinis, or start as children with Kool-Aid and move to sweet white wine and later to dry red wine, so do children start with burnt hot dogs. But with exposure to the "finer things in life," they will end up consuming rare filets as they watch their cholesterol levels rise.

Frustables First Posed in *Why Do Dogs Have Wet Noses?* and First Answered in *Do Penguins Have Knees?*

FRUSTABLE 1: *Does anyone really like fruitcake?*

We heard a disturbing report from Joseph Redman, of Lincoln, Illinois, about nutritional standards in the military:

> In 1968 and 1969 I served two tours in Vietnam as a helicopter ambulance medic. On many occasions we flew around the clock with no regular breaks for hot meals from the mess hall, which meant our option was to eat C-rations. The typical C-ration meal included a main dish of canned meat, sometimes with potatoes; a can of fruit; a can of cheese and crackers or crackers with peanut butter or jelly; and a can of cake.
>
> The three cakes I remember were pound cake (everyone's favorite), a nut-cinnamon cake, and fruitcake. The first two were always in short supply. This left great stacks of round, canned fruitcake available for the taking. When one is hungry, one will eat just about anything.

Our fighting men and women reduced to scavenging for fruitcakes! And they wonder why morale is bad in the military.

FRUSTABLE 3: *We often hear the cliché: "We use only 10 percent of our brains." How was it determined that we use 10 percent and not 5 percent or 15 percent?*

We heard from two professors who found academic studies that could have been the basis for the cliché. Prof. Michael Levin, of the City College of New York, did some calculations based on the work of neurobiologist Harry Jerison. We'll save you the gory details and focus on Levin's conclusions: "The human brain turns out to have about 8.8 billion more neurons than the typical mammal that weighs what a man does. The ratio of 8.8 billion to the total neurons in the brain is about 1/10." But Levin offers even more tantalizing evidence:

> According to Harold Jerison, the relation of brain mass E to body mass P in the typical mammal is given by $E = .12p^{2/3}$. This much brain is assumed to be necessary for housekeeping functions. Anything extra may be assumed to be used for "higher" cognitive functions.
>
> The *ratio* of an animal's actual brain weight to the brain-weight predicted by the equation is what Jerison calls its "encephalization quotient." It tells us how many times larger the animal's brain is than it needs to be for basic housekeeping functions.
>
> The average human male weighs 55,000 grams. Using the above equation, his "expected" brain weight is about 175 grams. The "encephalization quotient" is 7.79—call it 8, or rounding off to the nearest order of magnitude, call it 10. Roughly speaking, we need only 10% of our brains. Of course, what that means is that we need or use only 10% of our brains for the basic functions performed by all mammalian brains. Presumably, the rest is for "higher" functions.

Jerison's early research was conducted in the 1970s, after the birth of our cliché, but this is still fascinating stuff.

Robert P. Vecchio, Franklin D. Schurz Professor of Management at the University of Notre Dame, sent us a copy of some pages from a textbook he read as an undergraduate, *Foundations of Physiological Psychology*, written by Richard F. Thompson.

DAVID FELDMAN

Could this Frustable have stemmed from a misunderstanding of the physiology of the brain?

> ... Perhaps the greatest source of confounding in the analysis of whole brain tissue is the fact that the majority of cellular elements in brain are not even nerve cells. Ninety percent of the cells in the brain are *glial* cells and only 10 percent are nerve cells ...glial cells have often been considered as connective tissue, serving the same general kind of supportive function as connective tissue in most organs.

This textbook was reporting on research conducted by J. Nurnberger in 1958 and S. DeRobertis in 1961, well before any of the sources mentioned in *Do Penguins Have Knees?* To be honest, though, more than any insight into this brain stuff, we are dazzled by the fact that Professor Vecchio can remember anything from an old college textbook.

While these scientific studies could, theoretically, have provided the inspiration for the 10% figure, they aren't well enough known or disseminated to have hatched our cliché. So we continued our search for the phrase in popular culture.

We mentioned in *Do Penguins Have Knees?* that friends of ours swore they had read about the "10%" cliche in a Robert Heinlein novel, but James Gleick thinks he's now found the passage, and no numbers are involved. In *Citizen of the Galaxy* (1957), a fictional character says, "He proved that most people go all their lives only half awake." Same idea, but not the nail in the coffin.

That's why we were so excited when we heard from Allan J. Wilke of Toledo, Ohio:

> I've been involved in a Dale Carnegie course these last few months. Required reading includes *How to Stop Worrying and Start Living.* Mr. Carnegie frequently quotes the psychologist William James. On page 146 of this book, there is a paragraph that reads:
> "The renowned William James was speaking of people who had never found themselves when he declared that the average person develops only ten per cent of his or her latent mental abil-

ities. 'Compared to what we ought to be,' he wrote, 'we are only half awake. We are making use of only a small part of our physical and mental resources. Stating the thing broadly, human individuals thus live far within their limits. They possess powers of various sorts which they habitually fail to use.' "

As is his habit, Carnegie doesn't cite where he found this quote. But Carnegie's bestselling book was first published in 1944 and has been taught in courses for nearly fifty years. Who better to spread the word?

Unfortunately, we haven't been able to confirm the James quote, although in his letter to W. Lutoslawski, in 1906, James comes tantalizingly close:

> Most people live, whether physically, intellectually, or morally, in a very restricted circle of their potential being. They *make use* of a very small portion of their possible consciousness, and of their soul's resources in general, much like a man who, out of his whole bodily organism, should get into a habit of using and moving only his little finger. Great emergencies and crises show us how much greater our vital resources are than we had supposed.

Ultimately, it may not matter whether James actually uttered the words ascribed to him—for it is much more likely that Carnegie, and his disciples, spread the word than James, himself.

But perhaps our favorite new pronouncement on this Frustable came from Matthew Cope of Westmount, Quebec:

> Sorry, I don't know who first claimed that we only use 10 percent of our brains. But presumably, whoever it was, there's a 90 percent chance he was wrong!

FRUSTABLE 24: *Where, exactly, did the expression "Blue Plate Special" come from?*

We're hurt. We can't even convince some readers that blue plate specials were actually served on blue plates. Jan Gable, of Cedar City, Utah, insists that "blue" refers not to the color of the plate but to the collars of the workers who purchased inexpensive, complete meals in diners.

DAVID FELDMAN

Allison Berlier demurs. Blue doesn't refer to the plate, she chastises us, but to the food being served!

> During the depression, the most plentiful, and therefore, cheapest meal available, was the locally caught *bluefish* . . .

Honestly, Jan and Allison, there *were* blue *plates*. Many *live* people remember them. Authors even write about them. In fact, reader Jan Saul notes that Mary Higgins Clark, in her book, *Loves Music, Loves to Dance*, was so inspired:

> A blue plate used to be the special of the evening at a cheap restaurant. Seventy-five cents bought you a hunk of meat, a couple of vegetables, a potato. The plate was sectioned to keep the juices from running together. Your grandfather loved that kind of bargain . . .

Robert Klein, of Paramus, New Jersey, has conducted extensive research into the history of this phrase. He sent along a copy of John Egerton's discussion of the blue plate special in *Southern Food*. Egerton notes that restaurants featuring blue-plate specials "came early to the region, and many of the best of them have survived to this day, withstanding the fast-food revolution and other gastronomic upheavals." The typical blue-plate lunch, according to Egerton, consisted of a main dish, three or four vegetables, bread, and a drink, all for one low price. Klein concludes that the blue-plate special probably began in Tennessee or Kentucky during the 1920s.

FRUSTABLE 5: *Why does the traffic in big cities in the United States seem quieter than in big cities in other parts of the world?*

Nityanandan Ashwath, who first posed this Frustable, lurked in the bushes until he read our write-up in *Do Penguins Have Knees?* Now he offers three more reasons why foreign traffic seems noisier:

> 1. Most engines in vehicles on a U.S. street are large gasoline-powered four-stroke automobiles. These are inherently the

quietest type of engine ever invented. Most other places have a high percentage of diesels (buses/trucks), two-strokes (scooters), and small four-strokes (motorcycles) that are all much noisier.

2. The smaller vehicles overseas result in a greater density of exhaust population. That is, an observer on a street corner has more individual sources of sound within a 100-yard radius because bikes and minicars take up less street space per unit.

3. Most U.S. cars have automatic transmissions that limit the rpm buildup of the engine during acceleration. Drivers elsewhere have more opportunity for shrieking starts from a traffic light.

FRUSTABLE 6: *Why do dogs tilt their heads when you talk to them?*

In *Do Penguins Have Knees?*, we heard from readers arguing passionately whether dogs tilt their heads for better vision or better hearing. Reader Fred Lanting wrote with the best discussion reconciling these two viewpoints that we have seen:

> Dogs have a very poor focusing ability because the fovea (focusing depression) in the retina is less developed for that purpose than, say, the fovea of a hawk ... It's a tradeoff, since dogs have very good night vision and ability to detect motion better than we do. The dog tilts his head for the same reason we do: to get an almost imperceptibly different but significant new perspective—a better 3-D brain image of distance.
>
> The dog uses a *combination* of eyes and ears for this sharpening of the incoming sensory messages. Ears are set apart from each other for a reason: The tiny additional fraction of time it takes sound to reach the second ear tells dogs whence come the sounds. Thus a dog can find you in the dark or behind hiding places if you make a little noise.
>
> He tilts his head even if there's no noise *we* can hear because he wants to get the benefit of not only sight but any sound that *might* be forthcoming. He's trying to get all the sensory input he can because he's very interested in it.

One of our favorite correspondents, David Altom of Jefferson, Missouri, wrote to us about his cockapoo, Midnight, who he owned in the 1970s. Like many dogs, Midnight responded not only to the wail of police sirens outside their home but to the sound of sirens on television:

> Every time the sound of a police siren came on "Kojak," "Baretta," or "McCloud," Midnight would perk up his ears and tilt his head as if trying to understand that sound. His attention was directed to the speaker, not the picture. Once or twice, he went up and sniffed the TV speaker.
>
> Midnight also had two favorite songs: "Sister Golden Hair" by America and "One of These Nights" by the Eagles . . .

"Sister Golden Hair"? I thought dogs were supposed to have *good* hearing?

FRUSTABLE 7: *Why and where did the notion develop that "fat people are jolly"?*

Our 10-percent-of-the-brain expert, Prof. Michael Levin, took us to task for making fun of the validity of somatotypes, developed by William Sheldon about fifty years ago:

> There are three basic somatotypes: mesomorphic (muscular), ectomorphic (skinny), and endomorphic (fat). A good deal of valid research has established a correlation between mesomorphy and extroversion, aggressiveness and a domineering temperament. Criminals tend overwhelmingly to be mesomorphs, or slightly endomorphic mesomorphs.
>
> . . . ectomorphs tend to be introverted, inhibited, and restrained. So, comparatively speaking, endomorphs tend to be "jollier" than either mesomorphs or ectomorphs. They are relatively less inclined to try to dominate others, and are relatively less introspective and reserved. The perception of this is probably the origin of the (correct) stereotype of the jolly fat man. (The writer of this letter is mesomorphic, but has no desire to force his opinions on you.)

Sure, but because we are jolly endomorphs, we'll let you mesomorphic musclemen cram your opinions down our ineffectual throats.

FRUSTABLE 9: *Why does the heart depicted in illustrations look totally different than a real heart?*

In *Do Penguins Have Knees?* we mentioned Desmond Morris's theory that the heart was an idealized representation of the female buttocks. But reader Barth Richards, of Naperville, Illinois, offers a striking amplification of this theory.

During the Middle Ages, many Germanic and Scandinavian people, particularly pagans, used "runes," letters and symbols that had phonetic and often symbolic meanings. Runes were used not only in language but in magical rituals. One rune was our idealized conception of the heart. In the book *Futhark: A Handbook of Rune Magic*, the interpretation of the heart symbol is given as

> (actually an ancient representation of female genitalia and buttocks)—sensuality, eroticism, love. In Old Norse books of magic the sign often appears in spells of love magic; a symbol of sexual intercourse.

Richards theorizes that when Christians tried to subsume pagan culture, they retained the "love" connotation of the heart symbol, while eliminating the sexual components.

> The literal meaning of the symbol was altered to that of a "heart," which fit the Christian belief of the heart being the vessel of the emotions, including love.
>
> This also meshes nicely with one of the other suggested solutions you printed in *Do Penguins Have Knees?*, which said that the arteries of the systemic arch of many animals closely resemble the shape of the "heart" symbol. This coincidence would surely add to the Christians' sense of justification in referring to the pagan's love symbol as a "heart."

FRUSTABLE 10: *Where do all the missing pens go?*

Reader Jim Kasun claims to have accumulated about 4,400 pounds of them. ("At an average weight of .3 ounce, this translates to approximately 234,600 pens.") Although this doesn't account for every single lost pen, it surely explains the imbalance in Plano, Texas.

Jim believes that while countless pens have fallen out of pockets, as many are misplaced as lost. Look underneath sofa and chair cushions, Jim suggests—pens have a way of migrating deep into the innards of the furniture. Others are buried in overloaded drawers and cabinets.

Jim anticipated what was on our mind after reading his letter: "Why do I spend time doing this? I'm not sure . . . guess I just have a *pen*chant for it." Despite the pun, we can't be too mad at him. After all, he sent us a pen "from the 1980–1985 group. Who knows? Maybe you once owned it."

LETTERS

Letters

Maybe in the future we will publish a book of Letters to Imponderables. *Until that day, we have room to print only a fraction of the thousands of letters we receive every year. This section is reserved not for new Imponderables, conjectures about Frustables, or even words of praise, but rather for readers who want to vent their spleen about what we've written in the past.*

In August 1992, we republished all but the first Imponderables *book in paperback, incorporating many of the suggestions and corrections of readers. It can sometimes take years to validate objections and change the text on subsequent printings, but we do so regularly.*

We appreciate your suggestions and consider every one carefully. The letters published here are not the only valid criticisms or suggestions we received, just some of the more entertaining ones that we hope will appeal to a wide audience.

From now on, maybe we'll need to put an expiration date on Imponderables. In Do Penguins Have Knees? *we answered the question, "Why Are There Peanuts in Plain M&Ms?" Guess what? Hans Fiuczynski, external relations director of M&M/Mars, writes to tell us that the premise of the Imponderable is now moot:*

> Historically, M&M/Mars has used the same milk chocolate in both M&Ms Plain and Peanut Chocolate Candies. This milk chocolate contained a small amount of finely ground peanuts.
>
> At considerable investment in the plants producing these products, the chocolate production has been separated and the usage of any peanuts in the chocolate for M&M Plain Chocolate Candies eliminated, starting January 1992. However, as a precaution, we will continue to maintain the declaration of peanuts as an ingredient in M&Ms Plain Chocolate Candies. This is to provide protection to peanut-sensitive individuals in the event that a small

amount of peanuts may inadvertently appear in M&M's Plain Chocolate Candies.

We're also sad to report that the Imponderable from our first book—"What Is the Purpose of the Red Tear String on Band-Aids?"—won't make sense to kids in the next century. By the end of 1992, Johnson & Johnson will have phased out the tear strings altogether, substituting an adhesive strip.

But M&M/Mars and Johnson & Johnson aren't the only corporations dedicated to reform. Jena Paolilli of Chelmsford, Massachusetts, writes:

> In *Why Do Dogs Have Wet Noses?* you answered the question, "Why is there no expiration date on toothpaste?" by saying that there is none needed. I have found expiration dates on four tubes of toothpaste: two on Colgate for Kids (different sizes), one on Tartar Control Gel Colgate, and one on Colgate's Peak Baking Soda Gel . . .

We called the folks at Colgate, and they corroborated the recent appearance of an expiration date. "Why do you need one now if you didn't a few years ago?" we asked. The consumer affairs representative indicated Colgate probably didn't. The ingredients haven't changed, and it isn't at all dangerous to use toothpaste after the expiration date. But occasionally the flavoring or the fluoride in toothpaste breaks down chemically. The result is usually a watery consistency or a funny taste. In most cases, Colgate advised, the toothpaste is usable for at least a year after the date on the package.

In Why Do Dogs Have Wet Noses? we stated that, usually, the answer to "What vegetables are used in vegetable oil?" was: soybean oil. But canola oil has made great inroads, as Lauralou Cicierski, of the Canola Council of Canada, was pleased to inform us. Procter & Gamble's Crisco and Puritan Oils now both contain 100 percent canola oil, and other brands' ingredient lists increasingly say "canola oil and/or soybean oil."

The times, they are a-changin', we guess. And not only in the candy, oil, bandage, and toothpaste industries. It seems like

DAVID FELDMAN

there has been rampant inflation in Social Security numbers, too:

> In your book *When Do Fish Sleep?* you state that the highest numbers assigned as the first three digits of a Social Security number are 575–576 in Hawaii. I don't believe this is true. My wife and I both have SSNs that begin 585. In fact, most of the people I grew up with in Clovis, New Mexico, had 585 numbers.
>
> HAROLD GAINES
> St. Louis, Missouri

You're right. Historically, New Mexico's SSNs start with 525, but when they ran out of numbers, New Mexico, for a while, had the highest number, 585, of the fifty states. But several other states have been assigned bigger numbers since we wrote When Do Fish Sleep? *(Mississippi, 587–588; Florida, 589–595; Arizona, 600–601; and California, 602–626). The highest numbers that the Social Security Administration issues, 700–728, still belong to railroad employees, although new numbers in the 700-series have not been assigned since 1963.*

While we are focusing on geographical grumblings, we heard a chauvinistic chant from Ken Giesbers of Seattle, Washington. He asks us, "How dare you claim East Coast weather is weirder than ours?"

> In *Why Do Dogs Have Wet Noses?* you state: "Of course, the volatility of weather in the East makes the job of a weathercaster considerably dicier than his West Coast counterparts." You should be aware that the West Coast extends northerly past Southern California.
>
> Weather prediction in the Pacific Northwest is considered the hardest in the nation. Having lived in the Portland and Seattle areas all of my life, I was shocked, on a recent trip to Boston, to hear a forecasted high temperature of 82 degrees. In Seattle, no forecaster would ever be so bold. The forecast would be for "a high in the upper seventies to mid-eighties," and it would be wrong as often as right. The proximity of an ocean to the west, inland waterways, and mountain peaks with glacial networks all combine to make prediction very difficult indeed.

Heck, Ken, we think weather forecasting in the Northwest is a snap. "Cool, cloudy, chance of rain and showers" should work, oh, about 355 days of the year. And don't assume the weather forecast of 82 degrees in Boston was correct, either.

Larry Mills of Southfield, Michigan, attributes the presence of the oft-discussed ball on top of a flagpole to weather factors—lightning, in particular:

> The large ball is on top to greatly reduce the electrical tension that might build during electrical storms . . . this is opposite to a lightning rod, which comes to a sharp point to assure that electrical tension that may build at or near a structure will surely strike the rod.

We've never heard this theory before, and we've heard plenty on the topic.

But the flagpole ball Imponderable is a piker compared to all the letters we've received about why ranchers hang their boots on fenceposts, a staple of every Letters section. We are pleased to announce that we received only one new theory in the last year; perhaps we are starting to wean you from this topic. William Papavasilion, a teacher/folklorist from Lancaster, Pennsylvania, writes that in some areas, it was customary for folks to leave unneeded boots outside to be taken for the asking. Nowhere was this policy practiced more than at Boot Hill:

> If a deceased person had a good pair of boots, the undertaker (usually) would place his boots near the entrance of the cemetery. If a person took a kindness to a pair of boots, he simply would take the pair.

Speaking of death, J. Stephen Paul of West Monroe, New York, reports the rare sighting of a bird dying in flight. But he concurs with our analysis of what happens to dead birds: "By the third day, it must have been scavenged or resurrected itself." Paul's son also watched a bird "whop down" in flight. ("Threw a rod, I guess.") If Paul doesn't seem too sentimental about death, it may be because he is a hospital consultant, and

DAVID FELDMAN

he supplied another reason why surgeons wear blue or green uniforms (see Why Do Clocks Run Clockwise?*):*

> When medical personnel are operating, looking at red for a long time, a retinal imprint is established on the eye. When looking away, this appears as a greenish afterimage or "ghost image" wherever they look until it fades out. To counter this bothersome effect, which occurs any time a surgeon or assistant looks away to rest the eyes, the walls and clothing are colored a matching shade to render this effect invisible . . .

Can anyone confirm this theory?

Dead birds weren't the only feathered friends on your minds. Several of you tried to help us out after we confessed in Why Do Dogs Have Wet Noses? *that we didn't know how "turkey" came to mean a show business flop. Terry Pruitt of Gadsden, Alabama, hypothesizes that a bad show is like a turkey trying to fly—it may sputter aloft for a while, but eventually it will flop to the ground. But several readers, Daniel J. Drazen of Berwyn, Illinois, being the first, found citations of this very topic in various books. Drazen located an explanation in Harry and Michael Medved's* Son of Golden Turkey Awards. *According to the Medveds, the colloquialism was coined because vaudeville shows used to conduct Thanksgiving performances but attendance was poor. "Turkey Nights" were dreaded gigs for performers, and mediocre acts got stuck playing them. Such entertainers, without any clout, were called "Turkey Acts" and, eventually, simply "Turkeys." In a recent issue of* Variety, *Jeremy Gerard contended that "turkey" was originally a Broadway term coined to denote a poor show—one that was performed not during bad attendance times but good:*

> . . . "turkey" was coined to denote a show of dubious merit mounted between Thanksgiving and the New Year in order to ride out the seasonal tourist trade regardless of the [critical] pans.

In Why Do Dogs Have Wet Noses? *we tackled a couple of Imponderables about worms. "Are the nineties going to be the Decade of the Larva?" we mused about this obsession. Our joke* didn't sit too well with two of our Illinois readers, Neil B. Schanker of Palatine and Craig Cicero of Rockford. As both pointed out, worms are not larvae. They remain the same structurally as they grow. Schanker, by the way, is an assistant professor of biology at William Rainey Harper College. Craig Cicero is not yet a professor—he's thirteen years old.

While we're on the subject of insects, we have a ticklish issue to discuss. In When Do Fish Sleep? we quoted an entomologist as saying that crickets "chirp" by rubbing their legs together. In Do Penguins Have Knees? we ran an angry letter from another entomologist berating us, insisting that crickets rub the scrapers on their wings to cause the noise. We issued a groveling apology. Several readers have sent us textbooks, most with diagrams, indicating that the noise comes from scrapers on the legs. How can something so simple be in question? The final straw was when our eight-year-old nephew, Michael Feldman, found the following quotation in a book called Wings, written by Nick Bantoc: "Crickets chirp by rubbing their wings or legs together." We give up.

On second thought, we don't give up. How can we rest when we are presented with a new, unsolved mystery by reader Stephen Hostettler of Chico, California?

> I offer further evidence that fish do sleep. Several months ago, I got up to discover one of the swordtails missing from our tank. My wife found him swimming in a teacup on the far side of the double sink. Everything else on the counter and both sides of the sink were dry—proof positive that he was sleepwalking. The event so traumatized the little critter that he hasn't closed both eyes.

How do you know your fish doesn't take naps when you leave the room? Or don't the Hostettlers sleep?

Paul J. Breslin of Tuscaloosa, Alabama, took us to task for our discussion of the role of dalmations in firefighting in Why Do Clocks Run Clockwise? He thinks we left the impression that the main task of dalmations was to run in front of the coach to clear traffic. Although we did read first-person accounts

DAVID FELDMAN

(from the firemen, not the dalmations) of dogs clearing traffic, we probably did put too much emphasis on this task. Breslin summarizes their main duties well: "The dalmation's job was to keep the horses pulling together, to keep them from tangling the lines, to keep them apart, and to insure they were on the right lead."

Readers' objections to our treatment of animals extends to animated critters, too. Thaddeus J. Kochanny of Chicago, Illinois, proffers another explanation for why Mickey Mouse has only four fingers on each hand. He thinks the tradition dates back to

> depictions of trolls, leprechauns, meneuni, and other mythical "persons" that predate cartoons. In virtually all such carvings, the characters have three fingers. I believe this was done to show the image was nonhuman. This has nothing to do with the ease of drawing.
>
> I collect wood carvings of Anri, an Italian cooperative headquartered in the Italian Alps at Santa Christina, Italy. When the carving is a troll or mythic creation, it has three fingers and a thumb on each hand. When it is a person, such as a boy eating grapes, there are four fingers and a thumb on each hand of the figure.

Actually, we mentioned in When Do Fish Sleep? *that Disney had a habit of giving humans in his cartoons, or at least lead characters, four fingers and a thumb as well. But every animation expert we've ever consulted concurs with our explanation.*

While we're on the subject of hands, Dr. Jerry Tennen of Toronto, Ontario, wants to add another reason why most people wear wristwatches on their left hand: "If you wear a standard wristwatch on your right wrist, the stem eventually frays the cuff on your shirtsleeves. Too bad you didn't consult me first." Evidently so.

Jeff Reese of Mosinee, Wisconsin, wishes we had contacted him too—before we wrote in When Do Fish Sleep? *that dollar bills can't be counted by machines. We overstated the case. There are machines that count bills, but they are expensive and can't discriminate among different denominations. The expense of the bill-counting machines discourages many vendors from using machines that accept dollar bills.*

Now that reader Gabe Raggiunto is too mature to fling single shoes around his neighborhood (see "The Frustables That Will Not Die"), he sits back and reads the paper, luckily for us. He sent us an Associated Press newspaper story that recounts the same origins of the name Dr. Pepper, that we discussed in Do Penguins Have Knees? *But some citizens of Rural Retreat, Virginia, the real Dr. Pepper's home town, think otherwise. The town's mayor (and dentist), Dr. Doug Humphrey, claims that Dr. Pepper himself invented the drink (those medicos always stick together) and that a lovesick Wade Morrison (the hero of our story) stole the formula and sold it in Waco, Texas, as shameless revenge against Dr. Pepper, who would not let Morrison marry his daughter. We'll stick with our version, although we hear that Oliver Stone is trying to option the memoirs of Dr. Humphrey.*

Speaking of conspiracies, readers are still upset about disappearing socks. But have you ever wondered whether this is a problem in France? We guess not:

> At least one person has solved the sock problem to his satisfaction. I have read that Jerry Lewis never wears a pair of socks more than once and that he throws them away after wearing. That means no washing/drying/coupling or worry about the odd sock. He has been criticized for this extravagance by those who feel he should have the socks washed and then given to charity. But Lewis, being the lovable fellow we all know and adore, told the critics to perform a physically impossible act. You see what this sock business can generate in a person.
>
> DANIEL J. TIREN
> *Laurel, Maryland*

We sure do, Daniel. It can drive people to composing horrible puns: Tiren speculates that missing socks have gone into a special, merry resting ground in the sky—the hozone.

We heard from several engineers and technicians who had information to add about why the numbers on tape counters on

DAVID FELDMAN

audio and video tape players don't seem to measure anything. Electronics engineer Kevin Holsinger of Menlo Park, California, explains:

> In either a VCR or audio tape player, the tape is moved past the play/record heads when a motor turns the little wheel inside the cassette housing. The unit of measurement on the counter is related to how many times that motor has turned—but each count on the front panel might represent one revolution, five revolutions, one-tenth of a revolution, or whatever else they decide on.
>
> Although manufacturers did not agree on what the counts represent, they did agree on how fast the motors will turn. That doesn't result in a constant tape speed, though, because the reel the tape winds onto is getting larger as tape winds onto it. In one revolution, a reel with a larger diameter will pull more tape onto itself, which means that the tape is passing the read/write heads faster toward the end of the movie than it is at the beginning. You can't see or hear the difference in speed because it was recorded that way, too (and because the change in speed isn't really all that large, since an empty reel's diameter is still around 70% of a full reel). The motors, rather than the tape, run at a constant speed, because it is much less expensive to build things that way.

And while we're speaking of measurement, David Maier of Beaverton, Oregon, offers a simpler explanation (than we did in When Do Fish Sleep?*) for why gas gauges move faster as you empty the fuel tank of an automobile:*

> Most gas gauges are hooked to a float that measures the depth of gas. But because tanks don't have straight sides generally, volume doesn't vary linearly with depth. Consider a V-shaped beer glass—each time you drink an "inch" of beer, you are getting a smaller swallow.

Talk of beer always reminds us of baseball. How's that for a smooth segue into a discussion of why females "throw like a girl"? Anita Gertz of Farmington Hills, Michigan, felt we didn't cover all the bases in our discussion of the topic in When Do Fish Sleep? *Her genetics professor at Eastern Michigan University told her that when a person stands with the arms slightly away from the sides and the palms are facing forward,* the angle the bones of the forearm and upper arm make at the elbow (sometimes called the "carrying angle") is fifteen degrees in males and twenty-five degrees in females. Because the angle in males and females is different, so is their throwing ability. The explanation for the larger angle was that it evolved in females because they carried babies and small children much more often than males.

Our exercise physiologists still insist that girls could "throw like boys" if they were trained to do so. But let's not argue. We have more important things to squabble about. Like George Strait's hats ("Why Are There Dents on the Top of Cowboy Hats?" in Do Penguins Have Knees?*). Lee Denham of Warnock Hat Works in Pharr, Texas, sent us a picture of the country and western singer wearing a hat with "dents" (Lee recommends we call these "creases"), and says that all of Strait's hats have creases. We swear that we've seen George in a creaseless hat, but for now we'll concede the point, Lee, and hope we haven't forever tarnished Strait's reputation by implying that he has the same fashion sense as Hoss Cartwright.*

And any discussion of high fashion has to end on this high note: Why do old men wear their pants higher than young men? We shared many theories on this subject in Why Do Clocks Run Clockwise?*, but David Campion, MICP, wants to add two more:*

> Many older men experience deterioration or settling of the bones that comprise the pelvic girdle. It is possible that displacement of the iliac bones (the crests of which form the hips) may render the hips useless as a perch for one's pants.
>
> On close inspection, one will find that old men with high-riding pants are often wearing suspenders. I say "on close inspection" because old men frequently wear sport coats capable of concealing the suspenders. This combination may create the illusion of pants that are intentionally pulled up when, in fact, the underlying cause may simply be a snappy pair of suspenders.

Janyce E. McLean of Beeville, Texas, wrote to complain about our statement that Rinx Records was the first company to produce music specifically for skating rinks. Janyce says that her mother worked for a company called Skatin' Tunes, which

DAVID FELDMAN

produced organ music for rinks all over the country. The company was based in Babylon, Long Island, and "was begun sometime in the early 1940s by Hilliard Du Bois, who also used the professional name Allan Strow." Can any reader provide more information about this company?

Several readers, including Dr. John Hardin of Greenfield, Indiana, who first posed the Imponderable, found it hard to believe that the green tinge sometimes found on potato chips was the harmless chlorophyll we claimed it to be in Do Penguins Have Knees? *We've rechecked our sources and are happy to reiterate: Relax. Toxins can form on potato chips, but they reside on the peel. The toxins, glycolalkaloids, develop at the same time as the chlorophyll, but there is no connection between the "poison" and the green stuff on potato chips.*

In Why Do Dogs Have Wet Noses? *we declared that men's nipples were vestigial organs, ones that could conceivably disappear in the distant future. Bill Cohen-Kiraly of Lyndhurst, Ohio, took us to task for our sloppy, nonpoetic license:*

> Evolution does not necessarily rid bodies of things that are vestigial unless they offer some disadvantage to the evolutionee before he or she can reproduce and raise young to adulthood. So as long as nippleless men don't reproduce faster or better than nippled men, there is no reason for the nipples to disappear. Because of the sexual sensitivity of nipples, the reverse is probably true.
>
> But there is a bigger problem with your contention that they will disappear from men, however. Evolution is a genetic process and the genetic differences between men and women are relatively minimal, only one part of one chromosome. Many structural distinctions are the result of hormonal differences. In short, you could not eliminate the nipples on men without eliminating them on women because the genes that create them are not gender specific.

It's settled. No more government grants for research on male nipple elimination, then.

Sometimes we hear from correspondents who want to argue with other letter writers. One young reader from Interlochen,

Michigan, has a bone to pick with SUNY professor Noel W. Smith, who wrote in When Do Fish Sleep? *that the role of pubic and underarm hair was not primarily as a sexual attractant but as a lubricant to facilitate movement of arms and legs. Prof. Smith, meet Ben Randall:*

> If your lubrication theory is correct, why don't young kids get chafed when doing activities? Wouldn't they need "lubrication," too? I'm a mere eighth-grader and even I can see this.
>
> And another thing. Little kids move around a lot more than older, lubricated adults that I've seen.

Kids can be tough. But then so can adults. We recently received this letter from Paul C. Ward of Ligonier, Pennsylvania:

> I am currently reading your book *Do Penguins Have Knees?* with much pleasure and have enjoyed several of your other books. However, one thing bugs me. Why do you almost always answer a question in three hundred words or more when it could be answered in a fraction of that amount? Is this because authors are paid by the word?

Yes.

Do allow us one indulgence. In Do Penguins Have Knees? *we closed with a letter from a woman whose lover read to her from* Why Do Clocks Run Clockwise? *But we found even a better use for Imponderables in bed:*

> Norman Cousins attributed his recoveries to viewing laugh-provoking films. One of your Imponderables recently evoked a far more spectacular response. A friend suffered a stroke with serious sensorimotor deficits and was rendered aphasiac.
>
> During protracted hospital course, responses remained refractory. One afternoon, I was reading aloud from *When Do Fish Sleep?* and burst into laughter. Pausing for breath, into the silence threaded a wavering whisper, my friend's first successful attempt at communication. I bent closer, capturing the long awaited sound, borne aloft like a triumphant banner.
>
> My stricken friend crisply voiced, "Oh, read that again, read

DAVID FELDMAN

that again!," her face ablaze in smiles. All of us are glad your mother had you!

SALLI KAMINS
Venice, California

Thanks, Salli. You made our year.

And to all of our Imponderable friends, thanks for all of your support. We'll meet you again at the same place, same time, next year.

Acknowledgments

In every Imponderables book, the acknowledgments start with a thanks to my readers. Without your input, I wouldn't have such a wide range of mysteries to explore, answers to Frustables, criticisms that make the books more interesting and more accurate, and praise that often provides the author inspiration to rise from his stupor and trudge on.

If mail has become the lifeblood of the *Imponderables* series, it has also become the bane of my existence. As always, I am sending a personal reply to any reader who encloses a self-addressed stamped envelope, but I am behind, alarmingly behind, in answering correspondence. When I start writing the manuscript for the next book, my letter output dwindles. Please bear with me as I try to catch up, and be assured that I read and appreciate every word of every letter sent to *Imponderables*.

Is it karma or is it just dumb luck that I have the opportunity to work with such wonderful people? My esteem for my editor, Rick Kot, keeps rising as his voice keeps lowering—I have a recurrent nightmare that he will forsake publishing to sing bass for the Temptations. Sheila Gilooly, Rick's assistant, may have her soul in the rarefied world of verse, but she has been of immense help in solving my prosaic problems with great skill and charm. Craig Herman was forced to decide between a career in male modeling and publicity; luckily for me, he eschewed the superficial world of glitter. Andrew Malkin may have flown the HarperCollins coop, but his work in booking my last publicity tour was exceptional.

Imponderables books are produced on an extremely tight deadline, one of the many reasons I'm especially grateful to the production editing/copyediting team that renders my manuscript semicoherent: thank you, Kim Lewis, Maureen Clark, and Janet Byrne. And for her exceptional work on the last two jacket designs, my thanks to Suzanne Noli.

Even the muckety-mucks at HarperCollins have been exceptionally kind and supportive to me, and that starts at the top. Thanks to Bill Shinker, Roz Barrow, Brenda Marsh, Pat Jonas, Zeb Burgess, Karen Mender, Steve Magnuson, Robert Jones, Joe Montebello, Susan Moldow, Clinton Morris, Connie Levinson, Mark Landau, and all my friends in the publicity, special markets, sales, and Harper Audio divisions.

Jim Trupin, the Grand Pooh Bah of literary agents, is a neverending font of curmudgeonly common sense, while Grande Pooh Bette Liz Trupin, on the other hand, is a neverending font of common sense.

Kassie Schwan's illustrations amaze me with their inventiveness and good humor. This book's for you!

And thanks to Sherry Spitzer for her invaluable research assistance and dogged determination to root out Imponderability wherever she finds it.

Who do I run to when I can't moan or vent my insecurities at my publisher (neuroses do not flare only at office hours)? I bother my friends in publishing, of course. Thanks—for the wisdom, as well as the friendship—to Mark Kohut, Susie Russenberger, Barbara Rittenhouse, and James Gleick.

And to my friends and family, who offer both advice about and respite from my work, I thank: Tony Alessandrini; Jesus Arias; Michael Barson; Sherry Barson; Rajat Basu; Ruth Basu; Barbara Bayone; Jeff Bayone; Jean Behrend; Marty Bergen; Brenda Berkman; Cathy Berkman; Sharyn Bishop; Andrew Blees; Carri Blees; Christopher Blees; Jon Blees; Bowling Green State University's Popular Culture Department; Jerry Braithwaite; Annette Brown; Arvin Brown; Herman Brown; Ernie Capobianco; Joann Carney; Lizzie Carnie; Susie Carney; Janice Carr; Lapt Chan; Mary Clifford; Don Cline; Dorrie Cohen; Alvin Cooperman; Marilyn Cooperman; Judith Dahlman; Paul Dahlman; Shelly de Satnick; Charlie Doherty; Laurel Doherty; Joyce Ebert; Pam Elam; Andrew Elliot; Steve Feinberg; Fred Feldman; Gilda Feldman; Michael Feldman; Phil Feldman; Ron Felton; Kris Fister; Mary Flannery; Linda Frank;

Elizabeth Frenchman; Susan Friedland; Michele Gallery; Chris Geist; Jean Geist; Bonnie Gellas; Richard Gertner; Amy Glass; Bea Gordon; Dan Gordon; Emma Gordon; Ken Gordon; Judy Goulding; Chris Graves; Christal Henner; Lorin Henner; Marilu Henner; Melodie Henner; David Hennes; Paula Hennes; Sheila Hennes; Sophie Hennes; Larry Harold; Carl Hess; Mitchell Hofing; Steve Hofman; Bill Hohauser; Uday Ivatury; Terry Johnson; Sarah Jones; Allen Kahn; Mitch Kahn; Joel Kaplan; Dimi Karras; Maria Katinos; Steve Kaufman; Robin Kay; Stewart Kellerman; Harvey Kleinman; Claire Labine; Randy Ladenheim-Gil; Julie Lasher, Debbie Leitner; Marilyn Levin; Vicky Levy; Rob Lieberman; Jared Lilienstein; Pon Hwa Lin; Adam Lupu; Patti Magee; Rusty Magee; everybody at the Manhattan Bridge Club; Phil Martin; Chris McCann; Jeff McQuain; Julie Mears; Phil Mears; Roberta Melendy; Naz Miah; Carol Miller; Honor Mosher; Barbara Musgrave; Phil Neel; Steve Nellisen; Craig Nelson; Millie North; Milt North; Charlie Nurse; Debbie Nye; Tom O'Brien; Pat O'Conner; Joanna Parker; Jeannie Perkins; Merrill Perlman; Joan Pirkle; Larry Prussin; Joe Rowley; Rose Reiter; Brian Rose; Lorraine Rose; Paul Rosenbaum; Carol Rostad; Tim Rostad; Leslie Rugg; Tom Rugg; Gary Saunders; Joan Saunders; Mike Saunders; Norm Saunders; Laura Schisgall; Cindy Shaha; Patricia Sheinwold; Aaron Silverstein; Kathy Smith; Kurtwood Smith; Susan Sherman Smith; Chris Soule; Kitty Srednicki; Stan Sterenberg; Karen Stoddard; Bill Stranger; Kat Stranger; Anne Swanson; Ed Swanson; Mike Szala; Jim Teuscher; Josephine Teuscher; Laura Tolkow; Albert Tom; Maddy Tyree; Alex Varghese; Carol Vellucci; Dan Vellucci; Hattie Washington; Ron Weinstock; Roy Welland; Dennis Whelan; Devin Whelan; Heide Whelan; Lara Whelan; Jon White; Ann Whitney; Carol Williams; Maggie Wittenburg; Karen Wooldridge; Maureen Wylie; Charlotte Zdrok; Vladimir Zdrok; and Debbie Zuckerberg.

We contacted approximately 1,500 experts, corporations, associations, universities, and foundations seeking information to help solve our mysteries. We don't have the space to list everyone who responded, but we want to thank all of the generous people whose information led directly to the solution of the Imponderables in this book:

Randy Acorcey, Diversified Electronic Corporation; Jim Amanna, Mobil Oil Corporation; American Cat Association; Harold Amstutz, American Association of Bovine Practitioners; John Anderson, Borden's Glue; Joe Andrews, Pillsbury Brands; Richard Anthes, National Center for Atmospheric Research; Atlas Casket Company.

David Bahlman, Society of Architectural Historians; Ian Bailey, University of California, Berkeley; Jean Bailey, General Tire; Carol Barfield, United Animal Owners Association; Rick Barongi, San Diego Zoo; Marie Beckey, Perdue Farms; Lynn Beedle, Council on Tall Buildings and Urban Habitat; Denton Belk, Crustacean Society; W. J. "Buck" Benison, Southern Ambulance Builders, Inc.; Maynard Benjamin, Envelope Manufacturers Association of America; Randy Bergman, Colgate-Palmolive; Enid Bergstrom, *Dog World;* Barry Berlin, Goodyear Tire and Rubber Company; William Berman, Society for Pediatric Research; Kathy Biel-Morgan; Bill Biles, Gestetner Corporation; Peter Black, SUNY; Wallace Blanton; Richard Boon, Roofing Industry Educational Institute; J. Gregg Borchelt, Brick Institute of America; G. Bruce Boyer; Kimberly Boyer, Coca-Cola; Ben Brewster, Colonial Brass Company; Roy Brister, Tyson Food, Inc.; Richard M. Brooks, Stouffer Hotels; Lee Brown, Whitehall Products Ltd.; Don Byczynski, Colonial Carbon Co.

K. L. Campbell; John Carolson, Dixie/Marathon, James River Corporation; Jack Castor, San Francisco Zoo; Marc Chernin, Dwelling Managers, Inc.; Helen Cherry, Cat Fanciers Federation; Chesebrough-Ponds, Inc.; Kathryn Cochran, American Hotel and Motel Association; Roger Coleman, National Food Processors Association; Norma Conley, Pretzel Museum; John Corbett, Clairol, Inc.; James Cramer, American Institute of Architects.

Michael D'Asaro; Robert DeChillo, National Coffee Association of USA; Steve Del Priore, Pepsi-Cola Bottling Company of

New York; Diane Demee-Benoit, San Francisco Zoo; Michael DeMent, Hallmark Cards, Inc.; Thomas H. Dent, Cat Fanciers Association; Michael DiBiasi, Becton-Dickinson and Company; Tim Dillon, Cornell Laboratory of Ornithology; Robert J. Dinkin, California State University, Fresno; Brent Dixon, Paper Bag Institute; Richard Dowhan, GTE Products Corporation; Lynn Downey, Levi Strauss & Co.; Joe Doyle; Fred Dunham, Oasis Mobile Homes; William Duval, International Brotherhood of Painters & Allied Trades.

David Eagan, Eagan Associates; Eclair Bake Shoppe; Linda Eggers, Maytag Company; D'Elain Pastries; Raymond Ellis, Hospitality, Lodging and Travel Research; Sherry Enzweiler, Gibson Greetings; Jacob Exler, Human Nutrition Information Service.

Charles Farley, Brick Institute of America; Newton Fassler, Institute of Store Planners; Darryl Felder, University of Louisiana, Lafayette; Carla Fischer, GE Company; Robert Fischer, American Society of Bakery Engineers; Mike Fisher, Besam, Inc.; Hans Fiuczynski, M&M/Mars; Barry Floyd, Philadelphia Fire Code Unit; Edward S. Ford, Grayson Foundation; James B. Ford; Al Fowler, Heyer Company; Matt Fox; Gwendolyn Frost, Cornell Feline Health Center.

Dorothy Garrison, Cooling Towers Institute; Carl Gerster, Mobil Oil Corporation; Lennie Gessler, Professional Bowlers Association of America; Mary Gillespie, Association of Home Appliance Manufacturers; Megan Gillispie, The League of Women Voters; Ellyn Giordano, National Football Foundation and Hall of Fame; Paul Godfrey, Water Resources Research Center; William Good, National Roofing Contractors Association; Danielle Gordon, Kraft General Foods Corporation; Hy Greenblatt, Manufacturers of Illumination Products; Steve Gregg, Coffee Development Group; Mark Grunwald, Philadelphia Zoo.

Robert Habel, Cornell University; Daniel Halaburda, Panasonic Industrial Company; Dianna Hales; John Hall, American Bankers Association; John Haller, Robert Talbott Company; John Hallett, Desert Research Institute; E. E. Halmos, Construction Writers Association; Ed Hansen, American Association of Zoo Keepers; Megaera Harris, Office of the Postmaster General; John Hassett, International Bridge, Tunnel and Turnpike Association; Sylvia Hauser, *Dog World*; Jeanette Hayhurst; Donald Hazlett, Zippo Manufacturing Company; George Headrick, Construction Industry Manufacturers Association; David J. Hensing, American Association of State Highway and Transportation Officials; Jack Herschlag, National Association of Men's Sportswear Buyers; Bill Heyer, Heyer Company; Shari Hiller, Sherwin-Williams Company; Myron Hinrichs, Hasti Friends of the Elephant; Bruce Hisley, National Fire Academy; Sue Holiday, American Greetings; David Hopper, American Academy of Somnology; Tom Horan, American Irish Historical Society; Joe Horrigan, Professional Football Hall of Fame; Meredith Hughes, Potato Museum; Irv Hyatt.

Idaho Potato Commission.

Simon S. Jackel; Rand Jerris, United States Golf Association; William P. Jollie, American Association of Anatomists; Caroline Jones, Better Sleep Council; Chris Jones, Pepsi-Cola Company; Sally Jones, USDA; William Jones, Zippo Manufacturing Company.

Burton Kallman, National Nutritional Foods Association; Jack Katz, SUNY Buffalo Speech and Hearing Clinic; Leon Katz, Port Authority of New York and New Jersey; Kendell Keith, National Grain and Feed Association; Bruce Kershner; Donald Kieffer, National Hay Association; Sally Kinne, Poodle Club of America; Rodger Koppa, Texas Transportation Institute; Steve Korker, United States Postal System; Judith Kraus, FDA; Lucille Kubichek; Anita Kuemmel, Soap and Detergent Association; Karen Kuzsel, *Middle Eastern Dancer*; Linda Kwong, Bic Pen Corporation.

Richard Landesman, University of Vermont; Fred Lanting; Thomas Laronge, Thomas M. Laronge, Inc.; Thomas A. Lehmann, American Institute of Baking; George Lemke, International Brotherhood of Painters and Allied Trades; Joe Lesniak, Door and Hardware Manufacturing Institute; Edna Leurck, Procter & Gamble; Victor Liebe, American Traffic Safety Services Association; Judith Lindley, Calico Cat Registry International; Kick Lorenz, Gibson Greetings; Sally Lorette, Oakland Athletics; Kevin Lowery, Campbell Soup Company; Timothy Lynch, Kenneth Lynch & Sons.

Jane Macdonald-James, International Jelly and Preserve Association and Association for Dressings & Sauces; David Maier, Oregon Graduate Institute of Science and Technology; Kari Anne Maino, Best Foods Baking Group; Irene Malbin, Cosmetic, Toiletry, and Fragrance Association; Marlene Marchut, M&M/Mars; Joanne Marshall, Campbell Soup Company; Nancy Martin, Association of Field Ornithologists; Keith Marvin; Karen Mason, Recreational Vehicle Industry Association; Joe Mastrullo, Procter & Gamble; Doug Matyka, Georgia-Pacific Corporation; Susan Mauro, Pepsi-Cola Company; S. Michael Mazva, Eveready Battery Co.; Linda McCashion, the Potato Board; James P. MaCauley, International Association of Holiday Inns; James P. McCulley, Association of University Professors of Ophthalmology; Kay McKeown; Harry Medved, Screen Actors Guild; Barbara Meyer, Hallmark Cards, Inc.; Jim Meyer, United States Postal Service; Craig Michelson, Pfizer, Inc.; Bill Middlebrook, North American Philips Lighting Corporation; Mary D. Midkiff, American Horse Council; Mark Miller, American Bowling Congress; Stephen Miller, American Optometric Association; Steven Mintz; J. Robert Moody, GE Lighting Business Group; David Moore, Virginia Tech University; E. R. Moore; Randy Morgan, Cincinnati Insectarium; Marilyn Myers, Norelco Consumer Products.

Rosetta Newsome, Institute of Food Technologists; Irene Norman, Goldstein's Funeral Directors, Inc.; Jill Novack, Levi Strauss & Co.

Norman Owen, American International Electric, Inc.; Jane Owens, Western Trailer Park.

Andy Palatka, Business Forms Management Association; Rich Palin, Loctite Corporation; Joseph Pash, Somerset Technologies, Inc.; Wayne Pearson, Plastics Recyling Foundation; Philadelphia Zoo; Susan Pistilli, International Council of Shopping Centers; John A. Pitcher, Hardwood Research Council;

Ron Pominville, AMF Bowling Company; Barbara Preston, Association for Dressings and Sauces; Roy Preston, United States Postal System; Robert C. Probasco; Larry Prussin; Nancy Purtill, UCLA.

Howard Raether, National Funeral Directors Association; Jerry Rafats, National Agriculture Library; Lorraine Ramig, Denver Center for Performing Arts Voice Research Laboratory; Jean C. Raney, American Wool Council; Ginger Rawe, Kroger Company; Oakley Ray, American Feed Industry Association; Kelly Redmond, Western Regional Climate Center; Nan Redmond, Kraft General Foods; Richard Reynells, American Poultry Historical Society; Jim Richards, Cornell Feline Health Center; Chris Rieck, American Banking Association; Nancy Rivera, Greeting Cards Association; Caroline Robicsek, National Association for Plastic Container Recycling; Robin Roche, San Francisco Zoological Society; John Rockwell, National Center for State Courts; John R. Rodenburg, Federated Funeral Directors of America; Robert R. Rofen, Aquatic Research Institute; Alan Rooscroft, San Diego Wild Animal Park; Janet Rosati, Fruit of the Loom; Phyllis Rosenthal, NutraSweet; Kate Ruddon, American College of Obstetricians and Gynecologists.

John Saidla, Cornell Feline Health Center; Samuel Salamon, Cataract Eye Center of Cleveland; San Francisco Zoological Park; Ronald A. Schachar, Association for the Advancement of Ophthalmology; Robert Schmidt, North American Native Fishes Association; Jack Schultz, National Retail Federation; E. H. Scott, J. Hofert Company; Norman Scott, Society for the Study of Amphibians and Reptiles; William Scott, National Highway Traffic Safety Administration; Bert Seaman, B.J. Seamon Company; Keith Seitter, American Meteorological Association; Steven Shelov, Montefiore Medical Center; Hezy Shoshani, Elephant Interest Group; Scott Shuler, Asphalt Institute; Steve Sigman, Zenith Electronics Corporation; Dede Silverston, Eye Information; Harry Skinner, Federal Highway Administration; Brian Smith, U.S. League of Savings Institutions; Gary Smith, Agricultural Extension Service; Michael T. Smith, National Cattlemen's Association; Rose Smouse, National

Retail Federation; J. M. Smucker Company; Bruce V. Snow; Richard Snyder, Asphalt Roofing Manufacturers Association; Society of Plastics Industry; South Brooklyn Casket Company; Mark Spencer, Yellow Freight Systems; Sandra Spiegel, Gibson Greetings Cards; Margie Spurlock, Royal Crown Cola Company; George Stahl, Potdevin Machine Company; Bill Stanley; Elaine Stathopoulos, SUNY Buffalo Speech and Hearing Clinic; Henry Stehlingadam, Hydra-Shield Manufacturing, Inc.; Sunset Trailer Park; Swiss Bakery.

Jeanne Taylor, Milton Bradley Company; Frank Thomas, United States Golf Association; Tire Industry Safety Council; J. Donald Turk, Mobil Oil Corporation; William Turpin, Miles, Inc.

Edwin Uber, Bingo King; Mary Ann Usrey, R. J. Reynolds Tobacco Company.

Al Vanderneck, American Bowling Congress; Carolyn Verweyst, Whirlpool Corporation; James Vondruska, Quaker Oats Company.

Pat Wachtel, Maytag Company; Ann Walk, National Independent Bank Equipment and Systems Association; Iain Walton, D. D. Bean & Sons; Jeanne Washko, Borden, Inc.; Liz Wentland, Oster/Sunbeam; Thomas Werner, New York State Department of Transportation; Fred Wexler, Schick Razors; Larry Whitish, SAC Products; Beth Williams, American Association of Wildlife Veterinarians; Brad Williams, Levi Strauss & Co.; D. L. Woods, Texas A&M; Peter Wulff, *Home Lighting & Accessories*.

Peter Zando, Ebac Systems; Sheryl Zapcic, Lever Brothers Company; Caden Zollo, Specialty Bulb; Mike Zulak, San Francisco Zoological Park.

And to the many sources who, for whatever reason, wished to remain anonymous but still shared your expertise with us, our sincere thanks.

Index

calorie constituents in, 94–95
phenylalanine as ingredient in, 96
Dishwashers, two compartments of, 109–10
Disposable lighters, fluid chambers and, 92–93
Ditto masters, color of, 133–34
Dixieland music at political rallies, 234–36
Doctors and bad penmanship, 221–25
Dogs
 dalmatians and firefighting, 270–71
 drooling in, 34–35
 eating cat feces, 35–37
 eating posture of, 63–64
 head tilting and, 258–59
 miniature, 154–55
 poodles, wild, 207–9
 rear-leg wiggling, when scratched, 52–53
"DONT WALK" signs, lack of apostrophes in, 75–76
Doors
 double, in stores, 177–80
 in shopping mall entrances, 180–81
 "THIS DOOR TO REMAIN UNLOCKED DURING BUSINESS HOURS" signs, in stores, 202
Double doors in stores, 177–80
Dr Pepper, origin of name, 272
Driving on right side, vs. left side, of road, 248–49
Drooling, and dogs, 34–35
Drowsiness after meals, 138–39

Eating, and effect on sleep of, 138–39
Elderly, height of, 250
Elections, timing of, 41

Electric can openers, sharpness of blades on, 176–77
Elephants
 disposal of remains of, 196–97
 on Oakland A's uniforms, 14–15
English, driving habits of, 248–49
English muffins
 in England, 200–201
 white particles on, 49
Envelopes
 Christmas cards, paper bands on, 203–4
 size of, in bills, 81–83
Eyes
 pain, when tired, 159–60
 position, during sleep, 146

"FALLING ROCK" signs, purpose of, 72–74
Fat people and jolliness, 259
Fats, on nutrition labels, 142–43
Filters, cigarette, brown spots on, 112–13
Fire hydrants, freezing of water in, 150
Fish, sleep patterns of, 270
501, Levi jeans, origin of name, 61
Flagpoles, balls atop, 268
Flinstones multivitamins, Betty Rubble and, 4–5
Frogs and eye closure, when swallowing, 115–16
Fruitcake, alleged popularity of, 253
Frustables, 217–61
Fuel gauges in automobiles, 273
Funerals, and head position of deceased, in caskets, 8–9

Gasoline pumps, rubber sleeves on, 197

Gauges, fuel, in automobiles, 273
Glues, "super," vs. regular, 145–46
Golf balls and veering toward
    ocean, when putting, 107–8
Gowns, and caps, at graduations,
    99–102
Grading of cigarettes, 112–13
Gravel and placement on flat
    roofs, 153–54
Gravy skin loss, when heated, 58
Greeting cards, shape of, 70–71
Gulls, "sea," in parking lots,
    198–99

Hail, measurement of, 239–40
Hats
    decline in use of, 227–31
    dents in cowboy, 274
Haystacks, shape of, 47–48
Hearts, shape of, idealized vs.
    real, 260
Heat and effect on sleep, 137–38
Height of elderly, 250
Holes on bottom of soda bottles,
    187–88
Horses, vomiting and, 111–12
Hotel amenities, spread of, 118–21
Houses, settling in, 32–34
"Hut," as football term, 40

"I" before "e," in spelling, 219
Ice cream and thirstiness, 236–37
Imperial gallon, vs. American
    gallon, 16–17
Ink, color of, in ditto masters,
    133–34
Insects
    ants, and separation from
        colony, 44–45
    moths, and attraction to light,
        21–23
    roaches, and reaction to light,
        20–21

Jams, contents of, 140–41
Jars, food, refrigeration of
    opened, 171–72
Jeans
    Levi, colored tabs on, 59–61
    Levi 501s, naming of, 61
Jellies, contents of, 140–41
Judges and black robes, 190–92

Kissing and female leg kicking,
    218

Letters, 265–77
Levi jeans
    colored tabs on, 59–61
    origin of "501" name, 61
Light bulbs, air in, 199–200
Lighters, disposable, and fluid
    chambers, 92–93
Lips, upper, groove on, 42–43
Lobsters, ambidexterity of, 3–4
Lotion, after-shave, and stinging,
    161–62

M&Ms, peanuts in plain, 265–66
Mailboxes and postmaster
    general approval, 105–7
Mall, shopping, entrances, doors
    at, 180–81
Marmalades, contents of, 140–41
Matchbooks, location of staples
    on, 173–74
Matches, color of paper, 174–75
Meatloaf, taste of, in institutions,
    243
Meats and doneness preferences,
    252–53
Men
    dancing ability of, 218
    feelings of coldness, 218
    remote controls and, 217
Mickey Mouse, four fingers of,
    271

Milk, skin on, when heated, 58
Mobile homes, tires atop, in
    trailer parks, 163–64
Monitors, computer, shape of,
    129–31
Moths, reaction to light of, 21–23
Mottoes on sundials, 54–56
Movie actors, speed of speech of,
    241–43
Mustaches, policemen and, 219

Neckties
    direction of stripes on, 86–87
    taper of, 84–85
Nine-volt batteries, shape of, 104
Nipples on men, 275
Nutrition labels, statement of fats
    on, 142–43

Oakland A's, elephant on uniform
    of, 14–15
Orange coffee pots, in
    restaurants, 67–69

Painters and white uniforms,
    17–19
Pants, height of old men's, 274
Paper sacks, jagged edges on,
    117–18
Penmanship, bad, doctors and,
    221–25
Pens, disappearance of, 260–61
Pepper, and salt, as table
    condiments, 225–26
Perfume, wrists and, 90
Philtrums, purpose of, 43
Photographs, poses in, 218
Physicians and bad penmanship,
    221–25
Pita bread, pockets in, 98
Plastics, recyclable, numbers on,
    155–56
Pockets in pita bread, 98

Policemen and mustaches, 219
Poodles, wild, 207–9
Pot pies, vent holes in, 28
Potato chips, green tinges on, 275
Potatoes, baked, and steak
    houses, 127–29
Preserves, contents of, 140–41
Pretzels, shape of, 91–92
Pubic hair, purpose of, 275–76
Pudding, film on, 57
Purple
    Christmas tree lights, 185–86
    royalty and, 45–46
Putting, veering of ball toward
    ocean when, 107–8

Q-tips, origins of name of, 210–11
Quarterbacks and exclamation,
    "hut," 210

Rain, impending, smell of, 170–71
Ranchers' fenceposts, boots on,
    268
Razors, men's vs. women's,
    122–23
Recyclable plastics, numbers on,
    155–56
Refrigeration of opened food
    jars, 171–72
Remote controls, men vs. women
    and, 217
Restrooms, group visits by
    females to, 217
Roaches, reaction to light of,
    20–21
Robes, black, and judges, 190–92
Rodents and water sippers, 187
Roller skating rinks, music in,
    274–75
Roofs, gravel on, 153–54
Rubble, Betty, nonappearance in
    Flintstones multivitamins,
    4–5

Traffic signs
"DONT WALK," lack of
apostrophe on, 75–75
"FALLING ROCK," purpose of,
72–74
Trailer parks, tires atop mobile
homes in 163–64
Trees
bark, color of, 78–79
growth on slopes of, 141–42
Tumbleweed, tumbling of, 5–7
Tunnels, ceramic tiles in, 135–36
"Turkey," origin of term, 269
Turn signals in automobiles,
clicking sounds of, 203
TWIX cookie bars, holes in,
28–29

Underarm hair, purpose of,
275–76
Uniforms
painters' whites, 17–19
surgeons, color of, 269
Upper lips, groove on, 42–43

Vegetable oil, vegetables in, 266
Vending machines, bill counting
and, 271–72
Vent windows, side, in
automobiles, 13–14
Vitamins, measurement of, in
foods, 148–50
Voices, elderly vs. younger, 24–25

Vomiting and horses, 111–12

Watches (timepieces), 271
Water, boiling, during home
births, 114–15
Water temperature and effect on
stains, 77–78
Water towers in winter, 38–40
Weather
clear days following storms,
125
forecasting of, in different
regions, 267–68
smell of impending rain,
170–71
Whales, sperm, head oil in, 87–89
Whitewall tires, bluish tinge on,
192–93
Women
dancing ability of, 218
feelings of coldness in, 218
group restroom visits of, 217
leg kicking when kissing of,
218
remote controls and, 217
Wool, shrinkage of, vs. cotton,
166–67
Worms, larvae and, 269–70
Wrists as perfume target, 90
Wristwatches, 271

Yellow Freight Systems, orange
trucks of, 64–65

Help!

If you've read this far, you *know* that we need help, and not just psychiatric help.

We need letters and postcards listing your Imponderables, your answers to Frustables, and your comments, pro or con.

As always, we make two promises. If you are the first person to send in an Imponderable we use in our next edition, or offer the best solution to one of our new Frustables, we'll send you a complimentary copy, along with an acknowledgment in the book.

And if you send a self-addressed stamped envelope, we'll send a personal reply (even if sometimes it might take longer than we'd like). The SASE is necessary only if you want a reply —all correspondence is welcome.

Just mail your inspiration, along with your name, address, and (optional) phone number to:

Imponderables
P.O. Box 24815
Los Angeles, California 90024